THE FURNITURE LOVER'S BOOK

The Furniture Lover's Book:
Finding, Fixing, Finishing

L. DONALD MEYERS

A SUNRISE BOOK | E. P. DUTTON | NEW YORK

Library of Congress Cataloging in Publication Data
Meyers, L. Donald,
    The furniture lover's book.
    "A Sunrise book."
    Includes index.
    1. Furniture—Repairing.   2. Furniture finishing.
I. Title.
TT197.M49   684.1'044   76–54882
ISBN: 0–87690–234–4

Published simultaneously in Canada by Clarke, Irwin & Company Limited, Toronto and Vancouver.
Designed by Ann Gold
Illustrations by Rino Dussi

10 9 8 7 6 5 4 3 2 1

First Edition

CONTENTS

THE FURNITURE LOVER'S BOOK

1

THE JOYS OF REBIRTH

In the 1970s, being "born again" attained a height of respectability. People were being reborn physically, as well as spiritually, with transplanted hearts, kidneys, and other organs.

Less loftily, there has been renewed interest in the rebirth of old (and not-so-old) furniture. With prices for fine furniture woods soaring, and labor costs continually on the rise, good furniture is expensive. It is wise, then, to know how to determine which furniture is, indeed, "good," when buying it either new or used.

A knowledge of what to look for in furniture is helpful whether you're shopping in W. & J. Sloane, an antique shop, or the Salvation Army. The trained eye knows junk from a jewel no matter where it is displayed. The knowledgeable buyer literally sees through the artful deceits into the true construction methods. He can tell "built to last" from "built for quick sale." He not only knows when a piece has been cleverly contrived to look better than it is, but also knows when a would-be fixer or finisher has turned a silk purse into a sow's ear—and if it can be metamorphosed again. The trained observer can also tell when a sad-looking old chair or table has merely suffered from neglect and is salvageable, or whether it has "had it" and isn't worth another look.

The first four chapters of this book are devoted to exploring and explaining the furniture-making process, and what constitutes good and not-so-good construction. The types of woods used in furniture are described and evaluated. All-important jointing procedures are discussed and illustrated. Later chapters cover construction and finishing techniques in depth, as done at the factory and in the home. These chapters have a dual purpose—to help you buy quality merchandise when new, and to assist in picking out worthwhile pieces for repair and refinishing. Basic repair and upholstery methods are discussed; and for the person who likes to start afresh, plans are presented for building furniture from scratch.

It should be emphasized here that, while much of today's furniture is

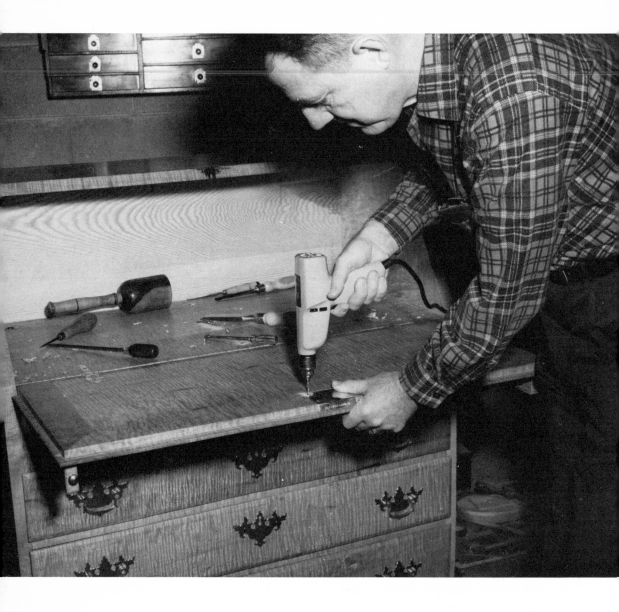

turned out on assembly lines like automobiles, better goods are still made by fine craftsmen out of fine woods. Yes, mass-production techniques are used by all furniture plants today, but much of the quality work is still done by hand. Makers of good furniture throughout the ages have considered themselves master craftsmen. The work they produce is designed for strength, long life, and beauty. A fine piece of furniture is built for appreciation, not for depreciation, as an automobile is.

That is why it is such a joy to find an old, forgotten piece in the municipal or bargain-store junkyard, to resurrect it and turn it into a Lazarus of beauty and strength. When the years of neglect are wiped away, the old joints are made strong again, and the musty finish refurbished, you've not

Here's a genuine antique, right? You can tell from the fine workmanship, the mahogany veneer, the inlays of satinwood, ebony, and boxwood. Wrong. It's a reproduction, although an authentic one. This desk-bookcase is an exact replica of a Williamsburg original made by Kittinger Furniture.

only gained a valuable addition to your household, you've rescued a fine piece of work from a premature grave. The reward is emotionally and spiritually as well as financially satisfying.

IS IT FOR ME?

Is it for you? Writers always hedge about these things. It's for you if . . . It isn't for you if . . . Well, that's true. Not everyone likes to do the type of work required for furniture restoration. It can be tedious. It can be messy. And sometimes it can be very difficult (but not usually). But you wouldn't have gotten this far into this book, either as buyer or browser, if you were not somewhat interested. And if you're interested, you can do it. The principal requirement is to have a love of fine things, and our guess is that you have. If your heart aches when you see what was once a beautiful piece of furniture, now beat-up, discarded, and/or broken up for firewood, you have the type of temperament necessary for the work described in this book.

Be warned, though, that there will be moments when you wonder how you got into this. My first experience with refinishing was not with furniture at all, but with an oak staircase in an older home I had bought. I had an interest in woods, and I wondered what was beneath the thick layers of white paint the former owners had piled on. The staircase was handsome, even painted white, with complicated moldings, and I imagined it would look even nicer in its natural condition.

I tried some paint remover on the top rail to see how it would look underneath. One try got off most of the paint, and two applications revealed some very nice English oak. Great, I thought, I'll do it all.

One year afterward, I had created a gorgeous natural-wood staircase for my daughters to walk down on their wedding day. At the landing, there were three huge stained-glass windows that glistened green, orange, and purple in the sunlight. I could see my daughters, dressed in white, the multicolored beams playing on their veils, and the whole scene framed in glistening oak.

But it was a rough year. Removers, paint, and old shellac spotted the rugs. Each baluster was hours of punishing work. The oak had never been filled, and the open pores clung stubbornly to flecks of white. I had to scrape each crevice with toothpicks, turkey skewers, beer-can openers, or whatever else was handy. Every time I applied remover—three and four times in most cases—the residue would become embedded in the pores and I had to dig it out again. Needless to say, my wife was quite unhappy with a staircase that was part oak, part white, and part in-between for twelve long months.

The worst part is that I moved out of town a few years later, never attaining my vision of daughters descending my wonderful staircase. But I do think the staircase helped sell the house.

There are a couple of lessons to be learned here. First, start on something portable, so that your mess doesn't assault the eye for months at a time. Second, don't tackle a big, long-term job until you've had some experience.

1.

2.

3.

4.

Fine craftsmanship at its best in the Kittinger plant. (1) shows perfectly matched checkerboard inlays and Carpathian burl elm drawer front; (2) illustrates hand-mortised hinges; (3) shows a carver at work on the legs shown in (4) At right in (4) is the leg as it comes from machine carving. Note the time-consuming detail on finished leg at left.

Basically, furniture repair and refinishing are not difficult jobs. If the joints are sound, they don't need repair. If they're not, they're easy to pull apart and fix. Today's chemical removers make short work of almost any finish, and a new one goes on rather simply and easily. If you have the interest, and the right tools and materials, you can do it.

HAND TOOLS (REPAIR WORK)

The number of tools you'll need for furniture repair and refinishing can be legion—or very few. It depends on the job and how heavily you're into the work. In more or less the order of essentiality, you'll need the following:

Claw Hammer—You probably already have one. If you don't, get one for a multitude of household tasks as well as furniture work. A 16-ounce, well-balanced model with a well-fastened head is worth the extra cost. (And save it for use on nails, not other things. The face of a good hammer is smooth and slightly rounded for maximum effectiveness and should not be chipped or blunted by use on concrete and the like.)

Screwdrivers—You probably have a couple of these around, too. Always buy high-quality screwdrivers with insulated handles (in case you want to use them for electrical work), and use them, too, for the purpose for which they were intended, not as prybars, etc. Quality screwdrivers are built for maximum torque in the screwhead, so don't ruin them by denting or bending them. Get several types (including at least one Phillips-head) in several sizes for all-around household use.

Pliers—Another common household tool. For furniture work, both the standard slipjaw type and the slim-nosed electrician type come in handy.

Saws—You probably have a saw around, too, usually an 8-point (8 cutting points to the inch) general-purpose crosscut saw. If you don't have a good one, get one. You will probably also need a "backsaw," usually 12-point—used for making finer cuts, especially in a miter box (see below). Other saws you might need are dovetail, veneer, and/or razor saws, which have up to 20 teeth per inch and are used for very fine work. A coping saw will be needed for curved cuts. Power equipment (see below) may substitute for many of these, but if you get into fine detail in making your own furniture or parts thereof, you'll find these small saws invaluable.

Clamps—Glue without clamps is like butter without bread—in furniture work, at any rate. The more you get into repair work, the more clamps you will need. Adjustable wood or "hand-screw" clamps are a must for holding wood together without marring the surface. Metal C-clamps are often needed (with wood shims to avoid marring) and bar or pipe clamps are necessary for long stretches. A belt or homemade tourniquet clamp is essential for repair of chair legs and similar jobs. (See Chapter 6 for more on the use of various clamps.)

Knives—A well-sharpened "Swiss Army," Boy Scout, or "stockman's" knife is a good investment, and you should also have an old, dull knife for cleaning out crevices and scraping off old glue.

Mallet—A large hammer with a wood, rubber, or soft plastic head for knocking apart loose joints and whacking them back together again.

Planes—The most essential is a smoothing plane, used for smoothing the edges of large boards. As you progress, you may want to pick up a block plane (for small work) and a jack plane (for making long, straight cuts).

Brace and Bits—An old-fashioned drilling tool that is still better for some things than an electric one. It can be controlled better for delicate work and large augers can be used more readily than in an electric model. Also good for removing tough or rusted screws (with the appropriate bit, of course). Overall, however, the electric drill is faster and easier.

Razor Blades or Razor Knife—Single-edge blades are cheap and useful for cutting veneers and other fine work. An X-acto knife is even better.

Folding Rule—Get a good one of these, with an extension for measuring inside cabinets, and the like. The ones that start from opposite ends on each side are more useful than the ones that measure the same way on each side.

Rasps and Files—For smoothing, rounding, and removing unwanted "gingerbread."

Scratch Awl—In general, more useful than a pencil for marking saw cuts. Also handy for starting screw holes.

Sanding Block—You can buy one, preferably with a pad, or make your own out of a piece of 2 x 4 if you don't want to put out the extra money.

Wood-Marking Gage—Used for marking boards lengthwise, scribing a line equidistant from the designated edge.

Nail Set—Purists will advise a center punch for the same tasks, but a nail set not only knocks out plugs and dowels, but is also useful, as the title implies, for setting nails. Get a small-diameter one to double as a center punch.

Glue Injector—A syringe or electric gun, very handy for forcing glue into hard-to-reach places such as under loose veneer, joints that need tightening but are difficult to separate, and other similar tasks.

Miter Box—A big help when trying to cut wood pieces, particularly molding, to an exact angle. Hardwood miter boxes are fine for 90- and 45-degree angles. The adjustable steel type is more accurate for these angles, and can be set for any other angle besides.

Wood Chisels—A necessity in joinery and other work.

"Surform" Plane—A rasp-type plane that is useful in curved work. One variety is made like a thin steel rasp for getting into holes, mortises, and other small places.

Woodworking Vise—Your third hand. If you have a regular vise, you should be able to buy or make woodworking jaws to cover the harsher metal jaws.

Nylon Rope—Used for making tourniquets to hold legs together, replacing a strap clamp, and for other holding jobs.

Spoke Shave—A small, razorlike plane that has handles or "ears" on both ends and is drawn toward the user. For exacting, close work.

HAND TOOLS (FINISHING)

Brushes, Old and New—The *sine qua non* of refinishing work. The old ones are used for applying chemical removers and other rough work. New ones are best for applying new finishes. An assortment of sizes, including a few artists' brushes for fine work, is a necessity. Animal (natural) bristles are best for most work. Nylon bristles should be used for latex paint.

Scrapers—Old, wide-bladed drywall knives and putty knives with rounded corners, so that they don't *really* scrape. If you have to buy new ones, grind down the edges and dull them with steel wool or emery cloth.

Toothbrushes—Again, use old ones if you have any. These are indispensable for getting into moldings, carvings, and other recesses where your scraper doesn't reach.

Steel Wool—A variety of grades, used for assorted chores such as final passes after scraping off removers, and better than sandpaper for fine abrasive jobs during the finishing process.

Orange Sticks, Toothpicks, and Poultry Skewers—Just the things for digging into tiny corners and pores. Toothpicks are easier on the wood but not as strong. Orange sticks are ideal. Poultry skewers may be necessary in many cases, but should be used with care to avoid scratching.

Rubbing Blocks—Similar to sanding blocks, but more flexible, used for curved surfaces and for "rubbed" finishes.

Rubbing Pads—For final finishes with abrasive powders. Actually hard felt about an inch thick.

Tack Rags—Available in many paint stores and auto shops, but you can make one if you wish (see Chapter 10). Highly useful as a final wipe to remove lint and dust before applying varnish and other finishes.

Pick Sticks—Usually hand-made as described in Chapter 10.

Spatula and/or Palette Knife—Used for applying patching materials and stick shellac. A palette knife is also used for mixing paint colors, although a putty knife can be used for the same purpose.

Alcohol Lamp—Since natural gas and other heating sources leave some soot, an alcohol lamp must be used when heating the spatula for applying stick shellac.

POWER TOOLS

Although most repair and refinishing jobs can be done quite adequately with hand tools, the power tools listed below will help speed the job and are usually more accurate. They are listed in descending order of importance.

Electric Drill—Invaluable for the quick drilling of holes, starting screw holes, mortises, and assorted other tasks. Accessories such as wire brushes and screwdriver attachments add to its versatility. The 3⁄8-inch models are now almost as low in price as the 1⁄4-inch, and the extra power is worth the small extra cost. Get one with variable speed.

Power Sander—A great time-saver when working with new wood or old surfaces that need a good smoothing. An orbital sander is more useful than a straight-line, although some models can be adapted for both uses. Don't use a rotary or disc sander on fine furniture.

Saber Saw—Indispensable for quick, fast cutting. Will saw any type of line, but best for curves and cutouts. Comes in some quite inexpensive models.

Radial-Arm or Table Saw—Terrific for all types of saw cuts, but considerably more expensive than the portable tools mentioned above. Very fast and accurate.

Electric Grinder—For keeping all kinds of cutting edges sharp and accurate.

Router—For making rabbets, dadoes, fancy edgings, and advanced joints.

Lathe—The ultimate tool for serious woodworkers. Most useful for making your own new furniture, but also very handy in turning new legs, rungs, and similar replacement parts for old furniture.

Jointer-Planer—Also best for new furniture, but comes in very handy for replacement parts.

Drill Press—For making a series of holes or for production drilling.

SPECIALTY TOOLS

There are a number of tools used for upholstery and other specialty work. These are discussed in the appropriate chapters.

MATERIALS

The first few materials discussed below, such as adhesives, sandpaper, removers, and some of the various finishing materials, are essential to any repair and finishing job. Others, such as fillers, sealers, and shellac sticks, may or may not be used depending on the type of wood and the tastes of the finisher. On the other hand, you should have at least a small supply of almost everything listed below for experimenting with the different types of finishing techniques discussed in this book. There is nothing more frustrating than finding that you can't carry on with the work because you don't have something on hand.

Adhesives—At the minimum, you'll need some "hide" (animal) or fish glue, white polyvinyl-resin emulsions such as Elmer's Glue-All, casein glue, and plastic resins such as Weldwood. (See Appendix B.)

Wood Putty—Comes in powder form. Mixed with water it is used for filling in cracks, gouges, holes, and other larger defects. Wood putty can be worked like ordinary wood and, most important, can be stained and finished like regular wood.

Wood Dough—Often referred to by the brand name Plastic Wood. Strong and workable, it is used to fill joints and other defective or broken areas where appearance is not important. Does not take staining and finishing well.

Sandpaper—Get a good assortment of the various grades listed in Appendix C. You won't need much of the coarser grades, but you'll be using a lot of the medium to superfine. Don't buy cheap flint paper, and avoid garnet paper if you can. The extra pennies spent for aluminum oxide or silicon carbide papers are well worth it in labor saved. They'll last longer, too.

Chemical Removers—There's a variety available, and you should have some on hand of the different types. You'll probably use the jellylike removers most, but see Chapter 8 for a full discussion of this topic. Especially read the section on lye, the most effective, but also the most difficult and dangerous to use.

Steel Wool—Start with a package of mixed grades 1/0 to 3/0, if available, then buy the grades individually when you find out which you use the most. Used for a variety of jobs, like mopping off after using removers and for fine abrasive jobs.

Denatured Alcohol—Many uses in removing and reviving old finishes, particularly shellac.

Oils—Various uses for both raw and boiled linseed oil, more frequently the latter. Tung oil is a favorite for pure oil finishes. Have at least a small can of each on hand. (See Chapter 10 for a complete discussion.)

Pumice—Used for rubbing. Get FFF grade, usually available in drugstores as a tooth whitener, if not from the same sources as your other supplies.

Rottenstone—A finely ground, decomposed, siliceous limestone with a slight odor of rotten eggs. Used for rubbing, and available from paint and hardware stores in only one grade.

Bleaches—May be necessary for some work. Various types are available, including household bleach (Clorox, et al.). See Chapter 9.

Stains—A multitude of types, discussed in detail in Chapter 9. For most woods, wiping stains are fine, although you may wish to use water or NGR (non-grain-raising) stains for specialized work.

Fillers—Needed only for open-grain woods such as oak and walnut, but a must when such woods are to be worked on. Buy paste types rather than liquid fillers.

Varnishes—Although natural-resin varnishes are still available and are used for some purposes, the modern polyurethane types are much better for all-around use.

Turpentine and Other Paint Thinners—Various uses, including brush cleaning.

Shellac—The best way to buy shellac is in flake form, for home mixing, but you can buy it premixed if you're sure it is fresh. Never use old shellac. You'll find several uses for shellac in chapters 7 through 10. "White" shellac is used much more frequently than "orange."

Lacquer—The new brushing and aerosol lacquers may prove very useful, but older lacquers are for application only with a spray gun and not recommended for home use.

Penetrating Sealers—A special finish that is easy to apply and is similar to old-fashioned "oil" finishes. Best for darker, open-grained woods.

Wax—Used for protecting and finishing. The best is paste wax with a high percentage of carnauba wax. See Chapter 12 for more details.

Opaque Finishes—There are hundreds of these, and there are times when you'll want to use one or more, but it is generally inadvisable to cover up good wood with paint, enamel, and the like. Softwoods and the poorer hardwoods may benefit from an opaque finish.

Veneers and Woods—For making new parts and new furniture, usually not available from lumber yards or other typical wood sources. These and other specialty items are usually obtainable by mail. Appendix D provides a list of mail-order sources. The best source for dedicated restorers is a garage full of old furniture and parts of your own.

THE PLACE WHERE YOU WORK

From the homemaker's standpoint, the worst drawback of furniture refinishing is the mess that surrounds it. Removers, finishes, and assorted tools need room for storage, and there should be a place to hide furniture in the state of repair or pre-repair. The finish-removing process is undeniably sloppy, no matter what remover you use. It is imperative that an obscure corner of the home be set aside for your work. Living quarters are impossible for this type of work, unless you absolutely have no other place to perform. Basements and garages are the most likely places, and even then, your workshop should be cordoned off from other areas such as the laundry or recreation areas. No matter how neat you try to be, the work area will be offensive to the eye and often to the ear. It will surely be an affront to the nose.

Which brings up the second must. The work area *must* have adequate ventilation. Most of the substances used in finishing require fresh air. Many of them are toxic if inhaled in a closed room, many are flammable, and a lot of them just plain stink. The more windows the better, and if you *must* work without them, install an exhaust fan.

A garage is probably the best place of all to work, mainly because you can easily move the work outside in nice weather. This helps in clean-up and for quick drying. The basement is more practical in colder areas. If you plan on using lye (see Chapter 8 for the many cautions on this), outside work is a must. And don't let any lye get onto any grass that you admire. There isn't a better grass-killer.

Your work area should have several items which will save time and effort. A workbench is one, preferably with lots of storage area and drawers. If possible, hang up perforated hardboard; and use a 2 x 4 backup behind the bench with holes drilled into it for chisels, screwdrivers, rasps, drill bits, and similar tools that are hard to store on perforated hardboard. The 2 x 4 also prevents things from falling out.

A work platform is another good idea. It brings low pieces up to workable height. You can build one with 2 x 4s and plywood (preferably ¾-inch). A good size is 4 x 3 feet and about 20–24 inches off the ground. It should be portable or built against a wall so that you can use the back wall to press against if you need pressure.

Make sure that the platform is level. If working on an uneven floor, use wedges or shims under the legs to make the surface level. The platform should be covered with a piece of old carpeting, tacked around and under the outside of the frame. If using the platform for stripping off the old finish, cover it with newspaper to make clean-up easier.

Another useful item is a wide "sawhorse." Two of them are even better. These come in handy when working with an awkward piece such as a high dresser or secretary. You can stretch the piece across the horses for easier manipulation.

2

WHAT MAKES GOOD FURNITURE?

When you are buying furniture, old or new, it is vital to recognize the good from the bad. This has little to do with looks, although generally a well-designed piece can be presumed to be well made and vice versa. But there is plenty of furniture that looks good to the eye, yet falls apart after a little hard use. The opposite also applies. Underneath an old and beat-up-looking piece, covered with layers of dirty finish or peeling paint, there may be fine mahogany or walnut.

Good furniture is constructed well and finished well. A really poor finish looks unnatural, and feels raw, rough, and wavy. It may be sticky, cloudy, or blistered. If the finish is merely mediocre, detection is more difficult. You may be able to get an idea by running a coin or other object over it, but the furniture dealer will be upset if you scratch it.

Construction is another matter. If you glance at a piece of furniture, one piece may look as good as another. So you have to snoop around a bit. One easy test is to jiggle it a bit. Are the legs even? (Move it to another part of the floor and try it again. The floor could be uneven.) Does it have a flimsy feel? Open the doors and/or drawers. Do they move easily without drooping? Drawers should open evenly and level with a light touch of a finger. You shouldn't have to use two hands or force. What kinds of drawer guides (tracks) are used? Wooden ones are used on most good furniture. The drawers should close easily, too, as should any doors. Check thickness. Thin doors are an indication of overall flimsiness.

While you have the drawers out, check to see if there's a "dust panel" (a thin piece of wood) between the drawers to catch the dust, as the name implies. Run your hand around the inside of the drawer. Is it smooth and free from burrs? What's the bottom panel made of? Real wood panels are used throughout in fine furniture, although a composition hardboard panel isn't necessarily a fatal defect. Bottom panels should fit into dadoes in front and sides with small wood wedges below.

Another good general test is to inspect the surface in a strong light at

13

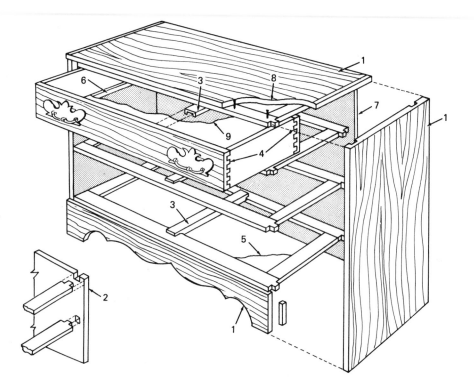

FIGURE 1. Some of the things to look for in fine furniture: (1) selected hardwoods, solid for legs, veneers for flat areas; (2) mortise-and-tenon joints; (3) strong drawer guides; (4) drawers dovetailed front and back; (5) dust panels between drawers; (6) drawer bottoms recessed into dadoes; (7) case backs recessed into sides; (8) well-mounted top and sides; (9) drawer interiors sanded and sealed.

an angle of 15 to 30 degrees. This will pick up shadows that indicate ir-regularities in construction or finish.

JOINERY

The best clue to any wood craftsman's work is in his joinery—the method of joining the wooden parts together. Although most joinery jobs are done now by machine, there are still quality ways and cheap ways of doing this. On older furniture, all this work was done by hand.

Beware if you see a lot of nails. There may be times when nails are ac-ceptable, but always where they aren't intended to be seen. The back of a chest may be attached with nails, and this is acceptable in a medium-class piece, but not in really good stuff. Screws are sometimes the only way to hold certain difficult joints together, but they should be few and well hidden.

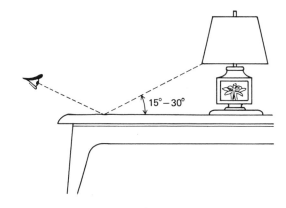

15° – 30°

FIGURE 2.

The only types of joints used by true craftsmen are those in which the wood is shaped so that it holds itself together—along with glue, of course. But the glue works only as a way to keep the joints from slipping apart. Most well-made joints would hold together, at least for a while, without any adhesive.

The art of joinery was known to the ancients, before the time of Christ. There has been little improvement since. Different types of joints are used in different places. The dovetail, for example, with its pins and tails (fingers

FIGURE 3. Various types of dovetail joints.

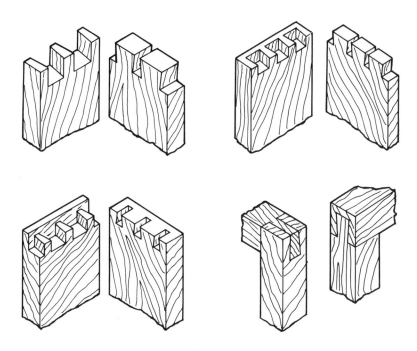

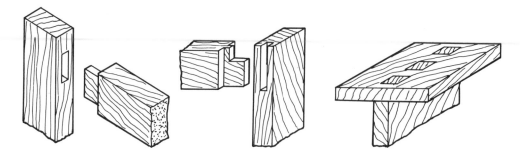

FIGURE 4. Several of the many types of mortise-and-tenon joints.

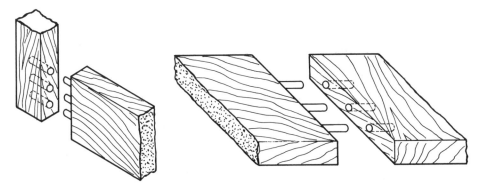

FIGURE 5. Just a few of the many ways dowels are used in joinery.

and interlocking cavities), is essential for good drawer work. For arms and other areas, a "mortise," or rectangular hole, is cut into one part, while a "tenon," a protruding section fitting snugly into the mortise, is cut into the other piece.

Another type of joinery that is used in fine furniture (but also in some cheaper furniture, too) is the doweled joint. Depending on where it is used, the pieces may be butted, mitered, or set at some other angle. In any case, holes are drilled into both sections and dowels (little round pieces of wood, preferably with spiral grooves) are inserted into the holes in one piece. The other piece is then pressed onto the protruding dowels.

A good example of a doweled joint (and which also illustrates the point above about joints holding without glue) is a table extension. The two halves of the table are separate. The male half is fitted with glued dowels, the other has holes drilled just a trifle larger than the dowels so that the dowels slide in and out without too much trouble. Better tables also have a mechanical lock to hold the halves together when not extended. The extension pieces are fitted in the same manner, but without any mechanical holding devices. When the two sides are pressed firmly against the extension, the table holds perfectly well unless pulled apart. (The dowels in this instance are rounded on the ends for easier insertion. Regular dowels have squared ends.)

GLUE BLOCKS

No matter how well a joint is constructed, there are certain parts of furniture that are subjected to severe strain and are improved by the use of glue blocks. A well-built table, for example, will have sturdy mitered pieces of wood where the legs join the top. These help to hold the sides, top, and legs together. Metal braces are sometimes used on good furniture as well as on mediocre. In any case, some sort of bracing is usually required in such high-stress areas.

All such bracing should be strong, tight-fitting, and hidden from view. If the blocking is not snug on all sides, it will do little good. The blocks are usually screwed into the wood as well as glued.

OTHER JOINTS

There are other types of joints that are not as strong. They are fine for such places as where panels are inserted into the sides and backs of dressers, for edge-gluing furniture core material (the centers of plywood-type construction), and for similar applications where stress is not a problem. Beware, however, if joints of this type are used for chair arms, table legs, bedposts, or other high-load areas.

Butt Joints—The simplest of all joints, the easiest to make, and the least satisfactory. Nails or screws are invariably used to keep butt joints in

FIGURE 6. Glue blocks are used at strategic stress points.

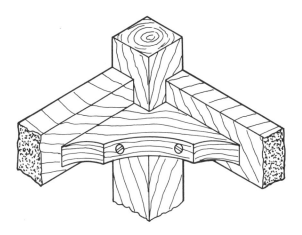

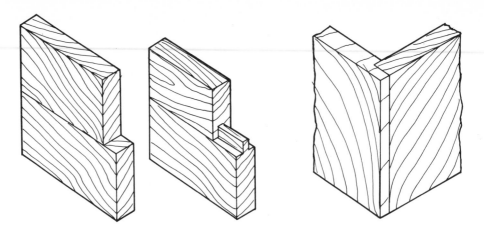

FIGURE 7. (*Left*) A butt joint is structurally weak, although its large surfaces are well suited for strong gluing and clamping. At right, the simple butt joint is strengthened somewhat by a tongue and groove. The best way to join two long boards edge to edge is with spiraled dowels, lots of good glue, and tight bar or pipe clamps.

FIGURE 8. (*Right*) Sometimes the rabbet joint is the only way to join two long, thin pieces of wood.

place. Generally not used in furniture, and a pretty sure sign of shoddy construction, if you find this type of joint.

A butt joint means simply that one piece is placed against another with glue and fasteners. If you buy a piece with butt joints, make sure that all edges are perfectly square without even a slight gap between surfaces. Even a minute space between the pieces means that there is no adhesion except for the nails or screws.

Rabbeted Joints—A rabbet is a long recess cut into the edge of one piece of wood and into which another piece is fitted. The rabbet is as deep as the other piece is thick. Sometimes both pieces are rabbeted to fit each other.

This type of joint is often used where two long pieces meet each other, such as table tops, and in kitchen and other cabinetry. Brads or staples are often used in addition to glue where visibility is not a factor. An acceptable and often the only way to join two long pieces of wood.

Dadoed Joints—A dado is a groove cut into one piece of wood, and into which another piece is fitted. Often used in shelving or where two pieces of wood are fitted with their wide edges together. Most shelves in modern furniture use adjustable hardware of some sort, but older pieces used dadoes to provide strength for permanent shelving.

Mitered Joints—Used primarily for picture frames and other places where two long thin pieces of wood join at right angles on outside corners.

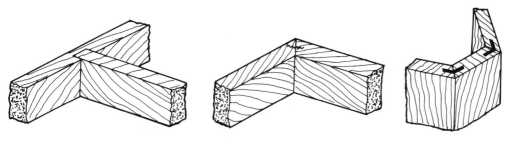

FIGURE 9. (*Left*) A dado joint is often used for shelving.

FIGURE 10. (*Right*) Miter joints should be used with fasteners or wood splines between the pieces.

Each piece is cut at a 45-degree angle and fastened together. A miter is actually a glorified butt joint, and glue alone will not hold without some form of bracing or mechanical strengthening. Small brads are often used in picture frames. Dowels, metal braces, or interior moldings are used to stiffen larger mitered pieces. More intricate stiffening methods include using dovetails, double rabbets, or a "tongue" or spline placed in grooves along the edges of both mitered pieces. These methods help to prevent warping as well as adding strength.

WOOD AND OTHER MATERIALS

In addition to construction methods, the other important feature to note is the wood itself. Of course, the furniture may not be made of wood. There are some very delightful (and expensive) pieces made from plastic, metal, and other materials. But wood is still the overwhelming favorite, and you should take a little time to study the woods used in furniture and how to recognize them. Even an expert won't be right all of the time, however, because one of the skills of good furniture making is to take a less valuable wood and make it look like something richer.

There is nothing inherently wrong with this. On the contrary, it is to your benefit if you can buy what looks like a walnut table for considerably less than what it would cost for *real* walnut. And the salesperson who tells you otherwise is not to be trusted. Much new furniture now comes with tags certifying the types of wood used.

WHERE WOOD COMES FROM

Everyone knows that wood comes from trees. But there is a little more to it than that. You should know, for starters, that the best furniture wood comes from deciduous, or broad-leaved, trees which lose their foliage annually. All hardwood trees are deciduous. Softwood comes from evergreen or coniferous (cone-bearing) trees. These trees do not lose their leaves in the winter. The wood from coniferous trees (spruce, fir, pine, etc.) is used mainly for rough construction such as house framing.

Actually, a lot of furniture is made from evergreen trees. Softwoods such as pine and cedar are often used for Colonial, or rustic-style pieces. But most softwoods are not very hardy and are easily damaged. There are other deficiencies in certain softwoods such as fir. The grain is "wild" and not very attractive.

Softwood is often the wood of choice for casual, painted, or built-in pieces by do-it-yourselfers. Fir plywood is commonly used for desk and table tops, shelving, and other uses where wide boards are needed. White and knotty pine are quite often the choices for those making their own Colonial-style furniture.

The reason that much do-it-yourself furniture is made of softwoods is that they are easy to work, as the name implies. Some of the denser hardwoods are extremely hard to penetrate, as you may have found out if you tried to attach drapery hardware to oak woodwork. If that doesn't convince you, try to nail into a piece of "hardrock" (an apt nickname) maple, or an ash or hickory baseball bat. For that reason, power tools are often required to work with most hardwoods. All nail or screw holes, for example, should be pre-drilled.

TREE STRUCTURE

A general knowledge of tree structure is valuable to the craftsman who builds his own furniture. Only the larger portion of the tree trunk, or "bole," is used for lumber. This portion is first crosscut into logs.

In most species, the "heartwood" at the center of the trunk is darker than the wood in the outer part (sapwood). The relative proportion of heartwood and sapwood in a tree varies with species and environment. Sapwood normally can be seasoned more easily than heartwood. It is more susceptible to fungus and insect attacks, but is more easily impregnated with wood preservatives. There is no difference in strength.

When tree growth is interrupted or slowed each year by cold weather or drought, the structure of the cells formed at the end and the beginning of the growing season is different enough to sharply define the annual layers or growth rings. In many species, each annual ring is divided into two layers. The inner layer, the "springwood," consists of cells having relatively large cavities and thin walls. The outer layer, or "summerwood," is composed of smaller cells. The transition from springwood to summerwood may be abrupt or gradual, depending on the kind of wood and growing conditions at the time it was formed. In most species, springwood is lighter in weight, softer, and weaker. Species such as the maples, gums, and poplars do not show much difference in the structure and properties of the wood formed early or later in the season.

Strength of wood depends on the species, growth rate, specific gravity, and moisture content. Extremely slow growth produces a weaker wood. Softwoods also are weakened by extremely rapid growth. Wood with low specific gravity or high moisture content is generally weaker. Defects such as grain deviation caused by spiral growth, knots, and burls also result in weaker wood.

Yet these structural defects frequently enhance the appearance of wood. Spiral growth results in a winding stripe on turnings. Butt wood shows the assembly of root branches, and crotch wood has a merging or diverging pattern. A burl produces attractive boards showing tissue distortion. The bird's-eye figures resulting from the elliptical arrangement of wood fibers around a series of central spots are valued highly and do not weaken maplewood appreciably. Some quartersawed woods show pronounced whitish flakes were the wood rays are exposed. This forms an interesting pattern, especially in oak and sycamore.

MAKING LUMBER

Lumber is sawed from a log in two different ways, with the plane of the cut either radial or tangential to the annual rings (see Figure 11). When the cut is tangential to the annual rings, the lumber is called plainsawed (hardwoods) or flat-grain lumber (softwoods). When the cut is in a radial plane (parallel to the wood rays), the lumber is called quartersawed (hardwoods) or edge- or vertical-grain lumber (softwoods). Generally, lumber with annual rings at angles from 45 to 90 degrees is considered

FIGURE 11.

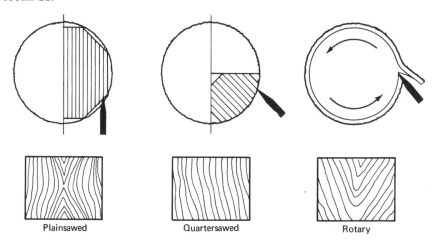

| Plainsawed | Quartersawed | Rotary |

quartersawed, while lumber with rings at angles from 0 to 45 degrees with the surface is considered plainsawed. Plywood is sawed with a rotary cut.

Plainsawed Wood—Is usually cheaper because it can be cut from the log faster and with less waste. It is less likely to collapse from drying; shakes and pitch pockets extend through fewer boards; round or oval knots affect surface appearance and strength less than the spike knots in quartersawn boards; figures formed by annual rings and other grain deviations are more conspicuous.

Quartersawed Wood—Shrinks and swells less in width than plainsawed lumber. It cups and twists less; does not surface-check or split as badly in seasoning and use; wears more evenly; raised grain caused by the annual rings is not as pronounced; is more impervious to liquids; most species hold paint better; figures resulting from pronounced rays, interlocking grain, and wavy grain are more conspicuous; width of the sapwood appearing in a board is no greater than that of the sapwood ring in the log.

As it comes from the sawmill, lumber has a high moisture content and is unsuited for furniture use. It is important that lumber be seasoned until the moisture content is in equilibrium with the conditions under which the wood will be used. When a condition of equilibrium moisture content is reached, the lumber has no tendency to shrink, expand, or warp.

Lumber can be seasoned by natural air-drying, by kiln-drying, or by various chemicals (common salt, urea, etc.) in combination with the other methods. The time available for drying, the species of wood, and the ultimate use of the wood are important factors in determining the method of seasoning. Kiln-drying is the common commercial practice. Chemical seasoning in combination with air- or kiln-drying is used for seasoning some high-quality lumber.

Certain characteristics are particularly desirable in wood used to make furniture. These include:
- stability, or ability to keep its shape without shrinking, swelling, or warping
- ease of fabricating, surfacing, and finishing
- pleasing appearance (which may actually include some surface defects in the lumber)
- suitable strength and grain characteristics
- availability

See Appendix A for details of the more common furniture woods.

PLYWOOD

Plywood is composed of thin plies or veneers that are glued together with the grains at right angles. Three-ply plywood has a center core faced

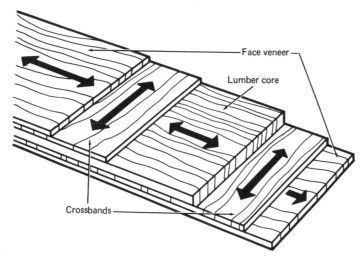

Face veneer

Lumber core

Crossbands

FIGURE 12.

with two veneers. Five-ply plywood has a core, two inner plies or cross-bands, and a veneer facing. Plywood provides strength in both length and width and has good resistance to splitting and moisture changes.

Lumber-core plywood is usually preferred for furniture construction. It consists of solid heartwood strips glued together and covered on each face with a thin panel of plywood. Certain types of joints are more easily made with this type of plywood.

Plywood is available in a variety of types and grades. For example, if a project is to be exposed on both faces, then plywood that has the best veneer on both sides must be purchased. But if only one face is to be seen, then a cheaper-grade "good-one-side" panel is used, with certain flaws in the veneer on the hidden side.

Hardwood plywoods, veneered with a variety of richly beautiful hardwoods, are preferred for the making of fine furniture. Most hardwood plywood panels have an extra-thick middle core with thin surface veneers.

HARDWOODS

When they are stained and finished, it is quite difficult to tell one hardwood from another. You should be able to tell if any wood is, in fact, hardwood, by digging a fingernail into an inconspicuous spot. Softwood will show the dent, but hardwood will not unless you've got an exceptionally strong fingernail.

The main object when examining furniture is to determine whether the piece is indeed made of hardwood. A secondary aspect is what type of hardwood it is. The favorite hardwoods over the centuries have been, and will no doubt continue to be, mahogany, walnut, cherry, pecan, hickory, maple, oak, and birch. All of these have natural grain patterns which are interesting (sometimes beautiful) to look at.

Most can be finished in their natural color, darkened with stain, or made almost blond by bleaching. All are strong and durable.

There are other woods which have approximately the same strength, but little grain pattern. These woods, such as gum, poplar, and cottonwood, can be stained to resemble the more expensive hardwoods and are often used in conjunction with them in less visible parts of the same piece of furniture.

The overwhelming favorite for better furniture remains imported mahogany. Make sure, however, that it is tropical American, West Indian, or African mahogany. Other, less expensive woods are sometimes *called* mahogany, but aren't. Lauan, for example, is often called "Philippine mahogany." It isn't a *bad* wood, but it isn't true mahogany, either. Other foreign tropical hardwoods such as crabwood resemble true mahogany in texture and other properties when stained, and are being used more and more for fine furniture. But they are still not real mahogany. Nice as they may be, they should not command as high a price as mahogany.

The reasons for the popularity of mahogany are many. It is strong and has a very attractive, warm grain pattern, but so do many other fine woods such as walnut, cherry, and quartersawed oak. In addition, however, mahogany can be finished both light and dark. Mahogany is one of the least vulnerable woods to shrinking and swelling due to changes in humidity.

GRAIN

Grain provides a pattern or configuration that may or may not please the eye. The way a tree grows is what causes the grain pattern. As far as structure is concerned, the direction of the fibers is more important than the pattern they make.

Furniture parts that require strength, such as chair arms and legs, bedposts, and table legs, should have straight grain. If there is much crossgrain or sloping grain, beware. Parts manufactured from non-straight grain may fail.

Drawer fronts, table tops, and mirror frames should also have straight grain. Otherwise, they may warp with changes in humidity.

VENEERS

Veneered furniture made around the turn of the century was put together with glues that failed in high humidity. Some people still believe that veneered furniture is not as good as solid furniture. That is not true. Furniture today is almost always glued with water- and mold-resistant

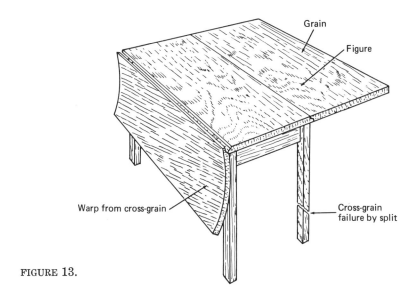

Grain

Figure

Warp from cross-grain

Cross-grain
failure by split

FIGURE 13.

Of all furniture woods, mahogany is the favorite. Some of the numerous grain patterns of mahogany are shown.

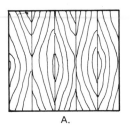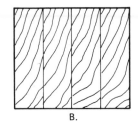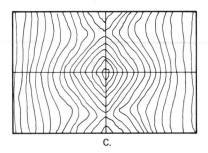

A.   B.   C.

FIGURE 14. Wood can be cut any number of ways to produce striking and beautiful veneers. "Matching" is equally important. (A) shows a "book" match, in which every other veneer sheet is turned over, like the pages in a book. In "slip" matching (B), the veneer pieces are joined side by side. True veneer art shows up in places like table tops, where the "four-way center and butt" (C) shows off the veneer at its best.

glue. Veneers seldom peel off, and make possible economical use of more expensive woods.

An advantage of veneered furniture is stability, because the layers of wood and veneer are so balanced that you get less change in dimension with changes in humidity than you would with solid wood.

Another advantage is the beautiful patterns that can be obtained in wood veneer by slicing burls or logs at angles and arcs not possible by conventional sawing of lumber.

One caution, however: Veneered parts should have an odd number of plies or layers—three, five, seven, or nine—with the grain direction of adjacent plies at right angles so that they will be balanced around the central core. An even number of layers may result in warping.

LAMINATED WOOD

Laminated wood is very similar to plywood, except that the plies are usually thinner and are all laid in the same direction. Laminated woods are used for forming curves and other formations which are difficult or impossible with lumber or plywood. A good example of this is in the formed chair backs of some modern furniture.

INLAYS AND MARQUETRY

Although rare in new furniture because it is an expensive process, fancy inlay is seen in a lot of good older furniture. An inlay is a piece of contrasting wood veneer set into the front or top of a piece of furniture. Dark woods usually had light inlays and light furniture had dark inlays. Since most older furniture is dark, the inlays are usually of a light-toned wood.

Marquetry is an art that has almost completely disappeared from factory-made furniture because of its prohibitive cost. It consists of making designs and even pictures with several types of veneers, usually expensive and exotic woods. Marquetry utilizes some of the very rare woods, which because of the small size of the mother trees, or the scarcity, cannot be made into regular lumber.

Some of the more popular woods used in inlays and marquetry are rose wood, satinwood, myrtle, yew, zebrawood, thuyawood, tulipwood, mulberry, and laburnum. Inlays found in modern furniture are ordinarily made of less expensive woods, or of unusual, more costly formations of regular hardwoods such as bird's-eye maple.

In the late eighteenth century, when inlay and marquetry were a high art, this English commode was decorated with East Indian satinwood, harewood, pheasant wood, sycamore, mahogany, and thuya. (*The Metropolitan Museum of Art, Fletcher Fund, 1929*)

Although marquetry has disappeared from store-bought furniture, you can learn the craft by buying a marquetry kit. The young lady is cutting out veneers and gluing them onto "marquetry-by-number" plans.

FINISH MATERIALS

If the lines of the piece suit your taste and the construction meets your standards, find out what kind of finish was used. Finishes of varnish, lacquer, and synthetic resins are all good if properly applied.

Ask for a guarantee that the finish will not water-stain under sweating glasses or discolor under a warm dish. That is especially important in dining and coffee tables. Many finishes are resistant to water, alcohol, and other things that may be spilled.

The most important thing about finishes is that the furniture should have some type of finish on all exposed wood parts, whether they are on top or underneath, inside a drawer, or inside the case.

That is advisable because moisture from the air moves into wood—even through the best finish—and causes wood to swell. If more moisture moves in one side than the other, the wood will swell unevenly and cause warping and tight drawers. Glue joints may open up or the wood may split.

When furniture goes into a very dry place, the opposite happens, and the shrinking of wood parts in furniture can cause just as many problems as swelling.

Most modern furniture finishes are spray-lacquered. This is a highly durable finish and one that is difficult for the do-it-yourselfer. Today's finishes are estimated to be 25% to 50% better than those used as recently as a decade ago. But the lacquer or synthetic coat is just the final finish. Afterward, this final coat is usually hand-rubbed and waxed. Most fine furniture receives over 20 different finishing steps. The finishing procedures suitable for do-it-yourselfers are described in Chapters 7 to 10.

FASTENING AND HARDWARE

As discussed above, the more all-wood and glue joints a piece of furniture has, the better it is likely to be. Screws are, however, necessary in many cases, and the presence of a few of them in obscure or structurally strategic places should not be a matter of concern. Be suspicious of nails and staples (except for upholstery, of course). When screws are used, check to see that they are drawn up tightly. Telltale gaps, whether screwed or glued, are a sign of poor workmanship.

Check all drawer pulls and other hardware to see that they are properly fastened and tight.

If you are buying a table with drop leaves or one that slides open to insert extra leaves, ask the salesman to turn it upside down so you can see that the hardware is fitted properly and tightly. Drop-leaf tables should have a long piano-type hinge or three or more hinges at least 3 inches long.

BUYING OUTDOOR FURNITURE

A lot of outdoor furniture is made of metal or other materials, but there is really no good substitute for well-made wood lawn furniture. Theoretically, any wood can be used outdoors if it is specially treated. But make sure you know what you're buying and that it is well treated with preservative if the wood is not of the outdoor-durable type.

Some woods are naturally weather- and insect-resistant, and these are the safest bet for outdoor use. The best of the best are the heartwoods (darkest, center sections) of redwood, red cedar, incense cedar, locust, and Osage-orange. Non-heartwood portions of the same woods are acceptable, but not quite as durable. Also quite weather-resistant, but not too often used in this type of furniture, are the heartwood portions of oak, walnut, mulberry, cherry, and mahogany.

Unless they are treated well with preservative (in which case they are quite acceptable and also lightweight) avoid woods such as gum, poplar, cottonwood, hickory, soft pine, and other light woods. Make sure, also, that all fastenings are of hot-dipped galvanized steel or aluminum. Plain steel nails and screws will rust and stain the wood. The more complex forms of joinery are normally not found on outdoor furniture, but if you find them, then it's a good sign that the furniture is exceptionally well made.

3

STYLE AND STORY

Decorating with furniture is easy—at least as this is written. For some years now, the prevailing style has been "eclectic," which means "selecting . . . from various sources," per Webster. In layman's terms, "anything goes." In former days, purists would raise an eyebrow if a French Provincial room sported a Hitchcock chair. Not anymore.

Eclecticism doesn't mean poor taste, however. Even if it pleases you (which it shouldn't), forget the Hitchcock chair in a room otherwise limited to French Provincial. But good taste does mean you can mix a French Provincial piece or two with an assortment of Mediterranean, Modern, Hepplewhite, Queen Anne, and/or even that Hitchcock chair.

A discerning eye and a little basic judgment, which is helped by study and experience, are the best guides to furniture selection. You can learn something about furniture styles by reviewing this chapter. If you feel eclecticism is beyond you, you're always safe decorating each room in one style alone.

MAJOR CATEGORIES OF STYLE

When an early furniture maker took his chisel to wood, he did not consciously say to himself, "I will now make a Chippendale chair in the English Traditional style." He made a chair (or whatever) in a manner which pleased him or—more likely—his customers.

A chair made by a particular furniture maker is one thing; putting it into a period and a certain style is another. So bear in mind that style is another word for "fashion," a fleeting and evanescent thing at best.

There are two major categories which can be distinguished with a fair degree of accuracy. They are based on the fact that there have always been two classes of people, the rich and the poor. In the beginning, only the rich had any furniture at all. The pharaohs of Egypt had beautiful inlaid and veneered caskets for their burial. The poor were fortunate to have a rough stool upon which to rest their weary bottoms.

This ornate mahogany armchair was made in England around 1815. (*The Metropolitan Museum of Art, Rogers Fund, 1967*)

While the rich had many fine pieces of furniture, the peasant was content with his coffer. This oak chest was used by an unknown American colonist in the seventeenth century. (*The Metropolitan Museum of Art, Gift of Mrs. Russell Sage, 1909*)

Monarchs, high churchmen, and others of the ruling classes during the Middle Ages rested *their* bottoms on ornate thrones. They dined on massive oak tables and slept in elaborate bedsteads complete with canopies and draperies (which had a very practical reason—keeping out drafts; the wing-back chair had a similar purpose).

During the same period, a peasant might have had one piece of furniture, usually a chest or coffer. It served many purposes. He used it for storage, sleeping, sitting, dining, and writing—if he knew how. Another piece found in less poverty-stricken homes was the hutch or cupboard, most often a crude variation of the coffer. The portable coffer had one outstanding virtue. You could always pick it up and cart it with you, a necessary feature in those nomadic times.

Furniture of the Middle Ages was almost universally Gothic in style, modeled after the architecture of the day. Made primarily of oak, it was characterized by deep moldings, pointed arches, wrought-iron locks and hinges, and an overriding heaviness.

The original division between rich and poor has continued throughout the centuries. It is, of course, sometimes blurred, but basically the two major style divisions throughout the years have been "traditional" and "country." Although "provincial" in many cases has been carried to a very high art form, the term was originally applied to the creations of country furniture makers from the "provinces," far away from the cultural glories of the large cities and gala courts. Provincial furniture is generally "country" in influence.

During the beginning stages of furniture design, virtually all styles were traditional, since the country style was limited almost exclusively to the portable do-all chest described above. For those who could afford it, however, furniture style as such really began with the Renaissance.

RENAISSANCE AND LATER STYLES

As humanistic values gained ascendancy when mankind moved out of the Dark Ages, a renewed interest in the classics gave an impetus to furniture styling.

The Renaissance influence began in Italy and soon spread to France and Spain. Ancient Greek and Roman values were imitated in furniture as well as the arts. As the new spirit was adopted in Germany, Holland, and England, it was embraced by the emerging middle class. This meant that there were more people ready to buy those artifacts for the home that were formerly reserved for the rich and powerful. During this period (sixteenth to eighteenth centuries) the basic types of furniture evolved. Tables, chairs, sideboards, were made and bought eagerly by the *nouveaux riches*. (The poor still lugged their coffers.) In those days styling was relatively the same throughout Europe. There was no "English" Renaissance furniture as opposed to "Italian."

In the years following the Renaissance, during the late 1600s, classical simplicity gave way to more individualism. Styles became increasingly elaborate. In continental Europe, the forceful, bold Baroque was popular, as was the more graceful and delicate Rococo.

In England, this period was characterized by styles that are more familiar to us. As in some other countries, the fashions were named for the reigning monarchs. Furniture of this era is interesting and valuable, but not as popular or as imitated as the eighteenth-century English Traditional that followed. Seventeenth-century English furniture styles are:

Jacobean or Stuart (1603–1649)—Covers the reigns of James I and Charles I. It was masculine, massive, and bold. Wood was extensively carved and primarily of oak. Square and rectangular lines were dominant, with heavy, ornate decoration. Gateleg and "cricket" (three-legged) tables made their appearances during this period.

Commonwealth or Puritan (1649–1660)—A violent reaction against the "corrupt" Jacobean, a reflection of the state of mind and morals during this time. Straight and severe lines dominated, with little or no carving or other decoration. Square shapes predominated, with high, straight backs and low seats. Stout, practical underbracing and somber-hued upholstery was the order of the day. Although "Commonwealth" is an accurate historical term, "Puritan" is more descriptive.

Carolean (1660–1688)—Also known as late Jacobean or Restoration. Elaborate, deep carvings returned. Spiral turnings or twirls appeared on legs and stretchers. The dominant wood was still oak, with some walnut beginning to appear. Cane seats and rich tapestried upholstery were other common features.

William and Mary (1689–1702)—Mary II married a Dutch husband, and William brought to England the craftsmen and styles of the Continent. More graceful and subtly styled furniture combined straight and curved lines in a harmonious manner that was as well suited for home use as the king's castle. Walnut began to replace oak as the most popular wood. Upholstery was much more extensively used than before. Decorations featured the "inverted cup" at the tops of legs, with flowers, cupids, and wreaths as carvings. Much of this was gilded, painted, and lacquered. Marquetry and inlays were incorporated into the craftsmen's decorative arsenal.

TRADITIONAL ENGLISH FURNITURE STYLES

"Traditional" English furniture reached its peak during the 1700s. Most of the furniture built then is still being imitated today. Authentic pieces in good condition—if you can find them—command a high price. The periods and their masters are usually broken down as follows:

Queen Anne (1702–1715)—Often referred to as the era of the "first modern furniture." The graceful cabriole leg with its knee curved out and foot curved in, was an omnipresent feature. Stretchers (between the legs) were eliminated or rendered insignificant. Elaborate decoration was eschewed, with the notable exception of the scallop shell which appeared, large or small, on virtually every piece. On some pieces, it took the form of a fan or sunburst, which the scallop shell closely resembles.

Curvilinear, undulating lines were predominant, and the "overstuffed" chair came into its own. Brocades and embossed leather were popular materials. In woods, walnut was the favorite, with cherry and maple second. There was still some oak, as well as ash, mahogany (which was scarce), and pine. Handsome tea tables and gaming tables made their appearance during Queen Anne's reign.

Georgian (1714–1795)—Named for kings George I, II, and III. English furniture making evolved to such high art that the period is better known for its individual craftsmen than for its monarchs. For the first time,

Several styles are illustrated in this Kittinger Williamsburg setting. At left is an exact reproduction of a Queen Anne chair made in Philadelphia circa 1735. Center is a replica of a Chippendale breakfront produced in England in 1750. Right is a wing chair, a copy of a Georgian original.

furniture makers were skilled and individualistic enough to have their names attached to their work, as described below.

This era is sometimes called the "age of mahogany," which became extremely popular once tariff laws allowed heavy imports of the reddish tropical wood. Other general features of this glorious, long period were the dominance of curves over straight lines, and the growing influence of French and Oriental styling. Rich upholstery became the rule, and there was a considerable amount of gilding and lacquering in the Chinese manner.

The great masters of this period, and the years of their dominance, are:

Thomas Chippendale (1740–1770)—Not only a superb craftsman, but author of *The Gentleman and Cabinet Maker's Director*, published in 1754 and the first important collection of furniture designs. His achievements were many, but perhaps the most important was his meticulous attention to careful fitting and joining. Chippendale was one of the first to make wide use of mahogany, which at first he stained to resemble walnut.

Chippendale's work was heavily dependent on carved decoration—delicate or intricate, or bold and lavish—whichever the piece demanded. His furniture exhibited a variety of motifs, many of them very English, such as lions, masks, and the familiar "egg and dart." But he also borrowed heavily from the Rococo embellishments of the French Louis XV, the Chinese, and the classical. There were elaborate curving lines, leaflike acanthus, acorns, scrolls, dolphins, the claw-and-ball foot, carved latticework, pagoda motifs, and bamboo turnings. He even borrowed Gothic elements such as pointed arches, fretwork legs, and quatrefoils.

Chairs were Chippendale's masterpieces. The backs of both arm and side chairs were distinguished by an amazing diversity. Vertical splats (the wood pieces down the center of the back) came in beautifully carved and intricate designs. Even ladder-back chairs were done in distinctive patterns. The uprights were molded, fluted, carved, or flat, but always different. The crest, or top rail, was usually scrolled and brought into points or "ears" at the corners.

The Adam Brothers (1768–1792)—Four brothers, three of whom were furniture makers. Robert, the eldest, was an architect, and his influence was strongest in that their furniture was designed primarily to fit specific houses he designed. Adam homes were classical and elegant, and so was the furniture that went into them. Graeco-Roman simplicity was the Adam trademark, with restrained, graceful, straight, and slender lines.

Decorations were sparse and in low relief. Dainty, carved moldings, featuring urns, wreaths, fans, and honeysuckle, were the most common feature. Surfaces were mostly flat, with the minimal decorative effects handled with great delicacy.

George Hepplewhite (1770–1806)—Noted for the grace, refinement, and slender lines of his works. Hepplewhite built on a smaller scale than others of the period. His chairs were distinguished by square, tapering legs and shield- or heart-shaped backs. Other works had oval shapes, serpentine fronts, and concave, cut-in corners. Graceful curves combined with sturdy construction.

Hepplewhite, too, liked mahogany, but his pieces were often set off with inlays and veneers of satinwood. His carvings were dainty and sparse, using wheat ears, bell-flowers, urns, rosettes, ferns, and other classical motifs.

Thomas Sheraton (1780–1806)—Delicate designs similar to Hepplewhite, but a little more rectilinear. Also fond of inlays and veneer. Inlays were so well applied by both Sheraton and Hepplewhite that most are still intact on surviving pieces. Veneers were thick, which prevented cracking and blistering.

The backs of Sheraton's chairs were rectangular with carved splats, often in the shape of three or four columns. Others featured a great deal of openwork. His later designs had a wide top rail and a wide, carved horizontal splat. The same type had "saber" legs, which flared out both front and back. Carvings utilized the lyre, urns, ferns, ovals, and floral swags. Table legs were reeded or turned. Narrow carved lines were common on most pieces.

Actually, Sheraton was more of an overall designer, teacher, writer, and bookseller than a craftsman himself. His designs were turned over to other skilled workers to produce. One of his inventions still common today is the drum table, a pedestal table with a round deep top in which several drawers were recessed. He was also somewhat of a fanatic, and was obsessed with such mechanical gimmickry as secret locks and trick springs.

NINETEENTH-CENTURY ENGLISH STYLES

After the master craftsmen of the eighteenth century, the later traditional styles that were in vogue in England are generally referred to as:

English Regency (1793–1830)—Not to be confused with the French Régence period discussed below. This marked a return by the British to simplification and functionalism, with a great deal of foreign influence. The French Directoire and Empire fashions were much admired and copied. The Orient, too, was extensively studied, with most of the pieces now being covered with lacquer in the Chinese style. Chinese motifs were widely imitated in carvings and in relief. Black was the favorite color, with white and ivory in second place. Gilding was common. Furniture was scaled down to quite small, intimate sizes. Curves were simple, bold, and combined with straight lines.

Victorian (1830–1890)—The long reign of Queen Victoria is well known for primness, solemnity, and sentimentality, as was the furniture. Designs were heavy, substantial, often clumsy. Both upholstery and wood were dark and sometimes dreary. Yet some of the pieces have a quaint charm, and the best examples are very good indeed. As far as woods are concerned, black walnut and rosewood overtook mahogany as the favorite.

One popular Victorian item was the marble-topped table. These find a ready market today, if only for the marble, which is often converted to other uses. Many other pieces, such as bureaus, sideboards, and commodes (a small chest with a tablelike top), had marble tops, and are often bought and sold on their merits as furniture.

The more valuable Victorian pieces today are side chairs and sofas. These are surprisingly comfortable, once stripped of their (usually) porcupinelike horsehair upholstery. The "whatnot," invented during this period to display Victorian treasures such as Staffordshire figures or Canton china, is a sought-after item. The platform rocker was patented during the 1840s. Another innovation of the era was the Morris chair, an adjustable wood-armed piece with a hinged back and separate cushions. Not exactly pretty, it was what poet William Morris intended it to be—comfy. Morris no doubt scribbled many of his works on the large, broad arms.

EARLY FRENCH TRADITIONAL

As with wine and art, French furniture is known for its delicate sense of balance and exacting attention to detail. The greatest skill appears in the carvings, inlays, and painted frills.

All of French art was influenced by the mores and political passions of the times. Furniture was no exception. During the reigns of the ostentatious Louis's luxuriousness abounded. After the Revolution of 1789, severity and simplicity reflected the tastes of the *directoires,* or new proletarian leaders.

Louis XIII (1610–1643)—One of the less elaborate periods, before the later, more flamboyant Louis's. Straight lines, squares, and symmetrical designs prevailed. Twisted columns, inlays, broken pediments, spiral legs, and turned balusters were featured. Carvings were elaborate, but not excessive. Various woods were used, principally ebony, walnut, and oak.

Louis XIV (1643–1715)—A long and lavish reign. For an outstanding example of the styling, noted for its luxuriousness, take a tour through Versailles, which was built for Louis XIV.

Straight lines were still dominant, although carving and ornamentation increased. The understructures of all pieces were heavy and elaborately decorated. Dominant woods are the same as for Louis XIII, with walnut becoming a little more popular.

Régence (1715–1723)—At Louis XIV's death, Louis XV was too young to rule. Philip of Orleans was the regent, or acting king, hence the name "Régence." The massiveness of the previous period began to be supplanted by a lighter, more airy feeling, with Rococo ornamentation. The straight lines of Louis XIV were replaced by elaborate curves. Intricate, often bizarre, decoration came into its own.

Louis XV (1723–1774)—Ornate and luxurious Rococo designs came into full flower during the half-century rule of Louis XV. Conversely, Louis XV furniture is smaller and more delicate in scale than that of earlier styles. The king's paramours, Mesdames de Pompadour and du Barry, influenced the trend to more comfortable, intimate, and feminine styling. Small desks, chaise lounges, and occasional tables made their appearance. The extremely "fancy" styling of this period included cabriole legs with carved knees and scroll feet. Louis's personal *bureau du roi* (king's desk) has been described as the most elaborate piece of furniture ever built. Its decoration included carvings, metal inlays, ormolu (imitation gold) mounts, painted panels, gilt, and lacquer. Favorite woods of the day were mahogany, oak, walnut, chestnut, and ebony.

Louis XVI (1774–1793)—The last monarch before the revolution. Archeological discoveries at Pompeii and Herculaneum prompted a revival of classical simplicity. Period furniture reflected a happy blend of the classical with its former flair, toned down just enough to bring out the best of each. Refinement and elegance were the by-words, with curves giving way to straighter lines. Classical motifs emphasized the authority and beauty of line. Mahogany was the preeminent wood, along with rosewood, ebony, and tulipwood.

Directoire (1795–1804)—The revolution changed both life and furniture styles radically, curbing the excesses in both. Under the rule of the five directors (*directoires*), the Jury of Arts and Manufacturers dominated public taste, in furniture as in every other art form. The trappings of royalty and aristocracy were replaced by classical and military ornamentation. Furniture became more streamlined, elegant, and graceful.

French Empire (1804–1815)—With Napoleon, furniture returned to the ponderousness and ostentatiousness of the "aristocrats." But the lavishness was tempered by classical restraint. Finishes began to receive new importance, with varnish and high polish replacing some of the more

Just before the French Revolution a master craftsman produced this very elaborate *secrétaire à abattant* (upright secretary). It is made of tulipwood, kingwood, holly, and mahogany veneered on oak. In addition, there is gilt bronze, marble, and leather. (*The Metropolitan Museum of Art, Gift of Charles Wrightsman, 1971*)

gaudy forms of decoration. Inspired by Napoleonic visions of a French "empire," Roman eagles, torches, lions, and wreaths were the dominant symbols. These were surpassed only by the more obvious "N" (enclosed in a victor's wreath). Rosewood and ebony were used in addition to the still popular mahogany.

"COUNTRY" OR PROVINCIAL FURNITURE

Country furniture is distinguished from Traditional mainly in that it evolved from artisans of the country or the "provinces." Most of it began as simple, often crude pieces with an eminently practical purpose. A chair —in most cases, a stool—was built to hold a person, and it was made strong and sturdy. A table was designed to hold what little food was available, and for nothing else.

As the local artisans became more experienced and specialized, they began to imitate the styles of the city. But they had neither the skill nor the patience to make intricate carvings and inlays, so they made their products plainer and less delicate. Instead of mahogany, rosewood, and other imported woods, they chopped down the trees nearby and used them. Depending on the country of origin, woods like ash, poplar, maple, and fruitwoods such as apple and pecan were used. Some of the fashionable woods such as oak, walnut, and cherry were also used if locally available. Many pieces were made of pine, which served the purpose of the local farmer very well.

In Europe, provincial furniture slowly evolved into a distinct and recognized art form. Some later French Provincial styles, in fact, are regarded more highly than their aristocratic counterparts. They are less gaudy, less pretentious, and more comfortable. The same applies to Italian and American variations of Traditional styling.

French Provincial (1650–1900)—Like all country furniture this style is less than exact in period and type. In its early years, the pieces were strictly functional, designed to meet the needs of the French peasant. As the centuries wore on, however, and cabinetmaking became an art as well as a necessity, furniture began to resemble Parisian styles, although the provincial versions were simpler and less gaudy. Ornamentation varied from province to province, but there were certain similarities in the paneling and carving, which largely replaced the fancier inlays and marquetry of the capital. Another common characteristic of French Provincial styling is the wide use of metal decorations, with large locks and oversize hinges.

Italian Provincial (1700–1850)—The derivation and development of Italian Provincial furniture was much like the French. Starting in rural areas and small towns, the style gradually began to copy the better features of furniture found in the big cities. There was no specific Italian Traditional style—except for the glory days of Rome—to follow, so French, English, and classical styling were adopted.

The Baroque style, which started in Italy, had the heaviest influence on Italian country craftsmen. They adapted the large, bulky scale to their own uses, eliminating the lavish decorative effects of true Rococo. Over the years, Italian Provincial began to follow rather rectangular lines. Legs were tapered and square. Curves were sparse and unornamented. Moldings and brass hardware were used for decoration, with some paint and enamel. Favorite woods were local fruitwood, walnut, and mahogany.

Biedermeier (1825–1840)—In early-nineteenth-century Germany, the rising middle class was satirized in the media of the day by the creation of a fictional character called "Papa Biedermeier." "Papa" was a typical bourgeois German, sort of a Teutonic Archie Bunker.

Since the German middle class had rejected the florid styles emanating from the rest of the Continent, the evolving simple furniture style of the time was named after the Biedermeier symbol. Local German furniture makers took the prevalent French Empire and Directoire furniture of the day and stripped it down to its functional lines. Although there was a wide variation to the various pieces, they had many things in common— plain lines, sparse decoration, yet luxurious cushioning and padding. What little ornamentation there was consisted of carvings of native fruits and flowers, with some painted details. Woods were primarily local— birch, ash, maple, and native fruitwoods—although there were some imported woods, mostly mahogany.

AMERICAN COLONIAL

American furniture falls under the general heading of country furniture. With the few exceptions discussed below, the colonists forged through their own rough designs out of whatever wood was available and in whatever style suited their fancy. Early on, the furniture was either crude and home-styled or a rather slavish copy of designs from Europe. English settlers adapted English styles, French settlers French styles, and so on.

As the colonies grew and became independent, reliance on "back home" diminished, but most "Early American" designs were patterned after what the settlers remembered from their homeland. As in other country furniture, however, certain native characteristics began to appear and individual craftsmen made their mark with many innovations.

Early Colonial (1620–1700)—Really a hybrid style, influenced by what the colonists brought with them and what wood happened to be on hand at the time. Pine was popular, as were birch, maple, and walnut. Most of the settlers at this time were English, and of Puritan upbringing. Their furniture was plain and utilitarian, a simplified and sturdier version of the Jacobean styles then in vogue in their home country.

Late Colonial (1700–1795)—Also known as "American Provincial." As the period began, the emerging American colonists began to reject the designs of local cabinetmakers and import furniture from England. American craftsmen in the cities began reproducing Queen Anne, Chippendale, and Sheraton pieces for the well-to-do, and some very fine work was created as the craft progressed. This type of furniture is formal and sophisticated and is really more Traditional than Provincial. The Windsor chair, with its spindle back and arms, was an "American innovation" of this period.

The great cabinetmaker of the later period was Duncan Phyfe. Phyfe's shop in New York City became famous for lyre-back chairs, pedestal tables, and curved-base sofas with flared legs and lion's paw feet. Phyfe drew his inspiration and his passion for excellence from the works of Sheraton, the Adams, and Hepplewhite, and later from the works of American Empire or Federal (see below). Phyfe used mahogany almost exclusively. His designs are finely proportioned as well as structurally sound. Prominent motifs, in addition to the ubiquitous lyre, were carved eagles, scrolls, cornucopia, lion's heads, medallions, wheat, and leaves of palm, oak, and laurel.

American Empire (1795–1840)—Also known as Federal in its early stages. Duncan Phyfe was the dominant influence here, but this style also drew on other models, mostly French Empire. The American versions of their European counterparts were heavier and sturdier. Motifs are similar to the Late Colonial except that patriotic motifs such as eagles became more and more popular. Mahogany was still dominant, but cherry was a close second.

Some furniture of this period is mistaken for Duncan Phyfe, but is actually the work of Charles Lannuier, also of New York. Lannuier's work followed French Directoire patterns and made heavy use of brass and giltwork. Other distinctive pieces of the period were the Hitchcock chair, with its painted wood and horizontal splats, and the "Boston rocker."

Pennsylvania Dutch (1680–1850)—This popular American style spans several centuries and is traced to the German immigrants (incorrectly called "Dutch" in a corruption of *Deutsch*) of eastern Pennsylvania, New Jersey, and southern New York. These were solid Germanic pieces, simple and plain. Decoration was primarily in the form of colorful painted motifs

A much-admired, truly indigenous American style is Pennsylvania Dutch (actually German). This example, made in 1780 of yellow pine and poplar, is painted with typical designs. (*The Metropolitan Museum of Art, Rogers Fund, 1923*)

similar to the "hex" signs so popular today. Woods were locally available varieties such as maple, walnut, pine, and fruitwoods.

Shaker (1776–1850)—The Shakers are a Quaker offshoot, and share the conviction of such groups against machinery, fancy frills, and almost everything nonreligious. Thus, Shaker furniture is severely functional, handmade, and totally lacking decoration. Paint or stain was occasionally allowed, but as often as not, a light coat of varnish was the only "decoration." By the same token, this devotion to hand work produced excellent craftsmanship, eye-appealing symmetry and line. Native pine was the main wood, with some maple and other hardwoods.

OTHER STYLES

There have been many other influences in furniture, notably Chinese, Turkish, and Moorish. Oriental designs, in particular, have been adopted by furniture makers ever since the first examples were brought back in the seventeenth century. The style has a classic, timeless quality that gives an impression of serenity and strength. Chinese furniture is direct and well proportioned, with heavy use of opaque lacquer and decoration.

Contemporary furniture can be said to have started in 1840 with the first steam-bent chair. Furniture made by that process became enormously popular and is still sought after today. With the success of "Bentwood," technology began to perfect other techniques for making furniture in factories. Since such furniture was necessarily limited in its use of carvings and elaborate decoration, designers made furniture that had beauty but could be turned out via mass production.

The greatest influence in contemporary design was the German Bauhaus, a school established in 1919. Its creed was that "form follows function." New materials were introduced to furniture design, such as chromeplated metal and plastics. Modular storage units were developed by members of the Bauhaus. Most kitchen furniture today is a direct descendant of the Bauhaus school.

Some of the more popular recent styles—in addition to eclectic—have been Mediterranean, a heavy handsome style which borrows from many other periods such as Gothic and the various Provincials; Danish modern, a spare, functional type with lots of oil-rubbed wood; and Modern, a continuation of contemporary styles, featuring metals, glass, vinyls, and other plastics.

As far as buying furniture is concerned, you can get almost any of the above-named styles in good and bad versions. Many of the so-called "new collections" are simply throwbacks to one of the older fashions described here. Now that you've read this chapter, you will be able to recognize them.

4

WHEN OLD AGE IS A VIRTUE

New furniture from a reputable manufacturer is likely to show good workmanship, and in some ways it's better than older furniture. The finishes, for one thing, are excellent, when properly applied. They can resist water, alcohol, even a mislaid cigarette.

But there are many things factory-manufactured furniture can't duplicate. The intricate carvings and fine decoration on some antique furniture are economically prohibitive to reproduce on today's pieces. And don't expect to find beautiful inlays or marquetry in the usual furniture store. It just isn't possible.

Most important, the wood in new furniture, though some of it is excellent for the purpose, isn't the same. Many woods, like walnut, mahogany, and rosewood, are simply too expensive to sell in the mass market. And what new wood lacks, no matter how costly, is the rich patina of older wood. Like the best Scotch whiskey, old wood has aged, mellowed, and acquired a rich, warm glow that cannot be duplicated in a raw, new state.

Fortunately, it does not require an expert eye to discern patina. You may have to look around a bit, but after you've seen some good examples of old wood versus new, you'll see it for yourself. It's something that's hard to describe and impossible to fake. The true furniture lover gets as much joy out of aged wood as the wine lover gets from a fine Burgundy.

WHAT MAKES AN ANTIQUE

According to the U.S. Customs Service, the official definition of an antique is an item made before 1830. If you import one, you pay no duty. Unofficially, an antique is generally regarded as something over 100 years old. Some antique collectors and dealers would stretch that definition to 50 years.

Sometimes an antique is loosely thought of as something that is collectable, an item that has value because of its uniqueness, or because it is hard

An old table—antique or junk? Although it's difficult for the layman to determine, this happens to be a truly valuable piece—an oak table from the Netherlands, created sometime in the seventeenth century. (*Rijksmuseum, Amsterdam*)

to get. The original Superman comic books, for example, are only a few decades old, yet command very high prices. Original Mickey Mouse watches date from around the same period, and also have a high value for collectors. A 1975 penny from the San Francisco mint is worth many times its face value because only a limited number were made.

In some ways, furniture follows that same general logic. A rare piece may have value simply because of its uniqueness. Louis XVI's *bureau du roi*, mentioned in the preceding chapter, is one of a kind. Even if it weren't so beautiful, it would have great value. It has even more value because it belonged to a king. (The same desk, if used by an unknown businessman, would be worth considerably less.)

Another consideration of value in an antique is the identity of its maker. This is a tricky one, however, and one that the buyer should be suspicious of. Porcelain, pottery, glass, silver, and other pieces usually are imprinted with the mark of the maker. Furniture ordinarily is not. If someone tells you a chair was made by Duncan Phyfe, how to prove or disprove it? There were thousands of imitators in Phyfe's own time—some inferior to, some as good as, and some superior to Phyfe himself. As a matter of fact, experts believe that the later furniture turned out by Phyfe was much inferior to his earlier work.

There are other dangers when searching for antiques. You may, for example, run across "authentic" Carver or Brewster chairs. The chairs were elaborate and thronelike, with many turned spindles. Many of those offered for sale look very old, and they probably are. But chances are good they were made during the Victorian era, when thousands of copies were made. After all, how many Pilgrims were there? And how many Brewsters or Carvers? How many authentic pieces are left today? Very few, and virtually all in museums.

BUYING ANTIQUES

The best way to buy a true antique is through a reputable antique dealer. That's hedging, of course, but it happens to be true. The problem is determining who is reputable. There is no easy way to tell who is reputable and who isn't. But there are certain clues:

- How long has he been in business? The longer the better.
- Will the dealer take back the piece if it turns out to be not as represented? Honest dealers can make honest mistakes and should cheerfully refund your money.
- Check the Better Business Bureau. It won't tell you exactly what you want to know, but it can clue you in on how many complaints, if any, have been lodged against the firm you're dealing with. Watch out for an outfit with more than a couple of complaints a year.
- Is the firm a member of one of the organizations of antique dealers? It's no sure sign, but it helps.
- Ask for references. Check with friends who have dealt with the dealer. What is their experience?
- Does the dealer level with you? Will he tell you, for example, that a certain piece is a reproduction, but a good one? It's unlikely that you'll find many genuine Chippendales or Tiffanies. Be suspicious if everything is "authentic" or "original." Have more faith if he tells you that a piece was made during a certain period, but is not necessarily an "original."

MAIL-ORDER FIRMS

A lot of unsavory people sell through the mails. Fortunately, these shysters are not too welcome when it comes to antiques. The various antiques publications try to be careful about accepting advertisements and generally you can trust ads in their pages. According to Ralph and Terry Kovel, whose antiques books are among the industry bibles, the mail-order firms that specialize in antiques are "99 percent honest."

AUCTIONS

Here we enter the world of *caveat emptor* (let the buyer beware). There are auctions and there are auctions. The large auction houses in New York City, for example, will send you illustrated catalogs and accept your bid by mail. Most are honest.

Local auctions are another matter. The vast majority of these are honest, too, but don't expect to pick up any great bargains. That country bumpkin who's selling off his great-aunt's relics may be a great deal sharper than you are. He isn't necessarily dishonest, but he isn't necessarily too candid, either. Often he may be as much in the dark as you are.

The rule here is to inspect the merchandise carefully before the auction. An honest auctioneer (who may or may not be expert in antiques) will allow you to come in a few days before the actual bidding to look over what he has for sale. You may not be able to tell whether a piece is authentic or not, but you can determine by careful inspection the condition of what you're bidding for. If the piece looks good, and it has the earmarks of what you're looking for, bid away. If it is in poor condition or doesn't appear to be what it is alleged to be, at least you will know ahead of time.

SOME TIPS ON AGING

If you plan on spending a healthy sum on a piece of furniture that is purported to be a true antique, it's worthwhile to make a few simple tests which will help verify its age. Here are some of them:

Fasteners—Somewhere in the piece there will probably be some nails and screws, if only inside (you may have trouble finding them without ripping the piece apart). Where fasteners do appear, you may get a clue as to the age. Screws were in use during the early eighteenth century, but they were hand-cut and quite imperfect. The threads were uneven and the slot at the top was off center and quite narrow. About 1818, machine-made screws appeared, but they had blunt ends until around 1845, when the modern, pointed-end screw appeared.

Until approximately 1820, nails were handmade. They, too, are very rough and wavy in appearance. Most had square heads. But the square head wasn't always used, and until around 1850, many of the new machine-cut nails were also made with square heads. So being square does not necessarily mean handmade. As a matter of fact, square-cut nails are being produced even now, and are available to the clever restorer. In general, however, rough-looking, square-headed nails are a good sign that the piece is pretty old. (Round-headed nails are a good sign that the piece is either new or was recently repaired.)

One caution here. Don't assume that the presence of new fasteners means that the piece is *not* an antique. An older piece has seen heavy use, and may have been repaired several times. New screws and nails would have been used to fix it. These are not objectionable as long as they are hidden from view. There is one thing you might do, however. Remove any new screws and check the screw hole. If it is a replacement screw, the screw hole will reflect the threads of the older one. Be wary if the screw-hole looks like a mirror image of the new screw.

Hardware—Many older pieces will have new hardware, and new pieces may have reproductions of old hardware. The hardware may help you to spot a truly old piece, but will not necessarily reveal a fake. It's a good idea to bring a magnet along (a small one you can put in your pocket and sneak out, if you're embarrassed). Try the magnet on the hardware. The hardware may look like brass or copper, but if the magnet clings to it, you have iron or steel.

Better drawer pulls are carefully beveled around the edges. If new hardware is used, check for plugged holes from the original. Older hinges were made of metal that was doubled over the pin; newer ones are a single piece on each side. Check the screws, as above, but you should know that there is some fine reproduction hardware that comes with the older-type screws.

Construction Details—You can't see the joinery details in good furniture, no matter what its age, except for the drawers. Pull out a few and look at them. They should be dovetailed, as discussed in Chapter 2, but now inspect the *number* of dovetails. The fewer there are, the older the piece. An eighteenth-century piece may have one large one, later antiques two to five. Also check the craftsmanship. If the dovetails were handmade, the pins and tails will be relatively rough and uneven. The spacing and size will be different. Smooth, perfectly spaced dovetailing is a sure sign of machine work. (But they were making machine dovetails in Victorian times, so the piece could still be fairly old.)

Check the backs of large pieces. In older furniture, large, thick boards were used, and in random widths. This is also the place to look for saw marks. The wood in most cases will have little or no "dressing" (see below). If the saw marks are straight, it probably dates to before 1850. If the marks are circular, it was surely made after that, because that's when the circular saw was invented.

Another clue to handmade furniture lies in the dressing. Instead of machine dressing, older cabinetmakers planed the wood by hand. No matter how skillful the craftsman, the plane left tiny grooves or hollows that a trained observer can feel just by running his fingers over the surface. You can try this yourself; or, if you can't tell that way, hold a straight edge across the grain and look at the light along the bottom. It should shine through the grooves.

Other tests of handmade work include checking two similar decorative features. A hand-carved chair finial (wood knob at the top of the back) is never an exact duplicate of the one on the other side. If it's made by machine, the parts will be identical. A handmade ball is never exactly round. A handmade table top is never exactly oval. There is, incidentally, a similar test that will tip you off to a fake. If you measure any rounded piece, such as a table leg, with a calipers (or even a tape measure), and find that it is almost exactly round, you know that the wood is relatively new. Wood shrinks over the years, and in only one direction. Anything that hasn't shrunk to at least slightly oval is of fairly recent vintage.

Another construction tip-off is the number of slats in a ladder-back chair, and the number of spindles in a Windsor chair. Here the rule is the opposite of the dovetail—the *more* slats or rungs, the older (and better) the chair. The oldest Windsor chairs have up to 13 spindles. Later ones had nine, the latest ones only four.

Wear—No matter how old a piece of furniture looks, be suspicious of anything that doesn't show some signs of wear. This doesn't mean it has to be beat-up to be old, but there are certain places that simply cannot escape symptoms of use. A chair seat, for example, should have a lighter color and be worn quite smooth from years of restless bottoms. The front rungs should be somewhat flattened on top from the soles of many shoes. A low cabinet door should have marks where it was kicked shut. The bottoms of chair legs should be worn from being dragged across the floor.

GOOD AND BAD ANTIQUES

It is not too difficult to distinguish an old piece of furniture from a new one. If it seems difficult at first, a little observation and reading can make it easier. The real difficulty comes when you want to distinguish a good antique from a bad one. Nearly all antiques have some value, but a particularly good one can bring a much higher price than an ordinary, or just plain bad, one.

This is where a reputable antique dealer is most valuable. If he knows his apples, he'll steer you to what is worthwhile, and you can do the same for yourself, if you want to devote the time and effort to research.

All we can do here is give you an example, so that you can see what the problem is (and how fascinating it can be). Take Queen Anne, for instance. This is a much admired and duplicated style. Assume that two hypothetical pieces were created around that period, both of them authentic. One is priced much higher than the other. Why?

Well, one was made in England, the other in America. The authentic British version is worth more, right? Wrong. It so happens that our American piece was made by the eminent William Savery, a Philadelphian who based his work on the early Queen Anne designs. These were simple, with graceful, clean lines. The later British cabinetmakers began embellishing the early designs with frivolous decoration, changing the classical lines, and in general creating a rather clumsy type of work. The pleasing curves of the original Queen Anne styling have been straightened, exaggerated, and bastardized in our hypothetical British version, rendering it of far less value than the American copy.

WHEN ALL IS SAID . . .

So, now we have a little insight into buying a true antique. But, when all is said and done, how practical is all this information? Not much, to tell the truth—at least not directly. The plain fact is that only a few of us have the wherewithal to buy a real antique. But it helps to have at least a background of knowledge so that maybe someday you'll be able to pick out a true gem at a garage sale, a Salvation Army store, or even the municipal dump. If you have some idea as to what it is you're looking for, you'll have a better chance of finding it.

We arrive now at the domain of the true furniture lover, those graveyards of the once-lovely but now downtrodden. All that's been said so far is merely background for the true quest—for a piece of furniture that can be rescued from the scrap heap and metamorphosed into something beautiful and useful.

Where do we begin? We could start in an antique shop. There are probably quite a few pieces there that could do with restoration, but the antique dealer wouldn't have them if they weren't worth something, and, in most cases, their cost is probably out of reach.

Most of us seek our finds in more pedestrian places—secondhand stores, Salvation Army and Goodwill stores, thrift shops, flea markets, and similar outlets. Auctions and tag sales are other likely spots. Even better are the cluttered basements and attics of friends and relations. They may be delighted to get rid of the clutter, and won't even charge you.

WHAT TO BUY

If Aunt Tillie offers you her old dining room set, or gives you free rein in her attic, the one thing you don't have to worry about is wasting money.

Not exactly a beauty, this old radio was found in a relative's basement. It can be sold for a fair price, or fixed up as a conversation piece.

You may lose a bit of time and labor carting the stuff home, but generally it's a good idea to take it regardless of whether it's what you want. Even if it isn't worth fixing up, parts may be useful as replacements on other pieces later. If you have never done any renovation, a piece from a friend's or relative's attic is a good place to start. Rather than practice on something valuable, test your mettle on something that isn't worth much to begin with. If it turns out badly, so be it. If it turns out well, you can probably find a place for it somewhere. Extra tables and chairs are always in demand.

It's a different story when you're laying out cash. Secondhand stores, Salvation Army-type outlets, and the like, are reasonable, but they don't exactly give things away. Here, caution is in order.

For your first attempt at repair and refinishing, it's best to try something small and easy. Look for a small end or night table. Avoid large, complicated pieces (or oak stairways). This is not to say that you can't do a decent job the first time around. If you see something more complex that looks like a good bargain, and you can't resist it, well, that's human nature. But if you're just looking for a suitable victim, choose something you can put in a corner somewhere if it doesn't turn out too well.

Whether you're a beginner or a seasoned hand at furniture repair, these guidelines apply:

- Buy something you can use. There's no point in going to a lot of work if you have no place for your handiwork, or it doesn't fit into your decorating scheme. You might be able to sell it, but not for anything approaching the value of your labor. (I once bought a beautiful Gothic chair, spent days restoring it, and had no place to put it. It was oversized, awkward, and out of place. When I moved, I sold it for peanuts.)
- Make sure it's repairable. A piece of furniture with an important part missing is a risky choice. If you're adept at the lathe, you can turn out a new leg or whatever, but most of us aren't that skilled.
- Don't buy something just because it's a good bargain. The original price is the least of the costs. The renovation materials cost something, but the most important factor is your labor. The piece may be a bargain because it's ugly, or too far gone for effective repair.
- Overlook fixable problems such as loose joints, crinkly finishes, and the like. It's your job to take care of those. Consider the finished product in your mind's eye.
- Look at design and construction. Are the overall lines good? Is it sturdy? If not, can these problems be overcome? You can saw off offensive finials, for example, or stiffen weak corners, but you can't do much for basic awkwardness or spindly legs.
- Can it be made into something else? You might not have much use for a highboy, but can it be truncated into a lowboy. Can a vanity be turned into a table? A high table into a cocktail table?

NOT DOING IT YOURSELF

It may hurt your pride to think that someone else can do a job better than you can, but if by some chance you happen onto something that's valuable, and you aren't sure of your abilities or experience, don't take a chance on ruining it. If Aunt Tillie's attic contains a real gem, don't experiment on it. Either wait until you acquire some experience, or turn it over to a professional restorer.

Perhaps you feel confident about one aspect of renovation, but not another. There's nothing shameful about that part of it being done profes-

Vanities like the one at left have little practical value in the modern home. All you have to do, though, is take off the mirror and casters, refinish, and—presto!—a very useful desk.

sionally. Wood refinishing is relatively easy, upholstery is not. So strip off the old upholstery, refinish the wood, then give the chair or couch to an experienced upholsterer.

Or maybe you just don't care for the mess involved in taking off the old finish. Take the piece to a strip shop. Most communities have one somewhere. The shop will probably have big vats of lye or remover, where the piece can be stripped quickly and fairly cheaply. You have only the fun part to do yourself.

5

A NEW LIFE MAY BE EASIER THAN YOU THINK

For the furniture fancier, a complete repair and refinishing job may be a labor of love, but it's labor nonetheless. Take heart, however, for a complete job isn't always necessary.

It is surprising, actually, what a little soap and water can do. You should always start your renovation with a good cleaning. It not only makes subsequent steps easier, but sometimes it may be all that the surface needs. (Structural repair is another matter entirely and is dealt with in the next chapter.)

If the piece is really grimy, you should go on to the next step and skip the wash, but where there is only surface dirt, it can be removed by scrubbing with white soap and water. Use the water sparingly, though, and dry the surface thoroughly afterward. Water is no friend of finishes, or of glue, either. A piece of old toweling will do as a tool here.

CLEANER-CONDITIONERS

A surface deeply embedded with dirt will take a stronger cleaner, one that is combined with healing oils, and is usually called a cleaner-conditioner or "Instant Furniture Refinisher." The label often promises that the product will restore furniture without stripping. If you can't find any, or don't want to pay the price, mix your own with three parts of boiled linseed oil and one part turpentine.

A cleaner-conditioner doesn't just clean. It helps restore natural color and grain, removes haziness, and often disguises small scratches. It will also take off most of the wax. (If the surface is heavily coated with wax, use pure turpentine or mineral spirits first, and rub hard to remove the wax.)

Apply the cleaner-conditioner with a lint-free cloth, such as an old diaper, and rub the liquid in thoroughly. Keep rubbing until the surface is clean and smooth. You don't have to dry it off because the ingredients are good for the wood.

In areas that are grease-stained or otherwise particularly bad, you may have to rub a little harder. If that doesn't do the trick, get some green hand soap from the drugstore and have a go with that.

By the time you're done with cleaning, you'll know whether or not you have to go any further. The cleaner may have done the job completely, or perhaps there are just a few spots remaining that can be fixed in one of the ways described in Chapter 7. If it looks okay as it, two or three coats of wax or polish will make it look even better.

If it still looks pretty bad all over, then complete removal of the finish is probably necessary. Or perhaps reamalgamation will work (see below). In any case, you haven't wasted your time. The finish remover or re-amalgamater will work better on a clean surface.

REAMALGAMATION

Reamalgamation is a blessed technique that can save a lot of time and effort on certain types of finishes and for certain types of problems. It works only for shellac and lacquer, however. It is *possible* to reamalgamate varnish, but it's so tricky and dangerous (acetone is the main ingredient) that you're better off removing the old varnish completely and starting over.

Obviously, you have to know what type of finish you have before you can try reamalgamation, but this isn't difficult (see Chapter 7). Use alcohol for shellac and lacquer thinner for lacquer. Regardless of whether the finish is shellac or lacquer, the process is the same.

The reamalgamation process is ideal for such problems as cracking, alligatoring, and haziness. Cracking, crazing, alligatoring, and crawling are technically different, but they all arise from the same cause. The finish is cracked in some type of pattern all over the surface, usually because of sitting in the hot sun or in a hot attic for a long period of time. Haziness, cloudiness, or blushing, all terms for an identical condition, occur when moisture, usually in the form of high humidity, creates a cloudy surface similar to the white ring that sometimes forms when a glass of water or mixed drink has been set down. Scattered haziness can be cured in the same manner as those white rings (see p. 101), but if it is widespread, reamalgamation is easier. And you can get rid of any accompanying alligatoring at the same time. (The two conditions often occur together.) A 2- or 2½-inch brush is the best size to use.

It is wise to experiment in a relatively inconspicuous spot, but the surface should also be as level as possible. A back or not-too-visible side is best. If you're doing this for the first time, and/or you're not sure the method will be effective, you might try a leg or rung, but the process works best when you have a large, horizontal surface to work on, and you might not be able to judge its effectiveness on legs or rungs.

Brush the solvent across the surface in long, wide, even strokes. Work first across the grain, then go over it again with the grain. What happens, in effect, is that you are dissolving the finish just enough so that it can be spread around again over the surface. The same finish is more or less "melted" and redistributed.

If one brushing against and with the grain doesn't work—and it probably won't for major damage—keep working the solvent over the surface a few times until the finish looks like new again.

You will find that shellac is considerably easier to work with than lacquer. Lacquer dries so quickly it's hard to deal with. Shellac dries more slowly, which means you can take your time. Sometimes, particularly in damp weather, shellac dries too slowly. You should generally avoid working with shellac when there is high humidity.

When working with either finish, you must be careful if the first two or three applications don't complete the job. As you add more and more solvent, you weaken the original finish, sometimes to the point where it is much too thin. Don't expect the surface to look perfect before it has a chance to dry. After the cracking or cloudiness disappears, there may be a few mild blemishes or brush marks. If you've already put on two or three coats, stop there, and let it dry. The minor blemishes may disappear upon drying. If not, try one more time.

When you're reasonably satisfied with the job, it is wise to lay on a coat of new shellac over the old shellac. If the lacquer coat looks pretty firm as is, leave it alone. If it appears rather thin, apply a new coat of brushing lacquer. After the last coat is dry, rub down the surface with fine 3/0 steel wool and add a coat of wax or polish.

You may run into a combination of shellac and lacquer that was used on some furniture between the Civil War and World War I. The solvent used for reamalgamation of this finish is three parts alcohol to one part lacquer thinner, used in the same way.

GOOD OLD-FASHIONED PAINT

If you find a piece of furniture with nice lines but a surface too beat-up to be refinishable, there's a very easy way to make it useful—with a coat of paint. This is not recommended where the wood is good and repairable. The natural color of wood is much nicer than any paint, in our opinion. But sometimes the wood isn't too pretty, either, even if it's in good shape. In such cases, the new, easy-to-apply enamels and semi-gloss enamels are just the thing.

Always sand thoroughly before painting and sand between coats.

If there are flaws, gouges, or whatever in the wood, they are easily repaired with a wood dough such as Plastic Wood. But don't use wood dough for clear finishing. It does not take stains well, and the patch will show.

ANTIQUING

Perhaps the most satisfactory treatment for a piece of furniture that has been through the wars is antiquing. This type of finish blends in well with traditional furniture, and can be used in any room, although regular enamels look best in kitchens and in modern settings. Antiquing is also an effective way of giving unfinished furniture the patina of old age.

Most paint manufacturers sell special antiquing kits with all the needed tools and materials. What the kits contain are base undercoat, a glaze finish, and usually some cheesecloth and a throwaway brush for application. The undercoat gives the piece its basic color, and the glaze (ordinarily a dark shade) is a thin, colored varnish. The antique effect is created by lighter applications of the glaze in the areas that are generally worn, giving the piece the look of being well used.

If the paint supplier has a color you like, there is not much point in making your own antique colors, but the choices are usually rather limited. In some stores, you buy your own base and a glaze of your choice, which gives you a wider range. Still, if none of these are suitable, it is possible to make your own glaze. (A wide range of base paints is usually available.)

For homemade glaze mix 3 tablespoons of gum turpentine, one tablespoon of varnish, and a teaspoon of the desired oil color or colors. The oil colors are available from artist supply houses, if not from your paint dealer. The most commonly used colors are the earth colors such as raw umber (grayish), burnt umber (brownish), raw sienna (reddish), and burnt sienna (reddish-brown). Any color that pleases you, however, is allowable.

When mixing, remember that oil colors are powerful, and a little goes a very long way. Err on the side of too little. You can always add more. Be sure to mix the ingredients thoroughly.

ANTIQUING TECHNIQUE

If you are using a kit, the manufacturer's instructions should be followed to the letter. The basic technique is about the same, but each brand may have its own peculiarities. Follow the steps below for homemade antiquing materials.

- Remove the gloss from the old surface with 3/0 steel wool, fine sandpaper, or liquid sanding solution, to provide tooth for the new finish.
- Wipe with a clean cloth, then a tack rag to remove the sandings, then apply the base coat as you would any other paint.
- With a wide, flat brush for large surfaces and a small one for turnings, coat one side of the piece with your glaze. Long even strokes, with the grain, are best. Paint any carved areas first, to allow more absorption

of the glaze. Flat areas should receive just a thin coat. Let the glaze stand for 10 to 20 minutes, then wipe with a clean, lint-free, soft cloth. Fold the cloth into a pad, and wipe with a circular motion, beginning in the center of each surface and wiping toward the edges. After each wiping, fold the cloth over and use a fresh side. Remember that the glaze is used to simulate wear, so leave those surfaces like chair seats and table tops with little or no glaze in the center, gradually increasing the tone toward the edges. Recesses and the lines in carvings get heavy doses of glaze because they get little wear. Don't try to remove too much glaze from them. Remove the excess with a dry brush.

- Go over the surface once again with a clean cheesecloth, then blend glaze with your dry brush. Wipe off excess glaze from the brush as you go along. These steps should be taken when most of the glaze has already been wiped up with your cloth. You'll find it easy to get the proper effect when there is only a thin film of glaze left to work with.
- If a wood-grain glaze is desired, instead of putting the glaze on and taking it off, dip your dry brush just slightly into the glaze and apply in long even strokes with the grain of the wood, using irregular lines to simulate the look of natural wood.
- Homemade glaze and some kit glazes (check manufacturer's recommendations) require a protective coat. After a day or so, when the glaze is completely dry, give the piece a coat of clear varnish. If using a certain brand of glaze, try to use varnish* from the same manufacturer. Two coats may be used if one doesn't seem tough enough.
- Treat the protective coat just like any other varnish finish (see Chapter 10).

LIMITED, SEVERE DAMAGE

Some furniture is in excellent shape, except for one part that is severely damaged. Sometimes a perfectly good table has a huge dent caused by an errant toy, for example, or a leg that has been chewed up by the family dog. The rest of the piece does not need refinishing, but it's unusable as is.

There are several things you can do. You can make a new part, find a similar one in your "parts pile," or find a way of covering up.

One way to fix a badly banged-up table top is to use a piece of contrasting inlay. But this is not easy for the unskilled, and the inlay should make some sort of pattern. If the damage is in the center of the table, you can

---

* To avoid confusion and repetition, the term "varnish" is used throughout this book to include natural and synthetic varnishes. The latter are called by a wide variety of names such as urethane, polyurethane, and plastic finish and are generally preferred to older types.

make a design there, but what if the damage is nearer the edge? You could repeat the design in undamaged parts to make it symmetrical, or redo the entire top (which is discussed below).

To install a veneer inlay, build up the damaged part below with wood dough or a piece of wood, but end just enough below the surface to leave room for the inlay (1/28 inch is the common thickness). Then glue in the new piece as described on p. 108.

There are, however, easier and simpler ways to repair or disguise this type of damage.

Distressing—An isolated dent or deep mark looks like an isolated dent or mark. A lot of isolated dents and deep marks look like distressed wood. New furniture is often distressed to make it look older. The wood is beaten with chains, hammers, bricks, and other objects. Figure out what type of dent yours was and what it was made by, and have a go at the whole piece with the same object.

Fancy Painting—Fill in the big gouge with some wood dough, then devise a pattern that will cover the repair and make it look like it was never there. You might run a wide stripe around a table top, or around a damaged leg that was filled with wood dough. Paint all the legs the same way. Ideal places for striping are in moldings or around the edges of a chair seat. If those parts are damaged or broken, fill them in first—or even replace the molding completely—and paint away. A large diamond, square, or circle can be painted right over a damaged area in a central spot.

If you're not sure how the design will look, draw it first in colored chalk. You won't get the full effect—which, admittedly, could be horrible—but you'll get a fair idea. If it doesn't look too bad, try it in paint. What can you lose? Actually, when it's done right, painted furniture can be extremely attractive, whether the furniture is damaged or not. The many techniques are thoroughly explored in *The Art of the Painted Finish for Furniture and Decoration* by Isabel O'Neil (Wm. Morrow & Co., Inc.).

When painting wider designs, which will probably be the case here, use a #6 sable brush. Smaller effects work out better with a #3. To use a brush free-hand, tap it carefully on the side of the container, and pull it along the surface with the arm fully extended. The shoulder muscle is the one that does most of the work. Hold the brush well up on the handle, with the bristles as far away as possible.

The worst thing you can do with an artist's brush is to be hesitant. The work will show it. Once you decide to paint something, go to it with gusto and courage. The strokes must be decisive, steady, and even. It helps to practice a little on some scrap wood. Confidence will come with time. But, if it doesn't, you can always outline your pattern with masking tape. You don't learn much that way, but you do get an even line.

One good technique with antiqued or other painted furniture is to use gilt that comes in a jar. It even looks nice, if used discreetly, on natural-finish wood. If the damaged spot is in the molding or a carving, you can build up the damaged section as described above, then apply the gilt with your finger over the damaged area and wherever else is needed for symmetry or to complete the effect. The gilt also comes in metallic colors other than gold, and may be used in conjunction with other finishing methods to add a touch of richness and color. You *can* use real gilt, but it's expensive and difficult. See Ms. O'Neil's book for details.

NEW TOPS AND SEATS

When a leg, rung, back, or other furniture part is missing or damaged beyond repair, a new piece must be bought or fabricated. This type of repair is beyond the scope of this book. Some types of repair, however, can be performed without any real knowledge of woodworking or structural repair.

TABLE TOPS

Replacement—The table top can be taken off, usually by removing screws in the frame that hold it down. You may have to pry off the top of a smaller table where the top is glued on. A new top of acrylic plastic, marble, or a part from another table can usually be adapted to fit the frame. You will find it difficult to get a piece of Plexiglas or Lucite large enough to fit a dining room table, but they're ideal for smaller tables. Acrylic plastic is sawn, drilled, and otherwise worked like wood. (Use a fine-tooth saw.) To attach it to the old frame, drill and countersink holes, and put in flat-headed bolts or screws. Glue will also hold the top down, but may loosen because of expansion and contraction of the wood beneath. The smaller the table, the better the glue will work. Follow manufacturers direction for type of glue and finishing the plastic.

Marble, granite, and other types of stone make handsome table tops. They are also available in sizes for large tables. Unlike acrylic plastic, these materials are very difficult to work with, and should be cut to exact size by the stone dealer. Place the new top over the old frame, and mark exactly where the bolt holes are in the frame. Drill holes into the stone with a ceramic bit, making sure to stop at least $\frac{1}{2}$ inch before you reach the top surface. Fill the hole with polyester glue and imbed bolts in this, thread-side out. When the glue has dried, attach the frame.

New Material over Old—Many new tables have laminated plastic tops, better known under one company's trade name—Formica. Though this material will never equal the beauty of genuine wood, it does come in surprisingly realistic-looking wood tones, complete with excellent grain simulation. For a table, dresser, or other top that is damaged beyond repair, a laminated plastic top will give an otherwise decent piece a new lease on life.

The old top should be prepared by filling all the holes and gouges, and sanding it down to make it level and to remove any gloss. A fairly rough surface should be left to provide tooth for the laminate. The surface must be free of all traces of wax, dirt, and any other substances that will interfere with good adhesion. A washdown with trisodium phosphate (TSP) provides good insurance.

The laminate should be cut with a fine-tooth saw with approximately ⅛ inch overhang to allow for edging (see below). You can clamp the laminate lightly to the table top and mark all around from below, or make a pattern if you find this easier.

Contact cement is the best adhesive for laminates, and for those who haven't used it before, be warned that the name is very apt. The adhesive is spread on both the surfaces to be joined, and is nonadhesive in that condition. But as soon as one cemented surface is placed onto the other, they are bonded together permanently. If the laminate is put down 1/32 of an inch off target, there's no way you can slide it over.

To prevent premature bonding, slick brown paper (available from your laminate dealer) is placed between the cemented parts. The top of the table and the bottom of the laminate are coated with cement and allowed to set, as directed by the manufacturer—usually for 15 minutes or more. The paper "slip sheet" is placed on the table top, and the laminate is placed carefully over it. The cement won't stick to the paper, and the laminate can be maneuvered into the exact position.

When you're satisfied that the laminate is in exactly the right position, pull out the slip sheet ever so slightly, holding the laminate down with your other hand. If the laminate moves, stop immediately and put it back into position. Keep pulling on the slip sheet until a small portion of the laminate sticks to the top. Check again carefully for positioning. At this point, if it isn't in the right position, you may be able to unstick the two and put them back together correctly. Assuming all is well, with one hand still holding the laminate, pull out the slip sheet a trifle more, all the time watching for any movement.

As the laminate begins to adhere to the top, keep pulling slowly on the slip sheet. When one edge is joined completely, you won't have to worry about the laminate slipping. You can pull out the slip sheet a little faster now, but still keep your hand lightly on the laminate. When about half of the surfaces are bonded together, you can pull out the paper entirely. Nothing in God's green earth is going to move it now.

Depending on the type of table, you may want to do the sides of the top too. You shouldn't need a slip sheet for this. Just make sure that the upper factory-cut edge butts against the top section.

A kraft paper slip sheet is placed between laminated plastic and table top to prevent adhesion of the contact cement before the top is properly positioned. (*Conwed Corporation*)

Once the job is done, the edges of the top are filed smooth. This looks better when the sides are done with the same material, but it'll be okay without. Tilt the file at a 45-degree angle, and go around the entire edge. A router bit is available to do a fast, neater job of this procedure. Just run the router around the top, and the bit grinds off the edges at the precise angle required.

You can, incidentally, hire a company that specializes in laminate work (usually a kitchen or bathroom supply house) to make an entirely new top for you. They will prefabricate the laminate with a particle board core,

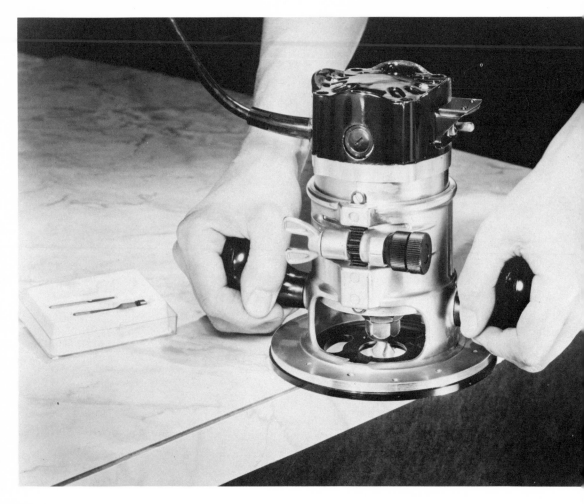

Laminate edges can be trimmed with a file, but it's much faster and more professional-looking when done with a carbide-tipped bit in a router. (*Black & Decker*)

much like a kitchen counter top. All you have to do is attach it to the frame. You pay for this convenience, of course.

A NEW CERAMIC TOP

Ceramic tiles make an interesting and carefree top, particularly for cocktail or other occasional tables. The tiles come in a wide variety of shapes, sizes, and colors at most dealers. You can use regular wall or floor tiles. For really interesting designs, however, the favorite is the one-foot square sheet containing small, 3/4-inch mosaic tiles on a paper backing. You can use the prearranged patterns, or make your own. Artistic designs are also available from the mosaic dealer.

Since the tiles will raise the table top ⅛ inch above the old surface, the table edges will have to be raised by that distance. One way of doing this is by also tiling around the edges, allowing the tiles to stick up ⅛ inch all around. Otherwise, you can glue thin wood strips around the edges, extending them above the old top by ⅛ inch. Use a compatible wood, wetting it first if it's to be used on curved surfaces. In any case, do the edging first. (Some tables already come with raised edges, in which case this step isn't necessary.)

LAYING MOSAIC TILES

Use special mosaic tile cement to attach the tiles. This same compound also serves as grout for this usage. Pour the cement powder into a shallow mixing bowl and trickle water into it slowly and carefully. Stir gently as you pour to avoid air bubbles. When the tile cement gets to the consistency of thick soup (check manufacturer's directions), tap the bowl lightly on the table to bring up any remaining air bubbles.

The mix is poured onto the surface to be worked and leveled with a small trowel, a flat knife, or your hands (if you don't mind that gooey feeling). The tile must be laid into the mix quickly and firmly. Smooth it down with the flat of your hand, starting in the center of the sheet and working out to the edges.

If you are working on a specialized design, you will probably be laying one tile at a time. In this event, lay the mastic only in that area you can lay before it dries. Check the manufacturer's directions for setting times.

Some squares have paper on the top of the tiles. Leave the paper on until the tiles are in place, then wet it with a sponge. Let it soak for about five minutes, then peel it off carefully. Wet the paper again if it doesn't come off easily. Try to avoid pulling up the tiles with the paper, but if they do come up, reset them. Remove any tiles that are set too low, add a little more cement on the bottom, and replace them.

Depending on the pattern and type of tile used, you may have to do a little or a lot of cutting. If just a few cuts have to be made, you can do it with a pair of slip-joint pliers. When extensive cutting must be done, a pair of special tile nippers will be needed. They aren't too expensive, and many tile dealers will rent or loan them to you. Either tool must be used carefully, taking off ⅛ inch or less at a time. Don't try to cut off large sections or the tile will surely crack.

If you're using large tiles, and a lot of cutting is anticipated, a tungsten carbide rod blade in a hacksaw frame will do the job. For many straight-line cuts, special tile cutters are handy. Always score the line well before breaking the tile, however. For just a few straight lines in a large tile, score with a glass cutter and lay the tile over a straight piece of narrow

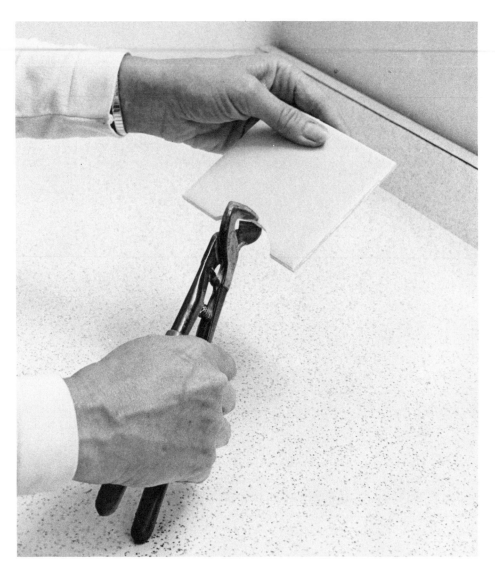

Tile is cut with special tile nippers shown. (*American Olean Tile Co.*)

metal like a nail or the long part of a coat hanger. Press down on both sides and the tile should break on the line.

For some types of tile (check manufacturer's instructions) enough cement should be laid so that the excess oozes up between the tiles. In this event, little or no grouting is necessary. If not, use the same mixture to grout between the lines. Some grouting will be unavoidable in any case, around the edges and other spots that aren't quite even. The grout used for flat surfaces should be level with the tile, because dirt will collect in the crevices. On vertical surfaces, the grout lines should be "tooled" with the back end of a toothbrush or a wet finger.

Most cement-grouts yellow with age, and a silicone sealer is necessary to retain the color. (Colored grouts, by the way, are available from some dealers, and make an interesting contrast.) If using mosaics, cover the entire surface with the sealer. Apply every few years to keep the grout from discoloring. Some newer grouts, however, do not turn color and may not need this treatment. Check with your dealer on this.

OTHER POSSIBILITIES

A fertile imagination will come up with other ways to cover damaged table tops. Leather is a terrific material for desks, but difficult to apply. Much easier, but satisfactory only for the short term, are adhesive papers like Contact and MagTag. Mirror squares, decoupage, and plate glass are other possibilities.

Wall coverings can be used to hide a badly damaged surface. This paper is made by Armstrong Cork Co. to go with its resilient flooring. (*Armstrong Cork Co.*)

CHAIR SEAT REPLACEMENT

Most modern dining chairs have a "slip seat," a piece of plywood or hardboard that is attached to the frame with screws. The wood is covered with upholstery or fabric. Many older chairs, and some modern ones, have woven seats of cane, rush, splint, or some form of twine.

Upholstered slip seats are easy to repair. They are usually attached to the frame with screws through the bottom. Remove the screws and the seat is loose. With a nail puller or the claw end of a hammer, remove the tacks that hold the upholstery in place. Staples can be removed with a staple puller or a screwdriver and pliers.

Gently lift off the fabric, being careful not to disturb the padding underneath. If the padding is pushed to one side, however, straighten it out as best you can. Replace any missing padding. (See Chapter 11 for more on upholstery.) Don't throw away the old seat cover, because that will serve as a pattern for the new one.

The old upholstery can be replaced with any fabric except one exactly like the old fabric. The wear and discoloration on the other chair seats will be even more noticeable by contrast. Try either for a complementary fabric or something entirely different. (This looks much better on the "host" chair than on a side chair.) Needlepoint makes an interesting variation, as shown in the photo opposite.

Cut the new piece as closely as possible to the old one, noting where the folds are, etc. Pull the fabric tightly all around and tack to the slip seat as it was before. When it is tight all around, screw the seat back on again.

CANING

Chairs with small holes drilled through the frame around the seat opening should have cane seats. A carefully woven cane seat is very strong and wears well. Seating cane, which comes from the rattan palm, differs from sugar cane and bamboo cane. Bamboo cane, which is shorter, straighter, and thicker, is used for furniture, walking sticks, poles, and the like. Neither bamboo nor sugar cane is suitable for chair seating.

You can buy cane at chair-seating and craftsmen's supply houses, at department stores, and mail-order houses such as the Cane & Basket Supply Co., 1283 So. Cochran Ave., Los Angeles, Calif. 90019. Buy long, select cane (from 15- to 18-foot lengths) for medium or large chair seats. Shorter lengths have to be tied more often. The best cane is smooth, glossy on the right side, tough, and pliable. The "eye," where the stem of the leaf grew out, should be smooth and unbroken.

Plastic cane is also available. It weaves easily, does not require soaking, is strong, and costs slightly less than other cane because little is wasted.

Needlepoint chair cover put new life into this Renaissance-type chair.

Its smooth, shiny texture is suitable for painted chairs, but does not look good on fine furniture.

If you are going to re-cane a chair seat, first cut away the old material with a keyhole saw. Clean out any nails, tacks, and pieces of broken cane or dirt from the holes and the seat rails. Drill through any holes that are plugged up. File down the inside of the frame so no sharp edges will cut the cane. Do any refinishing before starting to cane.

PREPARING THE CANE

Remove one strand of cane from the looped end of the hank, near where it is tied. Shake the hank as you pull to reduce the chance of tearing or tangling the cane. With the right or smooth side up, roll it up to fit into a soup bowl, fastening the ends with a clamp clothespin.

Fill the soup bowl with a cup of warm water and 1½ tablespoons of glycerine. Soak the cane in this solution for about 20 minutes, or until it is soft and easy to work.

WEAVING CANE

Weaving is done with the chair upright, working from the top of the seat. Vertical, or back-to-front, weaving is performed first; then horizontal (side to side), and then the diagonals. Beginning from the center each time helps insure that the rows of cane are woven in a straight line. Pegs are used both to hold the cane in place and to mark where the next roll of cane is to start.

First, count the holes in the back rail of the chair. If there is an odd number, begin in the center; if even, start in the row to the right of center. Insert a peg to mark the starter row. Now count the holes in the front rail and do the same thing there. The front rail will probably have more holes than the back, but worry about that when the time comes.

Remove one roll of cane from the bowl and wipe off the excess water with a cloth. Insert another roll to soak while you work on the first. Pull out the peg from the back row and push approximately four inches of one end down through the hole. Replace the peg to hold the cane. With the good, glossy side up, bring the roll to the front, remove the peg there, push the whole roll down through and refasten the peg.

Now push the cane up through the hole to the right of the peg, work to the back, and go down through the hole to the right of the back peg. Push the roll up through the adjacent hole, across, down through the next hole in front, down in back, etc. It's like lacing your shoes. Allow the cane to sag, however, just a little, so that it is slightly below the level of the seat frame. It should not be drawn tight. The right sag can be accomplished by pushing down lightly with one hand as shown.

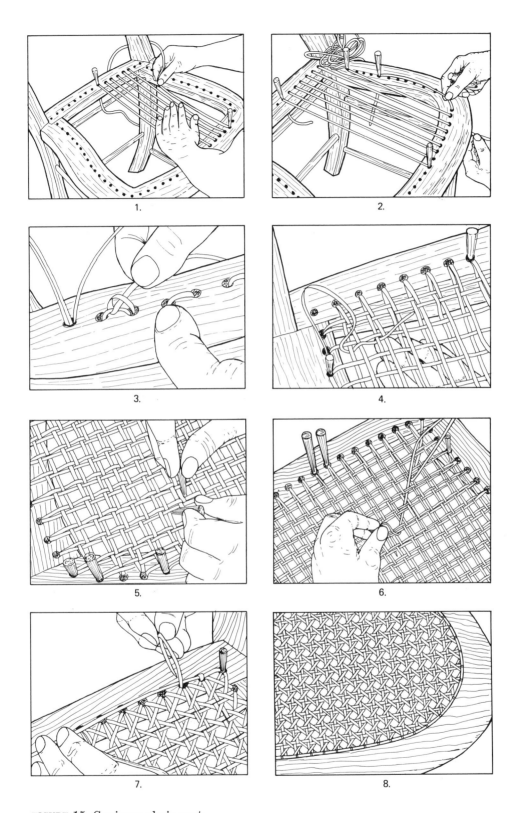

1.

2.

3.

4.

5.

6.

7.

8.

FIGURE 15. Caning a chair seat.

Continue weaving along the right side until you have gone through all the holes in which you can weave in a straight line from back to front. Never use corner holes at this stage unless they are big enough to handle eight pieces of cane. When you've covered all the usable holes, you will probably have cane left over on the roll. Don't cut it now. Push it out of the way and hold with a clamp clothes pin. Put a peg in the hole where you stopped.

Now do the left side of the chair seat in the same way, starting from the center and working to the left side. If you have extra holes in front, use separate pieces of cane between the front hole and a hole on the side that will give you a straight line.

SIDE-TO-SIDE WEAVING

Beginning at the right back corner, do the side-to-side weaving. Pull the cane up through the last hole on the right side (again leaving the very corner open), peg, and cross over the front-to-back cane. Go down through the opposite hole on the left side, back up the adjacent one, and over to the right again. All the horizontal cane in this step is woven on top of the front-to-back. Continue until you reach two opposing holes at the front. If there are extra holes because of a curving front, weave them with separate strands as directed above for vertical weaving.

SECOND ROW OF VERTICAL CANE

A second row of cane is now woven on top of the first vertical row. This series is done exactly like the first, except that it crosses over both of the other rows. Keep this row to the right of the first one as you go through the holes in the frame. Peg as in the first step.

When you reach the end of a roll of cane, or when tying separate pieces for curved areas, tie the ends of the cane to the loops formed on the underside of the adjacent holes. (see Figure 15C). Do the same for any other loose ends, so that all pegs are removed before beginning the next step. If necessary, moisten the ends of the cane so that they can be tied without breaking.

REAL WEAVING BEGINS

Although it's all part of the process, the steps so far have not been "weaving" in the technical sense. True weaving starts here, as you begin another side-to-side series. This time, start in the same corner as for the previous horizontal series, but insert the cane *over* the top row of vertical cane (the last one you did), and *under* the bottom row of front-to-back cane (the first row you did). As you weave, straighten the rows woven previously. When a third or so of the way across, pull the rolled length of cane all the way through, keeping your hand on top of the cane at a level with the frame. Lifting up may cause the weaving strip to cut the canes already in place.

Continue weaving in this same manner, following the same pattern as for the first row of side-to-side. Keep straightening and pulling, then restraightening, drawing the pairs of cane together as you go. You will now begin to notice a true caned look. The four strips of cane should all be interlocked as shown in Figure 15D. Keep pegs in the previous row until you complete the one beneath. When you finish each row, check to see that the second vertical rows of cane are on top and to the right of the first front-to-back rows.

Complete the weaving by using individual strips for curved front or sides, then soak the entire cane seat with a sponge or cloth. Restraighten all the rows and force the appropriate pairs together so that there are hollow squares throughout with interlocking rows of cane in each corner of the square. Pegs are convenient for this purpose, used as shown in Figure 15E.

DIAGONAL WEAVING

The next step is diagonal weaving. Starting at the right back corner, begin weaving, as above, toward the front left corner. This time, weave the cane *over* the *two* vertical rows and *under* both side-to-side rows. Weave with one hand on top and other underneath. Pull through, straighten, etc., as for the previous step. The next row goes to the left and back of the first row. You may have to moisten the cane to get it through the holes, since there are two cane pieces in each hole already. Continue weaving toward the left and back until you get about half of it done. Now check the number of holes left on each end. If there are more holes on the side than the front, which is likely, you have to improvise a little. Skip some holes in the side and/or double up on holes in back, "fishheading" the double-up hole so that the cane goes on opposite sides of the cane already woven.

When that section is finished, tie ends as previously mentioned and proceed to the front-right part of the seat. Start in the front left corner and weave toward the back right corner. This time, do the right and front holes in the same manner as the back and left.

When these diagonals are finished, start with the opposite diagonals— back left to front right. This time, weave *under* the pairs running from back to front and *over* the ones running from side to side. Use the same technique as for the other diagonals. Where holes were skipped or doubled-up, double up in previously skipped holes, and skip those that were previously doubled up.

THE BINDER CANE

The next and final step is application of the binder cane. Binder cane is slightly wider than the cane used for weaving. It is used to cover the holes and finish off the edges. If the seat is curved, use one long strip to go around the entire frame. If the corners are square or almost so, cut separate lengths, each six to eight inches longer than the distance between the corner holes.

The binder cane itself is not woven. Center it over the area to be bound, then push it down through a corner hole and peg tightly. Take a length of weaving cane that is wet and pliable, and push the weaving cane up and over the binder, then back through the same hole. Do this with every other hole if the holes are very close together. Choose a piece of weaving cane long enough to tie the entire binder in place. Since the holes will be quite full already, you will probably have to force the weaving cane through the holes with a scratch awl or a bone knitting needle. Keep the cane flat and tight. Also make sure that both weaver and binder canes are right-side up.

Repeat the same process on each side of the frame. If the corners of the binder cane do not lie flat, check to see that all of the cane—weaving and binder—is in place, then hammer in the pegs as far as you can without breaking the cane. Saw or file off the top of the pegs and sand down to the level of the frame.

Now it's done. If you've gotten everything right, you should be very proud of your work. When the cane is good and dry, sit down, relax, and pour yourself a drink to celebrate.

USING PRE-WOVEN CANE

One easy way to weave chair seats is with pre-woven cane. To use it, however, the seat must have a groove around the inside edge, with a wooden spline to hold the edges of the cane. You cannot use pre-woven cane for the typical caned seat with holes around the edges. The ends of pre-woven cane cannot be tied properly without a groove and spline.

With a groove-and-spline chair, first remove the spline. Save the spline if it's still in good shape. If not, buy a new one from your cane dealer. Set the pre-woven cane over the open area, tack it down temporarily, and cut it on all sides just slightly beyond the groove. A new razor blade or X-acto knife is best for this. Soak the spline in water meanwhile to let it get wet and pliable.

Fit the spline into the groove, and cut off the excess (if new) with a sharp knife. Check the old spline, if reusing, to see that it fits correctly. When satisfied with the fit, put the spline aside, but keep it damp.

Now apply an even layer of glue inside the groove. Dampen the ends of the pre-woven cane placed over the frame. Drive the ends of the cane into the groove with a wooden mallet and a scrap of hardwood wedge, beginning at the back of the seat. Leave the wedge in place at the center back, then drive the sides into the groove. Finally, drive the front of the cane into the groove, using additional wedges if necessary. Cut off any excess outside the edge of the groove.

After the glue dries, remove the wedges. Spread another thin layer of glue in the groove, then place the spline over the groove. Drive the spline firmly into the groove with a wooden mallet and an overturned wedge. Move the wedge all around the spline, striking firm, light blows with the mallet. When the spline is in place, let the glue dry and cut off any excess cane outside the spline.

"RUSHING IT"

If you're in a hurry for a new seat, don't "rush" it. Although it makes a beautiful chair, rushwork is time-consuming, and takes considerable skill and patience. It is used almost exclusively on spindle-and-post chairs, and requires padding in between top and bottom layers.

Splint (see below) is often used in place of rush, but rush looks better and is preferred for more formal settings. The difference in cost is very small when purchased (at the same supply centers mentioned above), and in many areas rush can be had for the taking. Uncured rush is available in marshlands of the northern U.S. and southern Canada, and in other lands with similar vegetation. It is gathered from cattails, whose "flower" is the familiar cigarlike "bob."

If you wish to pick up your own free rush from local wetlands, seek out the narrow-leafed cattail. Broad-leafed cattails, whose leaves are about an inch wide, are easier to find, but more difficult to work with. Search for the thinner leaves, in seven-foot or longer lengths. Late July, August, or early September, when the leaves are full-grown, is the best time for "rushing." Look for perfect leaves from stalks that do not have the bob, and cut just above the water (or ground). Leaves shrink at least a third as they cure, so be sure to gather an ample supply.

CURING AND PREPARING RUSH

Discard all stalks. Sort the leaves, placing those of the same width and length together, and tie them into loose, flat bundles. Be careful not to bend or break the leaves. Dry thoroughly for at least two or three weeks in a dark, airy room like an attic or storeroom. Do not put the leaves in a damp room, such as a cellar, where mildew might form on the leaves, or in a hot or sunny room where leaves might become brittle.

When thoroughly dried, dampen the rush until it is workable enough to twist and weave without cracking or breaking. This may take an hour's soaking. Fill a trough about three-fourths full of warm water. Add about one cup of glycerine until the water feels soft.

Rush is prepared by twisting two or more leaves into strands. Choose long, unbroken leaves of about the same length, width, and thickness. The number of leaves in each strand depends not only on the width of the leaves but on the size of strand you want. Usually, two leaves are twisted together; if they are narrow or thin, three may be used. A thin strand is best for a graceful, delicate chair. Lots of strands are needed to fill the seat, however, and the thicker they are, the faster the job.

Run the leaves through a wringer to take out air from the cells and to make the leaves workable. Set the rollers tight so that the leaves make a sharp, crackling noise as they are run through. Draw each leaf quickly over the edge of a letter opener or similar instrument, to remove any air that may be left in the cells.

FIBER RUSH

Fiber rush is made from a very tough, dark brown paper, twisted into a strand to resemble rush. It may be purchased in widths of $\frac{3}{32}$ inch, $\frac{1}{8}$ inch, $\frac{5}{32}$ inch, and $\frac{3}{16}$ inch to simulate antique rush seats, and in multicolored $\frac{3}{16}$ inch strands for new seats. It comes pre-twisted.

Buy the fiber in 1-pound or 2-pound lots or in quantity on a large reel. Pound lots cost a few cents more; reels take time and patience to unroll and rewind. Handle rush on a reel as you would wire; roll and unroll it rather than pull it. Take off about 25 yards to work with at one time. Tie the end to a nearby strand, and wind it in a roll about six inches across. Tie string in a slipknot around the roll so that it won't unwind or untwist.

SPLINT AND REED

True splint is narrow, very thin, long strips of wood from ash and hickory trees, as well as from the tropical palm (which, interestingly, also gives us cane, rattan, and reed). "Splint" is often used erroneously to refer to reed or wide cane. About the only type of chair that can be reseated with splint or flat reed (see below) is the spindle chair discussed above. It is best suited for simple chairs with few turnings, such as the Early American ladder-back. It is often used when the side rails are higher than those in front and back.

For those who have never worked with splint, flat reed (another tall grass) is similar and easier to use. Reed is not as satisfactory as splint, but will give you practice for working with splint. Wide cane also is often used for the same purpose.

Splint and flat reed are used interchangeably indoors. For outside furniture, flat oval reed and wide binding cane are substituted, using the same procedure. All of these materials can be purchased from the same sources previously mentioned. Paper splint is also available, but you really shouldn't bother with it, since it isn't very durable and not worth the small savings in price.

Whether you are using splint or some type of reed, one pound should do for the average-size seat of 16 inches across the front. Wide binding cane comes in bunches, with 500 feet ample for the average chair. Most of these materials come in varying widths, with the best size usually somewhere in the middle range. If it's too wide, the seat will look dumpy. If it's too narrow, it may take a much longer time than is necessary.

The exact procedures for working with rush, splint, and reed are rather complex. They are described in *Furniture Repair and Refinishing,* by this author and Richard Demske (Reston, 1974).

One last caution—all other repair and refinishing chores should be completed before repairing tops and seats.

Rush, cane, etc., should receive the same protection as any other raw material. A penetrating sealer should be applied to cane and splint. A mixture of half turpentine and half raw linseed oil is best for rush. Stains can be applied first to approximate the color of the wood if desired. Other finishing methods, as described in Chapter 10, can often be used. Check your dealer as to which finishing techniques may apply to your materials.

6

STRUCTURAL REPAIR

The preceding chapter dealt with some ways of restoring furniture without getting into a structural repair or removing the entire finish. Now we get into the nitty-gritty.

Chairs with loose legs and arms, worn drawers, warped table tops, and other problems caused by wear or poor original construction need structural repair. Many of these tasks are more difficult than those in Chapter 5 in that they require some woodworking skill. On the other hand, regluing joints takes less skill and effort than, say, hand-painting a gouged table top.

Whether you can tackle these jobs yourself depends on the type of problem and the amount of knowledge or experience you have. Anyone can take a chair apart and reglue it (taking it apart can actually be fun). There may be a few surprises in joint construction, but there's nothing that most people can't handle. If you've never handled a power saw before, however, don't attempt to cure a warp with wedged splines (see p. 95).

If you haven't read the section on joinery (pp. 14–17), by all means do so now. Those surprises mentioned above will not be quite so rude if you have an idea of what to expect. You'll have less chance of ruining a complex joint by pulling it apart if you have an inkling as to what type of joints are used where.

Fortunately for the furniture repairman, the better joints usually stay put. It's the simple joint that most often loosens, and is easier to put back together.

Unless the piece is otherwise in excellent shape, so that you know exactly what the problem is, it's a good idea to take inventory. Something salvaged from the junk pile or Aunt Tillie's attic may have a multitude of flaws. Put the piece up on your work platform and examine it carefully. Rock it a bit and note where the joints wiggle. Look for broken parts, missing hardware, surface gouges, warps, loose veneer, etc. Open doors and drawers and see if there is sticking or wobbling.

After you've made your list, decide the order in which things must be done. Missing hardware is the last item of business. Construction flaws are first. There's no point, for example, in doing a complete refinishing job only to discover that the table sways when you lean on it.

THE FUN PART

If your prospective victim has more than one or two loose joints, you may as well take the whole thing apart—or at least that section that's causing problems. A loose or broken chair stretcher, for example, usually means that the legs will be loose where they meet the seat. Check carefully to see how much overall looseness there is. Even if most of the joints seem solid, you will probably cause more looseness yourself when you spread the legs to remove the offending stretcher.

Chair rungs and legs are usually easy to take apart. They may be so loose that simply pulling on them will do the job. In the wooden kitchen chair shown on page 86 which has the type of construction often found on Colonial-style chairs as well as others, the stretchers are treated as one long, thick dowel (which, in fact, they are) and are inserted and glued into drilled holes. Other doweled joints, such as where the seat frame joins the legs, are similar. These joints can be easily knocked apart with a wooden or rubber mallet. If you don't have a mallet, wrap some rags around a claw hammer and have a go with that.

If you find that the joints don't come apart easily, you may find that you've overlooked a hidden screw. Check carefully to see if screws have been used. They may be covered with a wooden plug. Wood buttons often mask screw heads in cheaper furniture. The buttons are easily removed by prying them up with a screwdriver tip. Plugs take a little more work. If they are loose, they can sometimes be dislodged with an awl or a sharp knife point. Otherwise, they will have to be broken or drilled out. Obviously, you will have to replace them. A piece of hardwood dowel, as close a match as possible, should do the trick. Or use stick shellac for all or part of the fill (see p. 105).

Screws may come right out, or they may be a little sticky. Make sure that your screwdriver bit fits the slot exactly. Really stubborn screws will usually respond to a screwdriver bit in a brace, which gives you a lot more leverage. Give it a quick twist, first counterclockwise, then clockwise, to get it started.

Mortise-and-tenon joints should come apart in the same way. They don't loosen often, but when they give, as when older wood shrinks, they come apart easily. (See p. 91 for broken tenons.) A dovetail joint either holds or it doesn't. When a dovetail gives, the joint will fall apart by itself.

You may be surprised to find that, after you take certain joints apart, everything else just falls asunder. Take apart the frame of a dresser, for example, and all the panels simply fall out. Or, if you take apart the outer rails of a Windsor chair, all the spindles tumble to the floor. The panels that make up the sides of chests or other large pieces are allowed to "float" in their frames, to avoid warping or cracking due to expansion. Backrests of Windsor and other chairs follow somewhat the same principle. The outer frame is securely fastened to the seat, and the splats or inner spindles are attached with little or no glue.

If your spindle chair is fairly old, you may run into an unusual joint used by certain furniture makers. To make this type of joint, a piece of dry wood was shaped with knobs at the ends. The knobs fit into sockets in a part that was fashioned of green (unseasoned) wood, which later dried and shrank. As the green wood self-seasons over the years, the joint gets tighter and tighter. Eventually, however, there is a point of diminishing returns. The shrinking process stops, and wear and tear begins to take its toll. The joint loosens up, but the knob still prevents the rung from coming out. If you know there aren't any fasteners holding the joint together, but the part still won't come out by pulling or hitting with the mallet, you may have one of these joints. The only way to fix this is to force glue into the joint. Better yet, if you have one, use the glue injector recommended in Chapter 1.

ALL ABOUT ADHESIVES

An adhesive is something that holds things together. Sometimes it works, sometimes it doesn't, and some are better than others, depending on the two "parties" involved. There has been a bewildering influx of new types and brands over the past several decades, as any TV-watcher knows. Well, you don't have to hold up a man on a steel beam with one drop while working with furniture, and the super, crazy, or other fantastic glues can be left for those who need their cars raised into the air.

Most furniture work uses rather standard adhesives, and old-fashioned hide glue is as good as anything for most jobs. "White" or polyvinyl acetate glues like Elmer's have wide application for furniture use, as do caseins, plastic resins, and contact cements. Resorcinol glues are best for outdoor work, with epoxy resins a court of last resort when all else fails. (See Appendix B.)

The furniture lover is often confused as to what is best for what. There aren't any ready answers, but a consideration of the following factors should help you make up your mind:
  • Are the materials the same? If you are bonding acrylic plastic to wood, for example, the dissimilar materials expand and contract at different rates. The adhesive used must be flexible and "give," or the bond will break. Wood-to-wood bonds are usually easy, with several choices

available. When bonding other materials to wood, ask the manufacturer or dealer of the nonwood product what the best choice is.

- Is the material porous or nonporous? If you try to bond two metals together, for example, you must use an adhesive which cures by chemical action, or a contact cement, rather than one that releases a solvent. If the solvent cannot be absorbed, the adhesive cannot dry or set.
- What is the final use—and where? Outdoors, a waterproof adhesive, like the resorcinols, must be used. For veneers, which may be attacked by liquids, a water-resistant glue like casein should be used. Hide glue is inferior for this purpose, since it deteriorates from moisture. On any area where glue might stain, glues that dry clear must be used.
- What is the "glue line"? The glue line means the space between the two surfaces. Plastic resin glues, for example, cannot be used unless the two parts fit tightly and exactly together. They require a "thin glue line." Casein and white glues fill gaps well.

Follow these general guidelines:

All Purpose—Old-fashioned hide glue is hard to beat for general use, but choose something else where there is potential water damage.

High-Strength Areas—Where there is considerable strain on joints, and the joints are a little ill-fitting, use casein glue.

Medium-Strength Areas—When you want a quick and easy job, and great strength isn't a factor (not to imply that the glue is weak), white glue is perfect.

Edge-to-Edge-Gluing—In areas where you need a strong joint and there is a thin glue line, plastic resins like Weldwood are best.

Outside Use—Resorcinol is the only thing to use.

"Impossible" Jobs—Epoxy resins.

USING GLUE

Finding out which glue to use is not really difficult. For many jobs, several types will do. Be sure to read the manufacturer's instructions, though. Some of the older types of glue should be heated, some come in powders and have to be mixed, etc. Most are not difficult to prepare or apply.

Careful preparation of the wood is important. No adhesive will work properly when the surfaces are dirty, oily, or slick. Old glue is like yesterday's gardenias. Scrape or sand off all traces of the old stuff. If you use a sharp knife or power sander, be sure not to remove too much wood along with the glue, because that will leave a gap or widen the glue line. Also, don't try to leave the surface silky smooth—a little roughness provides better tooth. Use a medium-grade sandpaper, not the finer grades.

Two of the many ways of using a belt clamp are for holding drawers together (1), and for keeping strip veneer tight to the sides of a table top (2). A belt clamp may also be used instead of the rope tourniquet illustrated on p. 86. (*Adjustable Clamp Co.*)

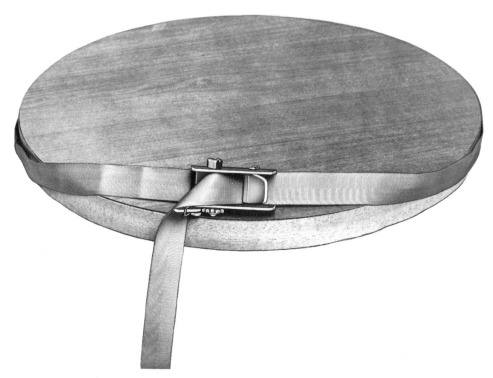

Another precaution is to stay away from cold temperatures while working with glue. Ordinarily, this shouldn't be a problem, but if you're working in a cold basement or unheated garage, move the piece to a warmer section of the house, at least until the glue dries. Most adhesives do poorly in cold temperatures. If moving your project into the house will result in protests from others in the family, buy or borrow an electric heater—or wait until summer.

CLAMPING

Although contact cement needs no clamping, because of its instant bond, most adhesives require some sort of pressure to be effective. You *can* work without clamps. But holding a chair together for two to 24 hours isn't most people's idea of a pleasant pastime.

Some jobs can be done without clamping. If downward pressure is all that's needed, as in gluing veneer, or legs into chair seats, heavy weights pressing down on the glued materials work well enough. Rocks, books, concrete blocks, or other heavy materials can be piled on and left overnight.

Another excellent non-clamp is the tourniquet. As a matter of fact, it is the best type of pressure-applier for some of the difficult repairs like the entire bottoms or tops of chairs. There are belt clamps available for this job, and they are easier to use, but an old cabinetmaker's trick is take a piece of rope, tie it around the legs or back of the chair, then apply even greater pressure by twisting a stick through the rope. The stick is kept from flying back by resting it against one of the legs or spindles. Insert some rags, newspaper, or other material where the rope bites into the wood to keep it from damaging the surface.

You can't do everything with rocks and ropes, though. You'll need at least some commercial clamps. The more work you do, the more use you'll have for bar clamps, wood clamps, and C-clamps. Pipe clamps are also handy to have around for extra-long jobs. For pipe clamps, you'll also need assorted lengths of pipes, threaded on one end to match the clamps. Clamps and pipe are available in either ½-inch or ¾-inch sizes.

Wood Clamps—Used to hold two smaller pieces together, or to clamp one piece of wood to a larger one where the width is not great. They can also apply pressure at an angle. Although they come in jaw openings up to 15 inches, the smaller ones are used more often. Bar or pipe clamps are used for longer stretches. At first, you may find the hand screws on wood clamps awkward to operate, but a quick and easy way is to grip one handle in each hand and swing the clamp around until the jaw opens or closes to the desired distance.

To use the wood clamp, open to a width slightly wider than the distance

To use a rope tourniquet, tie the rope around the glued parts (1), twist tightly, then let the edge of the stick rest against the chair leg (2) to prevent it from untwisting.

(*Adjustable Clamp Co.*)

to be spanned, then tighten the screws until the wood grips firmly and evenly. Tighten the outer screw one extra time for added tension. There should be no spaces between the jaws and the wood anywhere. Padding is unnecessary as long as you don't apply too much pressure.

C-Clamps—Used for small, spot jobs, such as repairing a broken chair rung or gluing down a chip. They come in assorted sizes, some very large, but for our purposes all you'll need are the small ones. C-clamps have harsh metal jaws, so a thin piece of wood must be placed in between the jaws and the wood being clamped.

Bar Clamps and Pipe Clamps—Come in very handy when spanning a fairly wide surface like the back of a dresser. The jaws of a bar clamp are

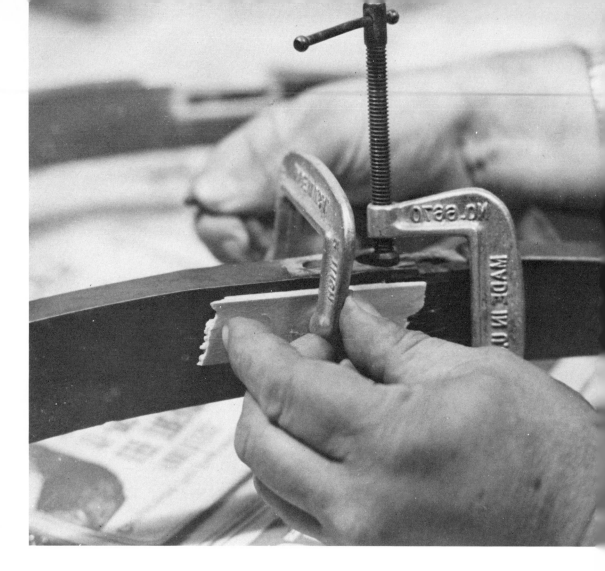

opened up by sliding the movable section down the bar until it is just a little larger than the span to be bridged. The screw-on end is pressed against the edge (again with a thin piece of wood inserted) and tightened until the proper pressure is achieved.

Pipe clamps are not self-contained, as bar clamps are. When you buy pipe clamps, you have to buy the pipe to match, from either a plumbing or hardware store. One end of the pipe is threaded to hold the stationary clamp. The other part of the clamp moves up and down the pipe to span whatever distance you need. Theoretically, there is no limit to the length of a pipe clamp.

Other Clamps—You can make your own wooden wedge clamps, which are useful for such jobs as edge-to-edge gluing. Wedge clamps are made of a rectangular piece of fairly thick stock ($3/4$ to one inch is best), which is marked a half-inch from each edge and cut down the diagonal to form two right triangles (almost). The pieces to be glued are laid on a wooden surface such as a platform, with the outside piece braced against a wall or other solid surface. Lay waxed paper under the glued area to prevent sticking. Put the two wedge pieces together as they were before cutting, then nail down the outside one, leaving the nail heads protruding slightly for later removal (or use double-headed nails). Then force the remaining wedge between the other wedge and the work by tapping with a hammer. If the wood to be glued is thin, weight it down to keep it from buckling.

There are also special corner clamps for gluing miters and other difficult joints.

Bar clamps are self-contained and are excellent for semi-long glue jobs. Pipe clamps (not shown) are similar at the ends, but utilize steel pipe between. (*Adjustable Clamp Co.*)

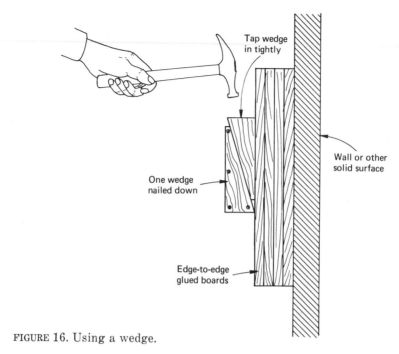

FIGURE 16. Using a wedge.

SPECIAL PROBLEMS

Given the right surface preparation, proper gluing, and clamping pressure, you should be able to repair almost any piece of furniture. There are a few special problems you may run into, though. Here are some of the most common:

Wobbly Chairs—Once the underpinning of a chair starts to go, everything seems to go with it. The first thing to do is to check and see if the parts will be tight when you glue them back together. The run-to-leg joints are usually all right, but often the joint where the leg is fastened to the seat will have widened due to friction from the errant leg. Ordinary glue won't hold this unless the gap between the pieces is narrowed.

Loose sockets can be filled up with toothpicks and wood matches. Another way is to saw a kerf down the middle of the leg top, filling it with a hardwood spline just slightly larger than the kerf. Tap the spline down until it expands the leg enough to make it fit tightly into the socket.

If the pieces to be joined are thick enough, you can insert a dowel through the socket and the leg. Drill the holes carefully with a hand drill or drill press. Use a bit of the exact diameter as the dowel, holding the wood carefully to make sure that the holes are vertical. A woodworking vise is advised here. Grooved dowels allow more glue surfaces and insure a tighter joint but straight dowels, roughened with a rasp or file, are fine, too.

Before gluing up the joint, test the dowels to see if they fit tightly without binding. If the holes are misaligned, plug up the existing holes and drill new ones. Trying to redrill the same holes is futile. Once alignment is satisfactory, apply a generous amount of glue (preferably casein) to both dowels and holes and clamp the pieces together.

When dowels were used in the original construction (or previous repair) and are broken, new dowels must be used. To remove old dowels, use an auger bit with a brace. If old corner blocks have broken, they must be glued back together separately, then reapplied. If the old blocks are in bad shape, you can try fabricating new ones. If nothing else works, wood or metal braces may be substituted to produce the required strength.

Using Dowels—There are many cases where a joint, split, or other defect can be repaired by the use of dowels. Some of these have been indicated here, and other uses will come to you as you proceed. There are times when dowel work does not require a high degree of accuracy, as in many end-to-side joints. The beginner is urged to try his luck there, and not attempt to use dowels in low-tolerance jobs such as edge-to-edge boards in a table top. When putting two boards together edge to edge, dowels are often helpful in adding strength and reducing warpage. To use dowels in this way, however, accuracy is vitally important. Any slight displacement of the dowel will result in unevenness which is difficult to correct. A dowel jig is invaluable in such cases to insure correct alignment, although dowel pins are also helpful if you don't have a jig.

After all the holes have been drilled in one side, insert dowel pins into each hole and very carefully line up the other side. When both pieces are exactly in place, press the undrilled piece onto the pins and the points will indicate exactly where to center the drill bit.

Holes on both sides should be countersunk to collect excess glue and provide greater strength. Use bar clamps or homemade wedges to press edges together.

Repairing Tenons—Since the mortise-and-tenon joint is usually a secure one, it seldom falls apart due to glue failure or other natural causes. If it does, the joint is simply stripped of old glue and put back together as described above. Sometimes, however, a tenon will break due to extreme pressure, weakness in the wood, or other causes. When that happens, the only real solution is to make a new double tenon (actually a large spline).

To make a double tenon, dig out the parts of the old tenon that remain in the mortise, and cut off the section that protrudes. Make a new mortise where the old tenon was, more or less matching the existing mortise. A blind mortise—one that does not extend to the top of the part—is best, but it is much simpler to extend the new mortise to the top of the part if you find a blind one too difficult.

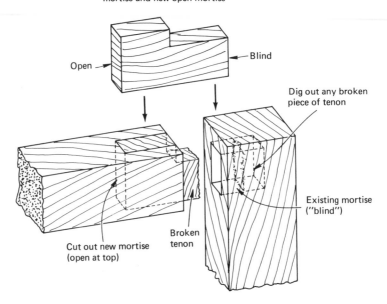

Double tenon cut to fit old blind
mortise and new open mortise

Open

Blind

Dig out any broken
piece of tenon

Existing mortise
("blind")

Broken
tenon

Cut out new mortise
(open at top)

FIGURE 17. Cutting a new double tenon to replace a broken one.

Fabricate a new piece to fit into both mortises. It should fill the mortises as precisely as possible, but don't worry if it's a little off. If you fill the joint with plenty of glue (hide or casein in this case), the glue will plug any gaps. Any joint that is subject to severe stresses may be reinforced by crossing the tenon with small dowels into each section.

Sticky Drawers—Cheaply made drawers will often stick or wobble because of poor or nonexistent glides (see Chapter 2). On better used furniture, you'll often find missing, broken, or worn runners (bottom edges). You can replace these easily with a piece of scrap hardwood and some brads. If the runners are not separate parts, plane down the bottom parts of the drawer sides till level, then install separate runners made out of thin strips of hardwood.

Sometimes drawers stick because of unevenness of the chest itself, which pinches the drawers. For an easy cure, check with a level and put something under the short legs. A little soap, candle wax, or paraffin on the sides and runners may be enough to cure minor problems.

You may find that the slides (the boards the runners ride on) are worn and uneven. To replace, rabbet out the old ones until smooth, then shim up to their former height with thin strips of wood. An easier method is to install thumbtacks, plastic bumpers, or tape in the worn areas.

When the drawer itself is wobbly, check for loose joints. Gently tap dovetailed joints apart, being careful not to break any of the pins. Scrape off

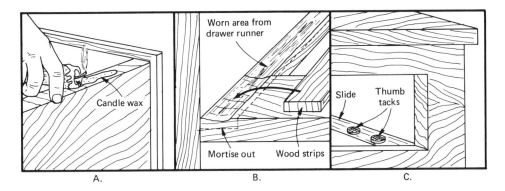

FIGURE 18. Dealing with sticky drawers.

the old adhesive, reglue, and clamp as described above. Corner clamps may be helpful to keep corners square. Other joints can be fixed in the same way, of course, but non-dovetailed joints will probably fall apart again under hard use. Such a piece may not be worth repairing, but if you believe it is, see if you can either dovetail the joints yourself or have them dovetailed for you.

Splits—Splits occur in large, flat parts, such as a dresser top, bureau side, or table leaf. They are caused by poor drying of the wood before assembly, or by being placed in an area with excessive humidity. The cure is approximately the same no matter where it happens.

Remove the part by unscrewing, removing glue blocks, knocking apart, or whatever. If there is only a partial split, you may as well crack it all the way, destructive though that may sound. A partial split is the very devil to glue properly. If you complete the job that nature will probably finish anyway, you'll have some good surfaces for gluing. Use bar or pipe clamps for thick pieces.

A couple I know (newlyweds) split the long side of their bed frame, right along the rail that holds the slats which, in turn, bore the weight of the springs and mattress, plus a healthy bride and groom. The wife insisted that they needed a whole new bedroom suite.

Anyway, faced with financial ruin, this very unhandy husband did a bit of research, bought some bar clamps and hide glue. Flying in the face of his pessimistic do-it-yourself friends, relatives, and assorted experts, he glued the whole long strip and let it dry for a couple of days.

That, dear reader, was 20 years ago, and the old bed still stands (although subject to less strain than two decades ago). Needless to say, our hero escaped monetary disaster and is now a pillar of the community. His wife still grumbles a lot about the old bedroom set.

The thin panels found in the sides of chests or in cupboard doors cannot be fixed in this way. Sideways pressure can't be applied. They are easily replaced, however, with a new panel of the same thickness. As discussed above, these panels "float" in their slots and are not glued. Simply lift them out of the frame after removing the top. One of the reasons these panels split, and thicker ones warp, is that the inside surface is not finished. To prevent such splits, give the inside a coat of linseed oil, sealer, varnish, or shellac. It's best to use the same finish as on the outside.

Sometimes you can close up hairline cracks by removing the panel and soaking the inside with wet rags for a day or two, then gluing a thin strip of wood over the back side of the split.

Warps—A warped board is like a warped mind—not too easy to cure. Warps usually occur in large parts like those subject to splits. The cause of warping is the same, too—that old enemy, moisture. It is good to remember when doing your own refinishing that most warps could have been avoided by the simple expedient mentioned above of applying a coat of some kind of sealer to the interior surface of the part. These finishing materials keep moisture out of the wood, or at least keep the dampness equal on both sides. You should know, however, that sealing the underside of a truly valuable antique may lessen its value. Antiques experts like to be able to examine the bare wood (to each his own).

In any case, it is the uneven moisture absorption that causes warping. The most effective cure is a fairly drastic balancing of the moisture, by wetting the unfinished side and drying the other at the same time, if possible. There are several ways to accomplish this. One is steaming, placing the piece over a radiator with wet rags on top. The easiest way seems to be laying the unfinished side over wet grass in the bright sun. Remember that the dry side is the one that curves in and should receive the dampness. While that side gets soaked, the sun is drying out the formerly wetter side.

If the warp is a "simple" one, in which the boards are curved in the same general direction, use the grass method (or some other wetting gimmick in cold weather). Sometimes the warp is more complex, however, with a "twist" longitudinally as well as a warp. If such is the case, put a big rock or other heavy weight over the part that is more out of shape than the others.

You should be able to see the effects of your labors in a few hours, or by the end of the day anyway. When the board is just about as straight as you can hope for, put it back where it came from, fitting it in as tightly as possible. Clamp any loose sections, such as a table leaf, to a couple of straight dry boards to help keep them from warping back again. When everything is dry, give the underside the sealer coat it should have had before. Some experts feel that it is acceptable to screw cleats to the underside of a table leaf that is prone to warpage, while others feel that this

Sealing the undersides and insides of furniture surfaces helps prevent warping. (*The Sherwin-Williams Co.*)

destroys the value of the piece, since cleats will be visible when the leaves are extended. You should really try all else first, and use cleats only if the case is hopeless. Apply cleats, if you use them, immediately after "dis-warping."

If the wetting doesn't work, and cleats are repugnant to your artistic sensibilities, there is yet another way, not an easy one. The warp in such cases may be caused not by moisture absorption but by internal stresses in the wood. This has to do with the way it is cut—radially, tangentially, etc. (see Chapter 2). With a power saw, cut a series of kerfs in the underside of the piece about 3 inches apart and to a depth about two-thirds of the thickness of the board. Make wooden splines to fit the grooves, preferably in a slightly wedged shape. If the part is curved so that the kerfs are in the concave (edges curled upward) side, then tap the splines in slowly, forcing them into glued grooves with a mallet. If kerfs are on the convex

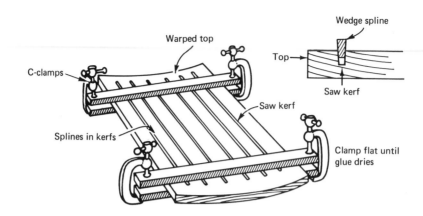

FIGURE 19. Sawing grooves and inserting wedged splines will cure warp. Whether the wedges are tight or loose depends on which direction the board is warped.

(edges curled downward), as most will be, cut the splines thinner and do not force them. Glue loosely and liberally into the saw kerfs. Clamp flat against some straight boards. Perhaps the most effective, but drastic, way to cure warpage is to cut the part into several small boards, alternating them as they are glued back together. This is not for amateurs, and may not look so good even if it's done right.

Since moisture isn't kind to many glues, you may find that in the wetting process, some boards have fallen apart. These will have to be glued back together as described under "Splits" above. This may be a good time to insert a couple of dowels in badly warped areas (see p. 91). Since this is a little tricky, however, with a chance of drilling crookedly through thin boards, you shouldn't attempt it without a drill press or drill-press attachment for a radial-arm saw. Minor warpage, by the way, is not always a bad thing. As a matter of fact, it is often prized in truly old antiques.

Loose Screws—Occur primarily at hinges, where the weight of a door, leaf, etc., exerts constant pressure and sometimes pulls the screws out of their original tracks. In many cases, the screws point into table tops, veneer, or other thin wood so that the time-honored trick of replacing loose screws with longer ones runs the risk of popping through the finished surfaces. Replacement will work sometimes, but it is risky—and you can't do it more than once. The use of fatter screws is also limited by the diameter of the hinge holes.

The best and easiest way to cure loose screws is to fill the screw hole with wood chips, matches, or toothpicks, etc., and glue, or to jam with wood dough or other filler. When the mix dries, the screw should go back in tightly again. When the wood is too dry or splintery, or you're screwing into end grain, you may have to cross-bore from a relatively invisible spot and insert a dowel into the screw area. The dowel, if tight and well glued, should afford the necessary solid wood for the screw to bite into. No further problem should be anticipated.

Broken Arms, Legs, Etc.—Almost any broken piece can be put together again with proper gluing. With a clean break, you don't have to worry about the old glue—but be sure the surfaces to be glued are clean and dry. Use an extra-strong glue for chair rungs, which are likely to have a heavy foot right back where the break was. Usually the break is at least partially longitudinal (along the grain) so that you have a fairly large surface to clamp together. C-clamps will hold the pieces together, one at each end of the break, with more in the center if there is room.

A broken part often loosens up the joints at either end of the part, so you may as well check them and reglue if necessary. If you let the repair go awhile, you may find that other parts have loosened as well. Tighten up everything at the same time, or your repair is doomed to failure. Don't forget to use thin wood shims on either side of your metal clamp jaws.

If a break occurs twice in the same spot, don't bother fixing it, since the second glue job will probably be weaker than the first. It's easier and better to make a new part. Rungs, legs, and other breakable parts are not difficult to replace. A plain rung can be fashioned from a dowel. More complex parts require a lathe or a professional cabinetmaker. Rungs are ideal candidates for your spare-part inventory.

New parts are fitted the same way the old ones are. You may have to shave the ends a little if they are too big or you may have to fill with scraps if the part is a little too small. Finish as any new wood (see following chapters).

Patches—Expert cabinetmakers can patch almost any part of a piece of furniture and make it look good. They can cut part of a chair leg, desk top,

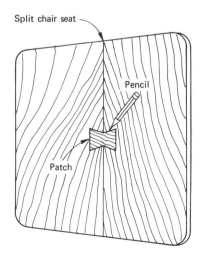

Split chair seat

Pencil

Patch

FIGURE 20. A patch for a split chair seat.

Lay patch across seat halves and trace around it. Chisel out space for patch.

or anything else, finish it, and make it look like new. If a structural part needs patching (see Chapter 5 for cosmetic patching), our advice is to take it to a cabinetmaker—or don't bother with it at all.

If you want to try your luck, however, a butterfly patch is one place to begin. Such a patch is often the only cure for such things as split seats. Although they may seem to be an eyesore, they are often prized in areas such as the top of a trestle table. First cut the patches in the shape of a butterfly (appropriately enough), then position on top of the two pieces as they will be when put back together. On a chair seat, use the underside, in case it doesn't look so hot. Trace the outline of the patch on the seat bottom and chisel out. Place the pieces together, glue all around, and insert the butterflies. Clamp the patches down and the pieces against each other. The seat should hold for centuries.

7

SURFACE RENOVATION

Chapter 5 dealt with ways of fixing up a piece of furniture without getting into involved repairs or refinishing. Chapter 6 was concerned with repairs to the structure, or the guts of the furniture. This chapter presents ways of curing surface flaws whether the surface is to be refinished or not, and regardless of whether structural repair is necessary.

Some of the methods presented here are used before, after, or during refinishing. Others can be used, with luck, without refinishing at all.

DETERMINING THE TYPE OF FINISH

Before you attempt surface renovation, you should know what type of finish you're dealing with. There are some finishes you'll just have to guess at, but after you've met them a few times, you'll be able to figure those out, too. The major types of finishes, however, have properties that make them easy to distinguish.

Both varnish and lacquer—indeed, almost all finishes—were invented during the twentieth century. Any piece which has been around longer than that is almost certainly shellacked or oiled. But remember that, unless a piece has resided in a museum all that time, the finish will undoubtedly have been refurbished at least once. Refinishers have their likes and dislikes, and the new finishes might well be shellac also. But then again, they may not. In any case, test for shellac first in any piece you think is a true antique. If it isn't shellac, chances are high that it has been refinished with varnish. (An oiled finish will feel either oily or unfinished.)

At the other end of the spectrum is furniture that you know is reasonably new. If so, then it probably hasn't been refinished, and the finish is almost certainly factory-applied lacquer. Pay no heed to the salesman who tells you that a new piece of furniture has been coated with a super "varnish" of some kind. He doesn't know what he's talking about.

There are also ways of telling whether a piece has already been refinished.

It may take you awhile at first to recognize the signs, but after you do a few pieces yourself, they will be unmistakable. Look for telltale signs of scraping or sanding. Or check underneath for signs of more than one finish. Check carvings and moldings for little pieces of steel wool or old removers. Examine chips or nicks in the finish. Is there another finish underneath the new one?

None of this is of any particular help in determining exactly what the finish is, but on refinished pieces, you can rule out certain ones like lacquer, which isn't used much by refinishers. And you can also conclude, with reasonable certainty, that any really old finish that hasn't been done over is shellac. (But test to make sure, as explained below.)

TESTING THROUGH THE WONDERS OF CHEMISTRY

If you flunked chemistry in high school, don't be intimidated. These tests are a lot easier. Finish X is dissolved by Solvent Y. Simple, huh? It really is.

Shellac—The solvent for shellac is alcohol. Whiskey won't do, however, since it is only half alcohol at best. Rubbing alcohol is no good, either, since it's only about 25% pure alcohol. What you need is "wood" alcohol, which is relatively pure, but denatured (poisoned, really) to prevent temptation.

Because of the same temptation factor, you'll rarely find wood alcohol labeled as such. It's usually called "shellac thinner" or a brand name with "sol" in it like Quakersol or Solox.

Take a piece of clean cloth and wrap it around the tip of your finger. Dip your finger into the alcohol, then rub it onto an obscure surface of the furniture. If the finish sort of melts, or comes off on the rag, it's shellac.

Lacquer—Use the wrapped finger again, but this time you'll need some lacquer thinner. Lacquer won't respond as enthusiastically to the thinner as shellac did to the alcohol. It will simply get a little foggy, as if the finish was suddenly scuffed or worn in that particular spot. There will be a reaction, though, which you can see. Soon after the fogginess occurs, the highly volatile thinner will evaporate, and the test area will look smooth and glossy again. What you've done is a mini-reamalgamation (see Chapter 5). If you have this type of reaction, the finish is lacquer.

Varnish—If neither of the above tests does much to the finish, you know you aren't dealing with shellac or lacquer. The odds are heavy that it's some type of varnish. Unfortunately, our little scientific experiment may go awry here. *Sometimes,* with *some* varnishes, lacquer thinner will cause the surface to crinkle up slightly. If however, the surface does not return to its former state or better, then it's varnish.

The only thing that will take off varnish is varnish (or paint) remover. You know that the finish isn't paint by looking at it, and a small application of varnish remover will verify whether the finish is varnish or not. To do this, put a dab of remover in an obscure spot, and the finish should wrinkle up in a few minutes.

How do you know the finish isn't sealer, linseed oil, or something else? Well, the other finishes will either have worn off naturally, or if not, they will not respond to the remover. Also, it is unlikely you'd want to remove sealer or other finish if it's still in good shape. Presumably, you've followed the advice already given in Chapter 5 to clean the piece thoroughly before doing anything else. Any remaining finish other than the ones discussed above will wash off if they haven't disappeared spontaneously.

WAX

Wax should never be used alone as a finish. It is usually put on over at least one coat of another finish to seal the wood. The testing solvents should cut through the wax to the finish, but very heavy coats may prevent it from getting through. If that is the case, remove the wax with turpentine or mineral spirits and some hard rubbing.

This is as good a time as any to tell you that whether you're refinishing or just fixing up a surface blemish, wax should be removed if it's built up to a point where it's gummy. After the wax is off, you can proceed to any of the steps in this or the next chapter. Chapter 12 deals with applications of new wax.

WHITE RINGS AND SPOTTING

White rings can occur on any finish, but it happens most often to shellac. Lacquer and varnish are relatively impermeable by water or alcohol, the culprits most often responsible for white rings or spots. To guard against damage from liquids, always give shellac a few coats of hard wax. It won't completely prevent problems, but it will cut them down considerably. At least you'll have time to wipe up spills before they get down to the surface.

To cure white discoloration, start with the easiest method and work up to the most drastic. You may know about rubbing in some cigar ash along with a little spit. Silly, huh? No, it isn't. It often works. Try that first on areas that aren't too badly affected.

Next up the ladder of effectiveness is fine 3/0 steel wool mixed with some oil. Actually any kind of liquid, except for water or alcohol, will do. Use whatever oil you have on hand—mineral, corn, linseed, vegetable (soybean), etc., or even some turpentine or mineral spirits. You may have to rub awhile, but don't rub too briskly.

This treatment should work in most cases. If it doesn't try some fine pumice and a little water, just enough to form a creamy paste. Mix the paste with some oil as above and apply gently to the surface. Don't rub too hard or too long, or you might scratch the surface. A padded sanding block may help, but be very careful about rubbing.

If none of the above works, there are commercial spot removers designed for this purpose. Use them carefully, however, and read instructions thoroughly. When the discoloration is gone, by whatever method, wipe the spot with a damp rag, let dry, and follow with a healthy coat of furniture polish.

It may be that the spot is gone, but the area affected now stands out like a sore thumb. A little more shellac or reamalgamation of the surface may help. But it's entirely possible that you'll have to give the entire surface the same treatment you gave the discolored area.

BRUISES AND DENTS

As discussed in Chapter 5, one dent in a piece of furniture looks like a dent. A whole bunch of them is called distressing. Furniture-makers distress furniture by beating it with chains, keys, bricks and other objects. You can do the same.

If, however, you prefer to remove the dent, there are several ways to accomplish it, none of them guaranteed. You will recall that moisture is the enemy of wood when it comes to warping. Here, we will use the same property—the fact that wood fibers act like sponges in soaking up moisture (witness swollen doors and windows during spells of high humidity).

Be warned that any of the processes used here will have a deleterious effect upon the finish, so it is wise to remove the finish from the surface to begin with, then go after the dents. If the surface is a table top, you may try removing the finish just from the top. But it will look newer than the rest of the piece when refinished, so you may have to do a complete refinishing job just to get rid of the dent. If you plan on it anyway, that's no problem, but if you hoped not to have to do that, you can first try removing the dent without taking off the finish.

The most effective way of removing a dent is to lay a wet cloth over the bruised area and lay a household iron on the cloth. Use the low or synthetic setting, and let the iron lie on the cloth for a half hour or more. The steam thus generated will send clouds of moisture into the wood, raising it, with any luck, to the former level. You can go about other tasks while the cloth is steaming, but keep an eye on the wood so that it doesn't swell too much. Chances are that it will swell too little rather than too much, but it's more difficult to get the swelling down than up, so don't fool around.

If the dent isn't removed that way, try again, but this time make some tiny holes in the depressed area with a needle, about $\frac{1}{4}$ inch deep. A light

The most effective way of getting rid of a dent in furniture is to lay a wet cloth over the area and steam the dent back up with an iron at a low setting. (*Minwax Co.*)

tap with a hammer will help if you can't push the needle in with your fingers. The needle holes will aid water absorption, and the swelling will either close the holes completely or make them so small no one will notice.

This method is dangerous near glue lines, by the way, and for old pieces with inferior adhesives. Try to stay away from any glued areas, but if you must work in areas where the glue might be loosened, a slightly different tack is recommended. Use pieces of wet blotter in the dent, and press a marble or similar object that might fit the depression on top of the blotter pieces. Turn the iron up to a higher setting (medium range) and hold the iron on top of the marble. This is a little tougher, because you have to stay with it, but it might work. At least the marble will prevent excessive heat from loosening the glue.

For very hard woods like hardrock maple, any of the above methods is rather futile. The fibers in such woods don't compress readily. When you manage to dent this type of wood (it isn't easy), the fibers are usually broken and won't come back up again. In such cases, the only thing to do is to sand around the area to feather out the dent, or fill it with a shellac stick as described later in this chapter.

GOUGES, SCRATCHES, AND SIMILAR WOUNDS

As discussed in Chapter 5, shallow scratches can often be obliterated with a cleaner-conditioner. You can also try a little nut meat from the same source (hickory nut for hickory, walnut for walnut, etc.). Rub the nut meat diagonally across the scratch or gouge a few times, and it should darken enough to be unnoticeable. Commercial scratch-healers and even shoe polish are other possibilities.

Another trick is to use a matching oil color or colors in the wounded area. The siennas and umbers make good starting base shades. Mix with the appropriate colors to get the corrrect tint. If you can find a matching or near-matching stain (see Chapter 9), that might work also.

Some filling may be necessary. There are several ways to do this, and each has its own champions. The best course here is to try each and decide which one you find effective.

The easiest materials to use are plain wax crayons, the kind you buy for the kids. These are melted over a sootless alcohol lamp and dripped into the wound. Many finish colors can be quite accurately matched by one of

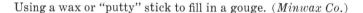

Using a wax or "putty" stick to fill in a gouge. (*Minwax Co.*)

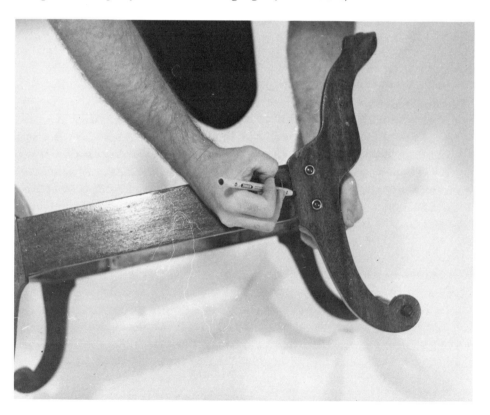

those big crayon assortments containing a lot of browns and reds. Mix these with some black, white, and/or yellow and you can arrive at a shade that will duplicate almost any furniture color you need.

Mixing itself is somewhat tricky. Shave off a few wax chips, heat them, and keep adding other colors until you get the desired shade. You have to heat up the mix each time, then let it cool, because you can't tell whether it's green or gray when it's hot. The stuff cools rapidly, though, and should take less time overall than other methods.

After the glop is exactly the shade you want, heat it up again and start dribbling it into the scratch. Scrape off the excess with a dull knife to the level of the other finish. Stroke the surface with your finger to blend the fill material smoothly.

Assuming all goes well, the next step is to coat the entire surface with a mixture of two parts alcohol and one part shellac. This prevents the wax from bleeding into any new finish. Then varnish the whole surface. If the scratch isn't on a surface where you'll be applying a new finish, the fill material can be left as is without further finishing. It may look a little prominent, though, in which case you may want to refinish as described.

If the repair doesn't match, or just looks bad to you, one virtue of wax is that it can easily be pulled right out again (a little heat will assist for stubborn fill). Either add more coloring to the old mix, or start afresh— or try another method.

It should be added here that you don't have to use wax crayons. Some furniture, hardware, and specialty shops sell precolored wax sticks made expressly for this purpose. You will have an easier time getting a match with these, but there's no guarantee you won't have to do some mixing on your own. Application is the same for both.

The truly professional way to fix up deep gouges is with shellac sticks. These give a more invisible repair, but are not easy to use. For one thing, a patch made of stick shellac is difficult to remove if it doesn't look quite right. If you're undecided on what method to use, try wax first, particularly for smaller wounds. Use stick shellac for larger patches and for areas of high visibility. But experiment on less conspicuous areas first.

Stick shellac is applied with a small spatula or a knife, heated in an alcohol lamp. The end of the shellac stick is also heated in the lamp until it melts, then a bit of the molten section is scraped off and applied to the gouge. When the hole is filled up, smooth it out with your spatula. For deep gouges, use several thin coats rather than one thick one. When the patch is wide, leave the center slightly higher than the edges. After it cools, shave it down with a sharp knife, razor blade, or the flat side of a chisel.

If the gouged-out area is at the edge of a table top or other surface, you'll have to make "forms" out of thin material such as a tongue depressor. Attach the form with masking tape and fill as outlined above. A really deep depression can be filled with wood dough or other material up to near

Stick shellac is applied with a knife or spatula, after both have been heated over a sootless flame. (*3M Corp.*)

the surface in order to save time and effort. Fill the remainder of the gouge with one of the other methods.

Stick lacquer is also available and is used in the same manner as stick shellac. It should go without saying that any repair must be made in a clean, fresh area, but this advice is so often ignored that we'll repeat it here, even at the risk of being monotonous.

BLACK SPOTS

Offhand, it would seem that black spots should belong with white spots. We have deliberately separated the two in order to emphasize the rather profound difference between them. White spots are usually superficial and easy to eradicate. Black spots and rings occur in the wood itself, almost always because water has penetrated the finish and collected underneath. (This is often caused by moisture condensing on a vase over a period of time.)

To treat black spots, the old finish should be removed completely. If you think you can get away with just the affected surface, fine, but the difference after refinishing may be so striking you'll have to do the whole piece over. In any case, you'll have to get to the bare wood to remove the problem. (See Chapter 8 for removing finishes.)

Once the surface is stripped, the black areas can be removed reasonably quickly by using a solution of oxalic acid. Unlike some of the chemicals used in refinishing, oxalic acid isn't as bad as it sounds. If you're careful, as explained on p. 123, you shouldn't be afraid of it. Household ammonia used undiluted will do the same job, but may require more applications.

Oxalic acid should remove the blackness without too much difficulty, but be sure to give the surface a bath with vinegar to remove tiny acid deposits. The acid will remove the wood stain, too, so you will undoubtedly have to restain the entire surface. (That's why we say you will probably wind up redoing the entire piece.) Finish as for any other piece which has been stripped for refinishing.

BURNS

The true furniture lover pays heed to the Surgeon General. Cigarette smoking is not only dangerous to your health; it raises hell with furniture, too. Cigarettes are by far the most common cause of burns in furniture surfaces.

A common question here concerns insurance. Since most homeowners' or renters' policies (the pure fire policy is almost obsolete for homes) have at least a $50 deductible clause, there isn't much point in filing a claim for cigarette burns. Furthermore, there is considerable question whether the damage is caused by "scorch" or a "burn." The haggling isn't worth it unless you have a real fire, destroying the whole piece—or more. If a valuable antique is burned, however, you should notify your agent anyway.

A burn can be treated as any similar wound. Use wax or shellac sticks as described above. First, however, cleanse the burned areas of all scorch marks by scraping or digging out the darkened areas with a razor blade. When the wound is clean, use the same repair methods as described for scratches and gouges.

A more serious problem occurs when the burn damages veneer or inlay. In this event, you will have to patch or replace the damage section as described below. If the piece has valuable inlays or marquetry, it may be time to call your insurance agent. You should know, by the way, that once the damage estimates are made and the claim settled, it's perfectly legal to keep the money and perform the repair yourself.

GREASE SPOTS

Most grease spots remain on the surface. This type of damage, as long as the finish is in good shape, can be easily removed by using soap, detergent, or a cleaner-conditioner as described in Chapter 5.

If the finish is itself weak or thin, however, the grease may penetrate to the wood below. When this happens, the grease must be removed. Strip the furniture down, and try various dry-cleaning fluids. If you don't know what caused the stain, you must use trial and error. Benzine will remove a lot of grease stains, especially those caused by animals. Acetone is better for vegetable oils.

Apply the cleaning fluid with a small brush, taking care not to spill it on areas other than the stain. Douse the spot liberally until the stain is gone, wiping with a tissue after each application.

REPAIRS TO VENEER, INLAYS, AND MARQUETRY

As discussed earlier, veneer has an odd and undeserved reputation. "Solid" wood is still preferred by most furniture buyers. Yet, veneer enables manufacturers and cabinetmakers to create beautiful surfaces that would be much too costly or physically impossible to duplicate with solid woods. The "cathedrals" or arch-like figures so treasured in mahogany, for example, are possible only when the wood is cut as veneer.

This same blindness often applies to used furniture. A Salvation Army special with crumpled and loose veneer is looked upon with horror by prospective buyers. Actually, it does look pretty bad, but repair is not that difficult, and the rewards for a job well done are both artistically and financially satisfying.

No matter how beat-up veneer may look, it can be refinished like other parts of furniture. You may have to remove the finish, and sometimes even sand down the veneer (a dangerous practice, since most are pretty thin), but it can be done.

Loose veneers can be glued back down in most cases. Older veneers were probably attached with fish or hide glue which had to be heated. As long as there isn't too great an accumulation of dirt underneath, you may be able to reattach the veneer by simply warming up an iron and remelting the old glue. Use waxed paper and a piece of toweling under the iron.

Blisters can often be reattached in the same way, but large ones may require slitting with a razor blade before they will flatten. Because such wood is probably swollen, you may find some overlap at the slit. Carefully pare off the part of the veneer that overlaps. Keep a steady eye and hand, and you will do a creditable job.

Veneer that is badly burned or damaged will have to be replaced. It may be that you can find a matching piece in your stockpile, but more likely you'll want to purchase new veneer. See Appendix D for mail-order sources, if none are available locally.

There are several ways of removing old veneer. Heat should soften most glues, or you can pry off veneers with a wide-bladed drywall knife or a similar implement.

Inlays and marquetry with pieces missing are relatively easy to repair. Real antiques should be turned over to a professional cabinetmaker, but the average inlay can be replaced by the amateur without too much difficulty. The slots have already been cut by experts. You may be able to purchase matching inlays from one of the sources listed in Appendix D, or you can replace the entire inlaid section with new wood. Marquetry pieces are usually small, so a replacement is seldom noticeable, even if in a different wood. Use a similar or neutral color so it won't stand out.

If one piece in a series of matching inlays is missing, it may be wiser to replace all the pieces of the series. A new piece will be obvious, but if they are all new, chances are that they will be less noticeable. You can buy entire borders and other common inlays from most of the sources mentioned.

To blend in the new pieces of inlay or marquetry, strip down the entire surface and refinish (see Chapters 8 and 9).

When cutting veneers, inlays, etc., use an X-acto knife, and don't try to cut right through the first time. Make a series of shallow cuts to prevent splitting the thin veneers (usually $\frac{1}{28}$ inch thick). If you do split the wood, it can usually be used anyway, since the split will ordinarily follow natural grain and should not be noticeable when glued down.

Old veneers which have split can be reglued for the same reason. Veneers which have lifted off at the edges are difficult to reglue properly, and it is better to break off the loose section entirely before regluing. That way you can get rid of all the dirt and old glue, too. Use clamps or weights. Needless to say, all old veneer should be scraped clean before regluing. This may take a somewhat delicate touch. If the veneer is split, treat as above.

RESTORING OTHER MATERIALS

Restoration of most non-wood furniture materials, such as hardware, leather, acrylic, vinyl, and laminated plastics, amounts to a thorough cleaning, and these processes are described in the care and maintenance section (Chapter 12).

Marble is one material that may deteriorate in spite of proper maintenance, because it is basically limestone and quite porous. When ordinary cleaning won't remove marks, it is probably because the marble is stained.

Restoration of stained marble is a pretty tough job. The only way to make it look new again is by literally grinding the entire surface down. If you're lucky, a rubdown with very fine abrasive paper such as 10/0 and rottenstone or tin oxide (available at drugstores) may do the job for stains that aren't too deep. Commercial marble-cleaning products are also effective.

Deep stains won't be affected by this, and if the fine-grit paper doesn't work, you will have to undertake a series of grindings using the same materials, but starting with coarser abrasive papers. A 3/0 grit should be used to start with, unless the surface is severely damaged, in which case you may even start with 1/0 paper. Keep rubbing evenly across the surface, then switch to finer and finer grits, until you've worked back down to the very fine.

Old marble pieces are quite highly prized, and it is suggested that a valued piece be taken to a professional marble refinisher. (Check the yellow pages.)

8

GETTING RID OF THE OLD FINISH

If you decide that none of the previously described renovation techniques will work for you (or if you've already tried them and *know* they won't work), the only course left is complete removal of the old finish. There is a lot of folklore and misinformation concerning this, and some of it can be extremely time-consuming and even dangerous.

Remember that the object of any furniture finisher is to apply a finish that will last. Be that finisher the original one at the factory or a subsequent refinisher like yourself, he has undoubtedly done his best to make the wood surface as tough and durable as he could. It follows, then, that his finish is not going to be easy to take off.

For a long time, the only effective way to remove stubborn old finishes was with massive applications of lye, a quick but hazardous—and messy—operation. Because of the dangers and the inconvenience, other methods came into being which were really never very practical.

SOME UN-RECOMMENDED REMOVAL TECHNIQUES

These methods have been tried over the years and are still recommended by some. They are ineffective, however, for the following reasons:

Sanding—Sanding *will* work if you have an orbital power sander, infinite patience, and are working only on large, flat surfaces. It is a rare piece of furniture, however, that doesn't have lots of curved and fluted areas which need hand sanding. Deep crevices are impossible for sandpaper, and you can't use larger-grit papers in any case, because they will gouge the wood. The finest-gauge papers can gouge the wood and/or ruin the patina if used improperly. Even if you make no mistakes, you'll be so exhausted once the finish is off, you won't want to bother with a new finish.

Heat—A blowtorch is the best way to remove old paint from wood siding, but don't try it on furniture. If you don't burn yourself or the piece, you'll

111

blacken and char it beyond repair. There have been warming irons and heating tools on the market for some time now, but none of them does a very good job.

CHEMICAL REMOVERS

There are several types of chemical removers, and technically lye, alcohol, ammonia, and the other removers discussed later in the chapter are chemicals, too. But the term is usually used to denote commercial "paint and varnish" removers, which came on the market a decade or so ago. Commercial paint and varnish removers come in various trade names (Bix, Zip-Strip, etc.) and may contain slightly different formulas, but the one thing they have in common is that they make fast work of virtually any type of finish you may find. That includes shellac, lacquer, varnish, and almost every type of paint.

If you've ever seen these compounds at your paint or hardware dealer, you've no doubt noted the skulls and crossbones, the "poison" markings in bold print. Some of the ingredients listed on the cans are methyl chloride, methyl alcohol, toluene, and acetone. These chemicals must be treated with respect. If they can shrivel up layers of paint and varnish, they can do a job on your skin and eyes, too.

But it really isn't all that bad. Paint removers can be spilled on normal skin without doing immediate harm. Unless you have an open wound or very sensitive skin, the removers don't even sting—not right away, anyway. Wash the remover off without too much delay, of course, and don't rub your face, but you don't have to make a mad dash for the sink as you would have to do with lye or certain acids. The one area you must protect is your eyes, but even here, you can rinse them out quickly with water and probably not suffer any serious effects.

Chemical varnish removers, in other words, are like power saws and aspirin. They can be dangerous to your health, but used with reasonable caution, they are very helpful.

SELECTING A COMMERCIAL REMOVER

There is no one brand of remover that is better than any other, but there are certain traits that should be looked for when buying. And some features are better for certain types of jobs.

In general, the paste-type (really more of a semi-paste or jelly) is preferred over the "liquid" because it doesn't run off when applied vertically. If, of course, you have a lot of large, flat, level surface, and/or you can turn the piece from flat side to flat side (a large chest may fit this description), the liquid is cheaper and a little easier to use. The waxless type is also preferable, even though it leaves a film that can be difficult to remove. If you have an area with lots of carvings and fancy work, you may prefer the wax type. Obviously, it depends on the job, but be sure to have the paste-type, waxless version for most all-around work.

One type of remover frequently recommended is the "water-rinse" type, and this is puzzling. If the piece must be rinsed with water, that means that the only place you can work is outside or in a basement with floor drains. Even though most of the water-rinse types have directions for non-rinse usage, there seems to be little point in buying them unless you're doing lots of work in a location with good drainage. Furthermore, we don't see how dousing furniture with water can do it much good.

The first time you use paint and varnish remover, try it on a small piece, preferably one that doesn't have a lot of fancy work. A night table or straight chair is an ideal candidate.

Once you've selected a victim, the next thing is to find a place to work. The work platform described on p. 12 is a good place, especially in winter, but in nice weather it's best to work outside. Wherever you work, be sure to spread a lot of old newspaper under the entire area. Removers are very messy. Make sure there is plenty of light and ventilation, and try to situate the work so that you'll be working on horizontal surfaces as often as possible. If you don't have a work platform, use boxes so that the piece will be high enough to prevent undue stooping.

If you haven't done so before, be sure to read the directions before you even open the can. Some removers should be shaken before opening, others not. Each product seems to have a little quirk. One manufacturer, for example, recommends putting the remover back into the can after scraping it off. (This saves money, but makes a bigger mess than usual.) Make sure that you know what to do after you scrape off the remover. Should you give it a once-over with water? If the directions don't say anything about this, you should probably give it a rubdown with alcohol. More on this later. Right now, just make sure you know what to do and have all the necessary tools and ingredients at hand.

APPLYING THE REMOVER

The economical way to buy removers (or anything else, for that matter) is in large cans, but these are cumbersome to work with. If you do use a big container, pour some out into a smaller coffee or peanut can big enough to accommodate your brush. You may want to wear goggles, at least at first, but you'll find that they're hot and cause sweat to drip into your eyes. You may also wish to wear gloves the first time, but this really isn't necessary unless you have cuts or sores on your hands. If you've followed our previous advice about saving old brushes, you'll have one on hand to use

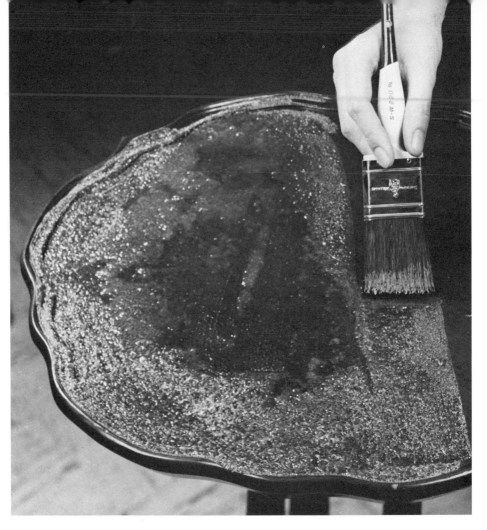

Chemical removers are applied with a brush. Just lay it on, don't brush out. Let stand until well "crinkled." (*Sherwin-Williams Co.*)

with the remover. Dip it into the remover and sort of lay it on the surface to be worked. Don't brush it around, as this dilutes its effectiveness. It is best to work one horizontal surface at a time, but for small items, you may want to work on the top and a couple of sides or legs. On exceptionally large surfaces, like a big table top, work in sections of about four square feet.

Now let the remover stand for at least 10 minutes, maybe 15 or 20, but at least until the surface is all cracked and crinkly-looking. If you know that there are many deep layers of finish on the piece, it may be wise to put on several coats of remover, one on top of the other, then cover the entire surface with burlap, letting it soak overnight.

One of the other tools you've saved is an old putty knife or scraper, the wider the better. Pick one that has rounded corners, or file them down if they're sharp, and use it to lift off the remover and old finish. The glop should come off in thick peels, which you will rub off onto old newspaper. After you've scraped off the big pieces, follow up with some burlap, rags, newspaper, or fine steel wool. Steel wool, starting with 1/0 and working to 2/0 or 3/0, can be used from the start, but it's a little expensive. Use it for legs, rungs, and other curved surfaces.

Thick coats will probably require another application, and very heavy or tough finishes may require three or more. It is best to finish one surface before going on to another, but you can go over the whole thing all at one time if you prefer, then come back for a second or third application.

MOLDINGS, CARVINGS, ETC.

It is plain that carvings, fluted moldings, and other fancy woodwork will not be cleaned by scraping. Steel wool will do the job on many wider crevices, as well as rounded surfaces, but deep and narrow recesses require special treatment. One of the best tools is a vegetable brush. It's marvelous for most moldings. But if you aren't fortunate enough to have one of those around, a toothbrush or any small brush will do nicely. Other acceptable tools for carvings and fine cracks are turkey skewers, orange sticks, tooth-

After scraping off the large surfaces with a wide-bladed scraper or putty knife, clean up the remains of the remover with a damp rag, burlap, newspaper, or steel wool. (*Sherwin-Williams Co.*)

Several implements can be used in grooves and moldings, including an old tooth-brush and a piece of steel wool wrapped around some string. (*Sherwin-Williams Co. and Minwax.*)

picks, and pieces of broken glass. Those bamboo skewers used for shish-kabobs are also excellent. So is steel wool wrapped around some string.

Sometimes none of this seems to work. Open-grained woods like oak, especially if unfilled, can give you a lot of trouble. You may also find some end grain, although most good furniture doesn't have it exposed. In these situations, the only solution is to try and dig out the stubborn finish with a sharp instrument dipped in alcohol. Try your skewers first, and resort to a sharp penknife if nothing else works. Brute force is sometimes necessary, and if that doesn't work, you may have to power-sand the area or simply allow bits of the old finish to remain.

When all of the finish is off, it is wise to go over the entire piece with a damp rag. Be careful when using water, however, as it can raise the grain. Use particular caution on veneers and inlays, which may loosen when wet. This is another reason to shy away from "water-rinse" removers.

The last step is to go over the whole piece with alcohol. This should remove all traces of remover, dirt, and bits of softened paint or varnish. If you used a wax-type remover, substitute turpentine or mineral spirits for the alcohol. Let the piece stand for about 24 hours to catch its breath, and you're ready for the next step in your refinishing project.

OTHER REMOVAL METHODS

Although commercial paint and varnish removers are best for all-around use, there are other removers that work as well or better in certain circumstances.

Alcohol—When you know that the finish on your piece is shellac, and only shellac (see tests on pp. 100–101), alcohol actually does a better and cleaner job than commercial removers. Some shellacs are mixed with a little lacquer ("tough" shellacs). To deal with these, add one part lacquer thinner to four parts of shellac. The mixture makes mincemeat out of the toughest shellac.

To use alcohol, pour some onto the surface to be removed and wipe with 1/0 steel wool. You don't have to wait, since the shellac should soften up right away. Remove the loosened shellac with a clean cloth, working small sections at a time. You will probably need a couple of applications so just keep adding alcohol and wiping until you get down to bare wood.

When working with alcohol, keep the windows open, since alcohol fumes can be quite toxic, especially in such large amounts. You can conserve alcohol by standing each chair or table leg in the container as you work on it. When the job is done, go over it all again with a cloth dampened in more alcohol.

Lacquer Thinner—Just as alcohol is the solvent for shellac, so lacquer thinner is the solvent for lacquer, and is the best remover when you know that your finish is lacquer. To make the thinner work more effectively, add some alcohol in the proportions four parts thinner to one part alcohol.

Half 'n' Half—Still another variation on the alcohol-lacquer thinner theme. This time stir up half alcohol and half lacquer thinner. Such a mixture works on finishes which are part shellac and part lacquer (often on top of each other) and even succeeds with some varnishes. The advantage of this and the other two combinations above is that if they work at all, they work faster and aren't as messy as paint remover. And they cost less.

TSP (Trisodium Phosphate)—A sort of mild lye which is a lot safer to use. It's recommended more for tough cleaning jobs than anything else. It'll also take the shine off concrete or wood before tiling, and it's good for removing old finishes from hardwood floors. It's not often used for furniture, but it might be used instead of lye where nothing else seems to work. Add a pound to about six quarts of water, and use like lye, as described below, except that you don't need a vinegar rinse. TSP is quite inexpensive, too.

Ammonia—Using this is like cutting open somebody's chest to massage the heart. It works like mad, but it's also mean as hell, worse than lye. You've probably gotten a good whiff of household ammonia at some stage in your life, and you know how strong it is. What we're talking about here is **pure** ammonia, which is many times stronger.

The only time ammonia is called for is when removing refractory (milk) paints or when all else fails, even lye. Even then, it should be used outdoors or at the very least with every window in the place open. Make sure there is plenty of cross-ventilation. You should also keep kids and pets away from the area.

To use, pour ammonia on the area to be worked and rub with a medium grade of steel wool. Do the whole piece at one time, then go back and do it all over again. You'll be disappointed the first time around, but the second application will restore the smile to your face. The finish should come off in big, satisfying sheets.

LYE

Lye is listed last and given a special section because it poses a lot of serious questions. It is undoubtedly a very effective finish remover, plus being fast and cheap. Many old pros use it, and you should know about it, too, if you're going into refinishing in a big way.

First of all, you should know that lye is a caustic alkali, the very stuff you put into your sink when it clogs up. Only there it's diluted for drain cleaning. Also, it must be washed off in a hurry before it "burns" the wood. Use buckets or the garden hose. This means working outside, or someplace in the basement with good drainage. But if you work outside, it has to be where you don't have any vegetation. Lye will kill it so that it may never come back. If you work inside, it has to be in warm spot and away from anything of value.

If all these "ifs" haven't deterred you, remember to pour the lye *into* the water instead of vice versa; otherwise it will boil up like Vesuvius. And don't use an aluminum pail because toxic fumes result from the interaction of lye and aluminum.

Now, if you're still game, it should be pointed out that lye is cheap, and it works wonderfully on stubborn old finishes, removing thick layers all at once instead of by degrees. If you're reasonably sure of yourself and super careful, you might want to try a can of pure lye or Drano (which *is* mostly lye), plus a little cornstarch, and mix up a paste in a big enamel or galvanized tin pail (the 10-gallon size is best). Fill the pail with about three quarts of cold water, then slowly pour in the lye, keeping your face away from the top of the bucket because it will boil up.

The first time you do this, be sure to wear rubber gloves, goggles, and clothes that cover most of your body. As you get used to using lye, you can shed some of these cautions, but never lose your respect for it. It is nasty stuff.

When the mix is bubbling nicely, take a handful or two of cornstarch or some powdered wallpaper paste and add that to the mix until it becomes thick and pastelike. A pound or so should do the job nicely. You may well ask what tool is used to mix this devil's brew, because it will make short work of spoons and fingers. The best mixer is a long-handled cotton mop, which will also be used for applying the mixture to the furniture.

Spread the mix lightly onto the piece and let it stand for about a minute for thin finishes and up to 10 minutes for very thick coats. Don't let it go any more than 10 minutes, though, because the wood will start to "burn" or turn back. To check progress, take off a little bit of the stuff from a corner with a scraper or putty knife. When it is "done," quickly rinse off the residue with the hose, or, if inside, buckets of water previously placed within range.

When you've removed all you can with water, it is time to go after the cracks and crevices. Using your toothbrush or similar tool, remove all traces of lye from these recesses before it has a chance to damage the surrounding wood.

Now that all traces of active lye are removed, the caustic effect is neutralized by using an acid. The cheapest and most available household acid is vinegar (preferably white). Give the piece a good vinegar bath, then let it stand for 24 hours or so.

If you did leave the lye on too long and darkened the wood, don't despair. The wood can always be bleached back to something resembling its true color (or any other shade, for that matter). Between the various stains and bleaches, almost anything is possible. The next chapter describes these techniques in detail.

9

BLEACHES, STAINS, AND ALL THAT

Now that you've removed all traces of the old finish, the victim of your cruelty will reveal itself in its natural glory (or misery). It may look fine as is. If so, and you're sure you like the color, the tone, and there aren't any large pores that need filling, there's nothing more you really need to do except brush on a finish—varnish, shellac, or whatever.

Personally, because I like the look of natural wood (and also because I'm lazy and like to do things the easiest way possible), I do very little bleaching, and use fillers only where necessary. I usually use stain, but often do without for really nice colored woods.

Put your newly denuded piece where you can look at it with a critical eye, ideally in the spot where it's going to be when it's all finished. Narrow your eyes a bit and ignore the bare look of the wood, imagining it as it will be once you've applied the finish.

Does it match the other pieces in the room, or will it provide a striking contrast—as is, that is? It may look too dark or too light. Remember that most finishes will darken wood slightly. Or you may not like the shade of the wood. In its native state, mahogany, for example, may look too reddish. Many of us like that coloring, but it may not work in your living room.

On the other hand, the wood may not look truly natural. Removers usually take off most of the old stain, but some may remain. Maybe you like it that way, maybe not. Or perhaps the remover has made the wood unnaturally dark. Lye, in particular, can discolor the wood. If you don't know too much about woods, you may not even know what the natural color of the wood is. The big question, nonetheless, is whether it suits you or not.

There are occasions when staining or bleaching is a necessity. The one outstanding example is when the piece is made of different types of wood, as many are. The various colored woods will look terrible without stain. If there's a big burned area, or places that show traces of surface defects or your renovation efforts, you should either stain the light areas darker, or bleach the dark areas lighter.

121

Bleaching is a matter of preference. Do you like the wood light (left) or dark (right)? (*Sherwin-Williams Co.*)

BLEACHING

Many refinishers routinely bleach their furniture. They just happen to like lighter woods. You, too, may like the lighter woods. You should also bleach a piece that is unnaturally mottled or dark-spotted, as mentioned above. Bleach any wood that is too dark for your tastes.

If you are bleaching the piece mainly to remove a darkened area, and do not really want to change the color drastically, the best way to start is with household bleach (Clorox or a similar product). Apply the bleach full strength with a cloth over the darkened areas until they lighten up to the approximate color of the surrounding wood. Then give the whole piece a once-over with the bleach, and remove with a damp rag once you've achieved satisfactory overall color.

There are other ways to do this, described below. But try the household bleach first. It's easier and quicker. Be sure to protect your eyes, and try to keep bleach off your skin. Wear rubber gloves if you have sensitive skin. The active ingredient in bleach is sodium hypochloride.

In household bleach the active chemical is considerably diluted, and the substance works too slowly for anything major. If you wish to alter the color drastically, more severe steps are necessary.

Oxalic Acid—The word "acid" frightens more people than "alkali," but there is good reason to feel the opposite way—at least for the refinisher. Lye, after all, is an alkali. Not all acids are as highly corrosive as nitric and sulfuric. Vinegar, once again, is an acid, and it doesn't scare too many folks. Tannic acid is one of the vital ingredients in wine, which is a precursor of vinegar.

Oxalic acid is one of those in-between acids. You wouldn't want to decant it and have it with dinner. On the other hand, it won't eat through your skin like battery acid does. As a matter of fact, in refinishing the problem with oxalic acid is that it may not be strong enough. It can be used effectively on open-grained woods such as ash, oak, and chestnut, but it may not do the job on close-grained woods.

The only way to use oxalic acid for bleaching is in "saturated" form. A saturated solution is one which has absorbed all the solid that it possibly can. The way to determine this is by adding the crystals or powder to a container of hot water until the water can no longer dissolve the acid. Since this is somewhat difficult to figure out, use one ounce of powder, or two ounces of crystals, to a pint of hot water, as a rough guide. If they stop dissolving before that, stop. If the acid keeps dissolving after the recommended amount has been added, throw in a little more "for the pot." Maple and some other very hard woods are helped by a pinch of tartaric acid, also available in drugstores.

Once your devil's brew is fully saturated, brush it on to the entire surface of your victim and let it stand for 10 to 20 minutes. The first time you use it, you'll feel (and be) safer with gloves, but they aren't really essential. Do protect your eyes, though. After the acid has whitened the surface to your satisfaction, it should be removed with a damp cloth. If satisfaction doesn't happen within the 20-minute maximum, wipe it off anyway and repeat the process until the wood is lightened sufficiently.

Two-Step Bleach—Called that, logically enough, because there are two steps to the procedure. Like many of the products discussed in this book, it comes disguised under various trade names, but you will recognize it easily enough by the two similar bottles or cans in one package. (It's basically hydrogen peroxide.)

It doesn't take much genius to know that you use bottle #1 or "A" first, then #2 or "B." As always, read the manufacturer's instructions. Usually, the first application is allowed to stand for about 20 minutes, then the second one is applied. The second liquid is allowed to stand for as long as needed to do its work. It is wiped off with a damp rag or whatever the manufacturer recommends.

Only one treatment by this method should make the darkest wood as light as you want it. It's pretty potent stuff and should be treated with respect.

Always wear rubber gloves, and protect your eyes. Be sure to read the label thoroughly *before* proceeding.

Lightener Stains—As the name implies, this product is really a light stain rather than a bleach, but is used for the same purpose. The effect is somewhat different, however, and may be just what you want. As with other penetrating or "wiping" stains, the softer parts of the wood absorb more of the pigmented oils than do the harder parts.

As explained below under "Stains," the different rate of absorption means that some parts of the wood will be lighter than others, but this is not necessarily undesirable. And since you are making the wood lighter rather than darker (as you do with most stains), the parts that are generally darkened by stains will be lightened by this type of stain. Follow the instructions given below for regular stains.

STAINS

Everyone knows that trees have annual growth rings, but not everyone knows that most species have two distinct layers in each ring. The inner layer consists of "springwood," with large cavities and thin walls. The outer layer is "summerwood," with smaller cells and thicker walls. Springwood is softer, lighter, and weaker than summerwood. When the wood is cut, and this too depends on *how* it is cut, the difference in these growth patterns accounts for the grain. Abnormalities such as burl, butt, crotch, and spiral growth are another matter. (See p. 20 for more on woods and how they are formed.)

In any case, this difference in grain accounts for the properties of stains and what they do to the wood. More stain is absorbed by the softer springwood, and less by the harder summerwood. There are other reasons, too, such as whether the wood is open- or close-pored, but mainly it is the difference in growth patterns that accounts for the grain and its absorption of stains.

If you look at the selection in a large paint or hardware store, you would think that there were a lot more different kinds of stains than there really are. Each manufacturer calls his stains by "unique" names and implies that his are the only ones that have such wonderful properties. But although there are some minor differences, basically there are only a few major types of stains:

Penetrating Oil Stains—More popularly known as "wiping" stains because of the way they are applied. These are by far the most popular among do-it-yourselfers and should not be sneezed at by the pros, either. Penetrating oil stains contain pigments which, when wiped onto the surface of wood, are absorbed into the fibers. The degree of absorption depends on the softness of the wood and, as explained above, the "contrastiness" of the grain. After application, the stains are wiped off the surface with a rag, hence the popular name. You can vary the depth of the stain somewhat by the length of time the stain is left on the wood before wiping.

Wiping stains are excellent for softwoods and most hardwoods. Pine, for example, responds well to a penetrating oil stain, as do basswood and poplar. Very close-grained hardwoods are not much affected by wiping stains, because of their very low degree of absorption. The vehicle for wiping stains is linseed oil, which doesn't raise the grain and cuts down on later sanding.

Any stain should be tried out in an obscure place, and preferably on a piece of scrap wood of the same species (almost impossible for refinishing, but easy if you're making one of the projects described in Chapters 13 and 14). If the piece is made up of different woods, you have a slight problem. There will probably be a slight variation in the way the stain is absorbed by the woods, but the overall effect should be acceptable once the piece is finished.

If you like what you see, proceed with a less prominent part and make sure it looks good to you. Then do the rest of the piece a section at a time. Wipe off the staining oil quickly at first, then leave it on for longer periods until you get exactly the desired effect.

Most large dealers have a wide range of stain colors, one of which should be just what you want. If not, the stains can be mixed. You can get practically any shade by the judicious intermingling of three basic colors—mahogany, walnut, and maple. But be sure to try out your combination before you apply it to the whole piece.

Combination Oil Stains—Manufacturers are coming out with new combinations all the time, and we're not sure, frankly, what to tell you about them. In general, be wary of them, or try them out on something you don't value too much. Sealer stains, for example, contain synthetic resins which lock in the color and can be used as a finish coat. This is fine if you're sure you like the shade and the finish. Once they are put on, the wood fibers have been penetrated deeply by the color and changes are almost impossible. Other combinations contain fillers and/or other materials. See p. 148 for more on this topic.

Non-Grain-Raising and Alcohol Stains—Non-grain-raising stains are dissolved in alcohol or other vehicles and are often abbreviated to "NGR" stains. NGR, alcohol, and water stains (see below) are aniline or synthetic dyes in the appropriate vehicles. Furniture manufacturers use these dyes because they are inexpensive and work very quickly. They also give the piece an attractive and bright color which is difficult to achieve with wiping stains. The sharp, brilliant color of dyes is much admired by real buffs, and they are a favorite of professional cabinetmakers and refinishers.

You'll have a difficult time finding dyes at the local paint store, and will probably have to order them from one of the mail-order firms listed in Appendix D. They come premixed or in little packages of powder (or larger quantities if desired) and are quite inexpensive. The usual mix is one packet of powder to a quart of alcohol, but that may be too concentrated for the darker shades such as ebony or walnut. Two quarts or more of alcohol should be added to the dark shades. NGR stains can be ordered premixed from most of the same sources. All colors can be mixed to create the shade you desire.

Alcohol evaporates rapidly, which has good and bad qualities for staining. Some NGR vehicles dry even more quickly. Because the stain dries so fast, you can apply several coats almost on top of one another. The bad news is that quick drying makes it almost impossible to go over your work. Once it's on, it stays on and cannot be brushed out or allowed to soak in, as wiping stains can.

Alcohol and NGR stains work similarly. They must be applied quickly and evenly, and usually a little on the light side. It's easy to darken the wood by adding another coat, but not so easy to lighten. Bleaching will probably be necessary if you lay it on too heavy. Another advantage, though, is that you can apply a different color on top of the previous one. If, for example, the first coat looks a little too red to you, you can mix up another batch, eliminating the red and adding a little more brown, or whatever. The second coat will blend in nicely with the first, and cut down on the red shading.

Alcohol stains tend to bleed through finishes, so give your piece a sealer coat after you're satisfied with the final result. A mix of one part alcohol to one part shellac does a good sealing job. It should be followed by at least one coat of varnish as soon as possible, and the final finish should be a hard varnish to prevent the stain from bleeding through.

Water Stains—These are the cheapest and probably the nicest-looking stains of all. The same dye powders are used as with alcohol, but this time they are mixed one ounce of powder to a quart of boiling water. This method is used by most furniture manufacturers. There are several problems, though, which make water stains difficult for the do-it-yourselfer. First, they are most effective when used with a spray gun. Second, they raise the grain of the wood, necessitating a difficult sanding job. After staining, all wood should be given a light sanding anyway, but water stains make it a chore. If you aren't careful, you may remove the stain from high spots.

For most stains, the surface need only be dry and free of dust. If you're using a water stain, the surface must be dampened first. You *can* apply the stain with a brush, but it's tricky. (So, for that matter, is application with a spray gun.) When the stain has been mixed to your satisfaction and tested in an out-of-the-way spot, it is put on with a two-inch brush in straight, long strokes. After each stroke, tap the brush on the edge of the container and go back over the part just done, picking up surplus stain. Then proceed to the next part and repeat the same process. Keep working until the surface looks nice and even without streaking.

You must work quickly, whether spraying or brushing, so that drips and blobs won't collect and sink into the wood, causing dark spots. The surface must be as flat as possible so that runs do not develop and cause similar problems. As far as we are concerned, this is just too much for the nonprofessional, and not worth the extra aggravation.

SEALER COAT

Be careful when the word "sealer" is used. "Penetrating" sealers are used for finishing, and are discussed in the next chapter. The topic here is the type of sealer used to cover stains and prevent them from reacting with the final finish. "Sealer" as used here goes between the stain and the finish, and is often called a sealer coat or a sanding sealer. There are slight variations.

You'll recall that in the preceding section under alcohol stains, we recommended using a sealer coat of half shellac and half denatured alcohol. Actually, this type of sealer can be used for any stain. It's *essential* for aniline dyes, and that's why it was mentioned above. If you're the dull type, like the author, you'll use it for everything. Purists, though, may recommend other types of sealers, feeling that the sealer coat should be a thinned-down version of whatever final finish you'll be using. If you wish to follow that advice, make your sealer coat out of one part of the finish (varnish, lacquer, or shellac) mixed with equal parts of its solvent. In other words:

Sealer for Shellac: ½ shellac, ½ alcohol
Sealer for Lacquer: ½ lacquer, ½ lacquer thinner (two coats are required)
Sealer for Varnish: ½ varnish (not urethane), ½ turpentine

Even easier to use than our half shellac, half alcohol mix is a "sanding" sealer, which can be used on anything, and is a mixture of shellac, varnish, and a lot of other things. It dries quickly and works very well, but is more expensive than the others. It's called a "sanding" sealer because it's used before sanding, the next step.

SANDING

After staining and sealing, the wood should be sanded (more accurately, steel-wooled). Whether you sand it thoroughly or not depends on whether or not you will be using a filler (see below). If a filler will be used, a light sanding with 3/0 steel wool should be sufficient.

When fillers are not used, you're close to the end of the ballgame. The next step is the final finish. With that in mind, you'll want the wood to be as glassy smooth as possible. Make sure that you use the right type of sanding material, either 4/0 steel wool or extra-fine (240 or 280 grit) abrasive paper, with silicon carbide or aluminum oxide backing, although garnet is okay.

The surface should be sanded thoroughly and completely, but this doesn't mean that you go at it with a vengeance. On the contrary, your touch should be light, but firm and steady. Make sure that the surface is gone over evenly and thoroughly, and be careful where there are corners and edges. Too hard a touch will cut through the sealer coat and into the stain. After sanding, wipe clean with a tack rag (see p. 133).

FILLERS

Wood fillers are controversial. Finishers have various theories about them, but there are a few things most agree on:
- Fillers give wood a smooth, mirror-flat surface.
- Fillers cause a somewhat poorer adhesion of the finish.
- Very coarse-grained, porous woods should be filled.
- Fine-grained, dense woods should not be filled.
- No one agrees about what to do about the in-betweens.

Whether you use fillers frequently or rarely is a matter of taste. If a hyper-smooth surface is important to you, then you will use wood fillers often. When you prefer your wood *au naturel,* you will avoid their use whenever possible. Our own preference is to err on the side of not using them. (See chart on p.130 for some guidelines.)

If you're *really* against fillers, those woods in the chart that should be filled can be finished with a penetrating sealer instead. Sealers either contain fillers or are formulated to make them unnecessary. The usual finishes such as shellac, lacquer, and varnish will not look well on these woods unless they're filled.

One advantage to fillers is that they can be pigmented, which means that you can use them for interesting effects with color. You've probably seen woods with certain colors in part of the grain, and this is usually done by using pigmented fillers. You can buy a neutral filler and mix in your own pigments, but there is a wide enough variety of premixed colored fillers to satisfy most tastes. The usual thing is to purchase a paste-type filler that is the same shade as, or slightly darker than the wood itself (after staining).

To use a paste filler, thin as directed on the container, or simply add turpentine until it reaches the consistency of heavy cream. After dampen-

When filler has set for about half an hour, wipe it up and force into pores at the same time by rubbing hard across the grain. (*Sherwin-Williams Co.*)

ing the part to be filled, apply the filler to the surface with a brush or squeegee. Give it a heavy dose, working it first with, then against the grain. Rub it around until you are sure that it has penetrated every pore of the wood.

After about 30 minutes, wipe the filler off with a cloth, a piece of cardboard, or a squeegee. Now, with a new, clean cloth or piece of burlap, work what filler is left across the grain. Keep wiping until all traces of filler have disappeared. Then, with yet another clean cloth, wipe slowly with the grain across the entire surface.

When the filler is completely dry (24 to 48 hours), go over it lightly with a worn piece of extra-fine abrasive paper. Be very careful not to make any gouges. Wipe up all traces of dust and apply a sealer coat as described above. One caution here: Use a varnish-turpentine sealer when applying enamel over filler; otherwise, the enamel won't adhere. Check the manufacturer's instructions (although you may find them confusing).

A word should be said about liquid fillers. This type of filler is designed mainly for fine-grained woods, but you shouldn't need a filler at all for fine-grained woods. If you want to try them, however, simply brush them on like any other coating. Repeat the application if some pores look unfilled. Sand first with fine 180-grit paper, then with extra-fine 240-grit, as above.

WOODS THAT ARE USUALLY FILLED

Ash	Locust
Butternut	Mahogany
Chestnut	Oak
Elm	Rosewood
Hickory	Walnut

WOODS THAT ARE NOT USUALLY FILLED

Basswood	Ebony
Beech	Maple
Birch	Poplar
Cypress	Sycamore
Gum	Willow

Any Softwood

10

APPLYING THE NEW FINISH

Take heart, gentle (if somewhat weary) reader, the end is near. As a matter of fact, the hard, messy part is done. Though the finish may take a little more skill and delicacy, you will at least begin to see the fruits of all your labors. That, in itself, will make the task more pleasurable.

There is a lot of balderdash written about furniture finishes. You can, if you wish, make it hard on yourself. There are some admittedly beautiful finishes that you can go into now, but you don't *have* to. The fact is that there are also some very beautiful finishes which are rather easy to apply. We suggest you try them first, then tackle the more exotic ones later. If you've followed the preceding chapters closely, you are no doubt anxious to culminate this project, and accept your reward of a handsomely refinished piece of furniture.

A word should be said here about unfinished furniture. Those who buy unfinished pieces often proceed on the assumption that they can take them home and put a finish on them immediately. If you like the color of natural wood, and it doesn't need filling, perhaps you can, but at least go over the last chapter and see if you missed anything. In all probability, your piece will need staining, anyway.

At this point you have already sanded down your refinished piece. Any new sanding is designed to get rid of any roughness caused by the refinishing materials. New wood will take a bit more work, and perhaps a lot, depending on how conscientious the manufacturer is. If the surface seems a little rough, give it a once-over with a medium 80-grit paper, then a fine 120-grit, and finally a 280-grit extra fine. Use a sanding block, and the better silicon carbide or aluminum oxide paper, although garnet is okay.

CHOOSING A FINISH

A review of all the counters in a large paint store will convince you that there are hundreds of different furniture finishes, all with their own distinct and competition-beating qualities. But there are nowhere as many generically different finishes as industry hyperbole would lead you to believe. It comes as a surprise, for example, to people who are hooked on tung oil, that many natural varnishes and penetrating sealers contain a great deal of that very ingredient.

I see no reason why the beginning finisher should use anything other than varnish, and probably a synthetic variety such as the urethanes. Those who object to the glossy look associated with varnish should simply choose the "satin" type, and rub it down if it still looks too "unnatural." Penetrating sealers are nice, too. But this hardly is the type of thing one gets tyrannical about, so we'll discuss all the various types, and you can choose for yourself.

VARNISH

Almost any type of varnish can be used for furniture, since all are basically the same, except for spar varnish. Natural varnishes contain resins (gums), linseed oil, and drying agents in a turpentine vehicle (to make them flow easier). They are tough and relatively easy to apply. The synthetic varnishes, mostly known as "plastic," "urethane," or "polyure-thane," substitute man-made for natural resins.

Spar varnish cannot be used because it is deliberately formulated so that it won't dry out in the sun. Since it is basically a marine varnish, it contains very little drier. This makes it tacky and long-lasting for boats, but not pleasant for sitting upon.

The chief disadvantage of regular varnish is that it is also rather slow-drying. Because of this, dust and specks have time to land on the surface and stick there. Tiny as they might be, these airborne particles tend to become dismayingly prominent on a table top. There are ways of ameliorating, if not preventing, this, as described below. Some of the newer varnishes demand less drying time, but it is doubtful that this problem will ever be completely eliminated.

Varnishing should be done in a warm room, at least 70 degrees. This, along with the need to minimize dust, may rule out the garage or basement, which is a serious drawback if that's where your workroom is.

There are ways to get around these difficulties. Basement dust usually comes from the floors above and from the concrete itself. If you haven't already done so, a ceiling should cover the pipes, joists, etc., where much of the dust originates. The concrete floor and walls should also be covered with one of the many finishing materials on the market. For warmth, use an electric heater.

Another way is to use the living quarters for the varnishing. It's not as messy and noxious as some of the other jobs here, and may be tolerated by the family. (But put down lots of newspaper or drop cloths over rugs *et al.*)

PREPARING FOR VARNISHING

If you haven't already given the surfaces of your masterpiece-to-be a thorough sanding with extra-fine paper, do so before varnishing. Wipe off all the dust with a clean rag, then give everything a once-over with a tack rag. A tack rag picks up the many minute particles of dust and dirt that can ruin an otherwise fine varnish job.

Another must for perfect varnishing is the pick stick. A pick stick consists of a thin piece of wood like a bamboo skewer or a cotton swab with some "burnt varnish" on the end. To make the burnt varnish, heat a small quantity of varnish in a small double boiler. Use a very small pan inside of another, or an old tin can inside of a larger one, if you don't have a regular double boiler. Add some crushed rosin, available as violin-bow rosin in a music store or in bags at a sports store, if not in your local paint store. Proportions aren't critical, but it should be about six to eight parts rosin to one part varnish.

After the materials are thoroughly mixed and begin to cool, dip the stick into the goo and leave a small ball on the end, about ⅛ inch in diameter or less. Now you'll need a little spit on the end of your finger. (Water just doesn't seem to have it.) Rub the burnt varnish around on the end into a pear shape. Roll and tap the ball in the palm of your hand until it feels good and sticky. Now set it aside until you've finished your first coat, when you will use it to pick up specks and lint with a gentle, tapping motion. (A fine sable artist's brush will also do for this, but not quite as well. In an emergency, use a plain toothpick.)

Another optional gadget that you can make, if you've a mind to, is a varnish pan. Take an old pot or pan, and bend the handle so that it fits

---

HOW TO MAKE A TACK RAG

Although tack rags are available at most hardware and paint stores, some refinishers prefer to make their own. Materials needed are a clean, lint-free cotton cloth like a diaper, oxford-cloth shirt, or handkerchief; gum turpentine, and natural varnish. Heavy cheesecloth is preferred by many to regular cotton.
- Dip the cloth into lukewarm water and wring out.
- Soak the damp cloth thoroughly with turpentine and wring out.
- Lay the cloth out on a clean surface. Drip small drops of varnish onto the surface until covered.
- Fold up double, then wring tightly.
- Repeat the process until the cloth is uniformly coated after you wring it out and open it up.

around your thumb. Attach a wire across the pan. The varnish pan prevents you from dipping the brush too far down into the liquid, and provides a convenient place (the wire) for tapping the brush.

One further note: Although shellac is recommended as a first coat in most instances, you can start off with varnish and use it all the way. Thin the prepared varnish a little first before using, however (first coat only), adding about one part turpentine to six parts varnish. The one time you *must* use shellac as a first coat is if the wood has been recently stained. Even then, you may find that some synthetic varnishes will not adhere well to shellac, so check the label before using shellac as a first or sealer coat.

APPLYING VARNISH

A *sine qua non* for varnishing is a quality, two-inch bristle brush. Even more important is that the brush be relentlessly clean. If you have any doubts about the cleanliness of the brush, buy a new one, preferably one that has a cover on the bristles so that it hasn't picked up dirt at the store. Sure, a good brush isn't cheap, but there's no point in going to all this trouble and spending all the other money if you spoil it with a dirty brush. Varnish can also be applied with a pad, if you prefer, but you'll probably find brushing more satisfactory.

A big problem with varnish is that it tends to bubble. The bubbles can ruin the surface. To prevent this, never stir varnish. Treat it as if it were nitroglycerine—gently. And never drag the brush across the rim of the can as you would for other coatings. Dip the brush about a third of the way into the varnish. Tap the bristle tips lightly against the inside of the container just above the surface of the liquid (or use the wire on your varnish pan).

Now we're ready to go.

When brushing on varnish, don't bend the bristles, but "flow" the liquid on. Use only slight pressure on the handle. Start off with parallel strokes along the grain, then cross over them immediately, brushing at right angles to the original lines. Work as quickly as possible without rushing. Start brushing in a wet area and work into the dry to avoid "stab" marks from the brush. When the surface is covered completely, "tip off" by stroking lightly with just the bristle ends of an almost dry brush. Pay particular attention to bubbles, brush marks, and runs. To minimize runs, make sure the surface is as level as possible. Work in a strong light so that you can locate dry spots, runs, and other defects.

Once you've completed the above steps, don't try to repeat them. Rebrushing causes more problems than it solves. Any runs or bumps can be rubbed off before the next coat. Keep your pick stick handy to lift off specks as quickly as possible.

Varnish is "tipped off" with just the tips of the bristles of an almost dry brush. (*Benjamin Moore & Co.*)

Even quick-drying varnishes take longer than most other finishes to dry, and that's why the surface collects so much dust and other airborne debris. Every once in a while, as it dries, go over the surface with your pick stick. Allow to dry as directed by the manufacturer, or at least 48 hours, before proceeding to the next step.

HOW MANY COATS?

This is another of those questions that furniture finishers debate incessantly. It depends on a lot of things. If you've used a shellac sealer, one varnish coat may be enough. That also depend on how many coats of shellac and the type of varnish. It depends, too, on whether you use glossy or satin varnish. Many satin finishes contain "flatting" additives, which tend to discolor and cloud up if more than one coat is used. In such cases, you can apply a glossy coat first, then a satin finish on top. Ordinarily, two coats of satin are enough. Check manufacturer's instructions in each case. If you like the looks of what you've done, it may be time to stop, because further coats could spoil what you've already achieved. Experimentation and personal taste are really the only guidelines here. In any case, unless the manufacturer insists that his product requires only one coat over bare wood, you should apply at least two coats of *something* to protect the wood.

Assuming you will apply at least one more coat of varnish over the first, you have to use extra-fine sandpaper or 4/0 steel wool between coats. Most varnishes do not adhere well to glossy surfaces. Besides, scuffing the surface will eliminate runs and other defects, as previously discussed. Use a good grade of sandpaper and always sand with the grain to avoid scratching. What you are really doing here is dulling the sheen and providing tooth for the next coat, so don't really "sand" the surface. Just go over it lightly.

It's difficult to see how you're doing with all that sanding dust around, so brush off an area to see if you've achieved a smooth, satiny look. When it looks like the job is done, dust thoroughly and give it another go with the tack rag before proceeding with the next coat. Repeat this procedure before each successive application. Apply the next varnish coat in the same manner as the first, and if it's the last coat, be particularly careful about runs, specks, and other defects.

THE FINAL STEP

After you've laid on your final coat of varnish and allowed it to dry as specified, the last coat should be "rubbed" to give your piece that highly desirable glassy-smooth finish. Actually, you should wait longer than the manufacturer directs before rubbing—a whole week, if you can stand the suspense. The finish will then have hardened sufficiently.

Powdered pumice does most of the work here, the finest grade you can find. Recent forays to paint stores indicate that pumice manufacturers no longer grade their product, which is a shame. You can assume that it is fine enough if it's intended for wood finishing, but we'd all feel a lot better if the box said FFF or FFFF. The pumice is made into a paste by mixing with a light oil such as machine or motor oil. Don't use linseed or drying oils for this procedure. You can do almost as well, by the way, by using plain 5/0 steel wool, if you can find it. Always rub parallel to the grain, no matter what the rubbing procedure. Use straight, moderate strokes, and check the effect by wiping off a portion to see how it looks. When it looks and feels perfectly smooth, use a clean dry cloth to wipe off all remaining powder and oil.

The rubbing operation will leave the surface very smooth but a little dull-looking. If you prefer a higher luster, repeat the same type of procedure, but this time use rottenstone and oil. A felt rubbing pad, reserved for use with rottenstone only, is the tool for this. (A blackboard eraser will do almost as well.) When the surface has been polished to the desired sheen, wipe off all traces of the paste by wiping repeatedly with clean cloths until

Professional hand-rubbing with pumice and oil at the Kittinger factory.

the surface is so dry that it "squeaks." The surface should then look and feel as smooth as glass.

PENETRATING SEALERS (INCLUDING TUNG OIL)

This finish is considerably different from the others in this chapter, and logically it should be considered at the end. But we're doing this in order of recommended techniques.

Once you're hooked on varnish, it's a hard thing to kick. Much as I like penetrating sealers, I find myself using varnish more or less out of habit. Penetrating sealers are actually easier, and they impart a very lovely, natural, hard finish. You can get into arguments over whether pure tung oil *is* a sealer, but it works the same way and is applied similarly.

In addition to being easy to apply, penetrating sealers (except for pure tung oil) dry quickly, reducing the problem of airborne dust. Sealers resist alcohol, chemicals, moisture, heat, cold, scratches, burns, and grease. They are simple to repair, with a quick extra coat renewing the surface instantly. You can also renew small areas without telltale lines of demarcation.

Sealers are made from a base of either synthetic resins or tung oil (a derivative of a Chinese tree which is now grown in the southern U.S.). The elastic quality of these materials allows them to sink into the pores of the wood, actually becoming a part of the surface, rather than just a coating. Sealers don't run, or leave ridges which must be sanded down.

Why not use a sealer for everything if it's so wonderful? Because its "natural" look doesn't work with many types of furniture. The wood should have a soft, mellow sheen to begin with. Although there are open-grain sealers, they work best on furniture made of close-grained woods. The surface must be very smooth and well sanded, with no holes or defects. You must like the wood the way it is. Penetrating sealers are completely invisible, imparting no sheen whatever unless you use a dozen coats. The furniture will look, in other words, like it doesn't really have a finish on it. For the better-looking woods, this is great—but not so good for the poor relations.

When you have a piece that you think will look nice with a sealer, go to your paint or hardware store and look through his probably meager stock. Read all labels carefully. You'll want a sealer that contains varnish instead of wax. Most antique or modern furniture looks best that way. Exceptions are Early American style furniture, which may look best with a wax type. Open-pored woods don't take too well to sealers. If you want to try it, though, use a thick sealer, and don't use filler.

USING PENETRATING SEALERS

A peculiarity of some sealers is that they should be strained before use (check the label). The best way to do this is by stretching a piece of nylon stocking over the top of the open can, and dip a cloth in the part that oozes through.

Apply the sealer with a circular motion of the cloth, working across the wood grain. Let the sealer sit for about 10 minutes and wipe off any excess with a clean, lintless cloth. Here we have some fun. The next step is *hand* rubbing. This should be done as soon as the excess is wiped off. Simply rub your hands over the just-finished surface, warming the mix and helping absorption into the pores of the wood. This also removes air bubbles and ensures even lapping of the finish.

Continue that same process over the other areas of the piece. Be sure to wipe off any excess that is not absorbed. Allow the piece to dry for 24 hours before smoothing. With a piece of 3/0 steel wool, buff gently. Wipe with a clean cloth and then a tack rag. This process removes bubbles and provides tooth for the next coat.

Penetrating sealer is applied with a clean cloth, using a circular motion. Hand-rubbing warms it and helps absorption into the pores. The sealer actually becomes part of the wood, resulting in a mellow, hard finish. (*Minwax.*)

SUCCEEDING COATS

There are those who, after the first sealer coat, would go to wax or varnish. This really defeats the purpose, but try it if you like. Penetrating sealer addicts, on the other hand, prefer to apply several more coats of sealer. Succeeding coats are applied the same way.

If you're going the sealer route all the way on dark wood, you'll want to try a little *crocus cloth* on the second coat. Available at a few hardware and paint stores, crocus cloth is impregnated with jeweler's rouge (iron oxide), a powder that turns light wood fibers reddish. This coloring agent, if you decide to use it, cannot be removed once it's applied.

Use crocus cloth instead of the lintless cloth for the second coat. Wrap it around a wood block for the best effect. This gives the surface an extra smoothness, as well as the reddish tint that enhances the beauty of dark woods. Don't use it on light woods.

Allow the succeeding coats of penetrating sealer to dry for 24 hours in good weather, at least 36 in high humidity. Since penetrating sealers don't alter the color of the surface, you may not be able to tell when the job is done, but apply at least two coats. A third coat is usually desirable. Some sealer addicts use a dozen coats or more. A practical rule of thumb is to keep adding coats until the piece looks good to you.

Whenever you conclude that you've put on as much sealer as the surface will take, you'll want to give it a rubdown. The easiest way is with 4/0 or 5/0 steel wool. Or, after the final coat has dried for about a week, use the pumice-and-oil mix as discussed above for varnish. This should be the end of it, but you can use wax or varnish over the last coat if you wish to make the sealer last longer. Varnish over sealer seems a little self-defeating, since one of the virtues of this finish is that it can be touched up or resealed so easily. Wax is another matter, although it may impart a sheen that you don't particularly admire. But at least wax is easily removed with turpentine.

SHELLAC

If you are "into" natural products, shellac is a "natural." It's made from the secretions of the lac, a strange insect that inhabits the banyan and fig trees of India. The secretions are processed and sold either in solution or as flakes. In either case, the flakes are immersed in alcohol. (Here, the natural bit breaks down, because pure alcohol is hard to come by. You must depend on the "denatured' variety, as discussed earlier.)

It's too bad that shellac isn't more durable. A properly shellacked piece has a warmth that is hard to duplicate with other finishes, but its vulnerability to water, alcohol, and almost everything else makes it a poor choice for final finishing of table tops, chairs, or anything else that can expect any kind of rugged duty.

This does not mean that shellac has outlived its usefulness. Far from it. As already discussed, shellac is a beautiful, fast-drying material that is unbeatable for sealer coats. It is often used as a base coat (or two) for the other finishes, notably varnish. A secret of the professional finisher is to use shellac as the basic finish on a piece, then give all the vulnerable areas, such as tops, a final coat of varnish. The rest is left as is.

Shellac is also an excellent choice for things which do not receive a lot of wear. Ideal candidates are wooden display boxes, mirror and picture frames, bookcases, etagéres, clocks, and similar objects. Even chairs, settees, and benches can be successfully shellacked. Shellac is contraindicated, however, as the doctors say, for any surface where someone may set down a martini or a vase.

BUYING SHELLAC

Although shellac does come in liquid form, it has a short shelf life because of rapid evaporation of the alcohol base. Unless you know that your supplier has a steady turnover of premixed shellac, steer away from the prepared mix and buy the flakes to make your own. People like to make it seem very esoteric, with talk about "three-pound cuts" and the like, but it's really not half as complex as it sounds. A three-pound cut means that the ratio is three pounds of lac per gallon of alcohol. The lower the cut, the more alcohol is used.

Those who have never used shellac before should start with a "thin" mix such as one-pound cut. As you get used to working with it, heavier cuts may be used. Three- or even four-pound cuts are used most often by journeymen finishers. Virtually all premixed shellac bought from the store will require some thinning. See the accompanying chart for the approximate quantities. Ratios are by volume. Use a cup, pan, or similar object to mix. Don't get exercised about exact proportions. They are not critical. As a matter of fact, you can start off by simply mixing the usual three- or four-pound commercial cut with half again as much alcohol to achieve a workable thin mix. As you progress, add less and less, but always add at least a little alcohol to assure an even flow.

"White" shellac is generally used for furniture, although some like the darker glow of "orange."

GUIDE TO CUTTING SHELLAC

To Get	from	Store-Bought	Parts Shellac	to	Parts Alcohol
3 lb.	—	5 lb.	Two	—	One
2 lb.	—	"	One	—	One
1 lb.	—	"	One	—	Two
3 lb.	—	4 lb.	One	—	Two
2 lb.	—	"	Four	—	Three
1 lb.	—	"	One	—	Two
2 lb.	—	3 lb.	Five	—	Two
1 lb.	—	"	Three	—	Four

USING SHELLAC

To thin shellac, use a clean two-inch bristle brush and stir the ingredients together in a coffee or peanut can or soup bowl. If you can afford it, you should buy a new brush each time. If not, wash the brush thoroughly, first with alcohol, then soap and water. Go easy when you stir. Although it's not as critical as with varnish, the bubbles that are generated by stirring will hinder your work.

Prepare the surface in the same way as for varnish, wiping with a dry cloth, then a tack cloth. Set the piece on your work platform and start working on the largest surface.

Dip your brush into the previously prepared mix, stir it slowly a few more times, then apply the fully loaded brush to the surface. Use long, even strokes, lapping over the last line just a little bit as you move along. Although you don't have to brush with the grain, it's a good habit to get into. The brush strokes may look obvious, and you'll be tempted to go over them, but don't. One advantage of shellac is that such defects work themselves out as the liquid dries. When you've covered the surface completely and evenly, put the brush down and relax a bit.

Now turn your piece to another side and do whatever you can from there. Keep turning until the entire piece is done. Now let it dry for an hour, maybe less, until it is dry to the touch.

After the first coat dries, rub down with 3/0 steel wool. Wipe with a dry cloth to remove all traces of steel fragments, etc., then apply a second coat. Three coats of shellac are usually recommended, although two will do in many cases. If the shellac is to be followed with varnish as a final finish, two coats are plenty. Use a 3/0 steel wool rubdown, and dust thoroughly with a clean cloth and then a tack rag.

After the final shellac coat, the high gloss should be rubbed down a little with steel wool. How much gloss you rub off depends on the grade of steel wool. To take off just a bit of the shine, use the finest grade you can find, 6/0, 5/0, or whatever. To produce the more popular "satin" (dull) finish, 3/0 is best.

When the steel-wooling is complete, rub thoroughly with a clean cloth and put on an application of wax (see p. 166).

LACQUER

For many years, lacquer was strictly a pro's material. It's used almost exclusively by furniture factories, which have the tools and facilities to spray it. It's still better sprayed, but the expense and mess of spray equipment make this method prohibitive for the do-it-yourselfer. And spraying isn't as easy as it looks.

Brushing lacquers have been continually improved by manufacturers, and now these are within the scope of the handyman. Lacquer's chief virtue is also its chief fault for the home finisher. It dries extremely fast, which makes it great for speedy work, but also means that you must do it right the first time or it's too late to correct mistakes. Lacquer literally dries as you apply it, and it's very difficult, if not impossible, to go back over it and smooth it.

Actually, lacquer is very much like shellac (they both start with lac secretions, as the names imply). The thinner for lacquer is acetone, however, which dries even faster than alcohol. If you've ever done any body painting on cars, you know that lacquer mixed with pigment imparts a hard, fast-drying finish to metal. The same type of spray lacquer in clear form can be used for furniture, but it's expensive and messy. For small objects, though, aerosol cans are handy and do a nice job.

When you buy brushing lacquer, purchase twice as much lacquer thinner. The lacquer should be mixed with equal parts of thinner, and you'll need extra thinner for cleaning yourself, the brush, and whatever else you've messed up. Always buy thinner from the same manufacturer, because there are crucial differences between brands. And always read labels, as usual. A separate lacquer brush is a must, too, of natural bristle, since acetone dissolves nylon.

If you plan on using lacquer for your final finish, pay close attention to the stains, fillers, etc., that you use. Many of them are dissolved by acetone. Make sure that all the preparatory products are lacquer-compatible. And avoid lacquer for certain woods like mahogany and rosewood. Acetone eats up the natural dyes in those woods. A good sealer coat should prevent this, but it's easier and safer to use another finish.

APPLYING LACQUER

As always, clean all surfaces thoroughly and wipe with the tack rag. Mix lacquer and thinner in equal parts, and dip the brush until it is moderately full. Brush the lacquer on with long, bold, full, and continuous strokes, working from the unfinished area into the finished, and lapping the strokes slightly onto the wet edge. Don't go back over prior strokes unless they look really bad. Be careful not to let the liquid accumulate in carvings or turnings. Tip off the excess quickly and lightly only where necessary.

One of the nice things about lacquer is that scuffing between coats is necessary only if there are surface defects. Two coats are all that should be needed. Additional layers will only gum up the first two. Since the coating is quite shiny, you will probably want to give the final coat a rubdown. Use the procedure described for varnish (p. 136).

LINSEED OIL FINISH

It should be emphasized at the outset that when linseed oil is discussed in conjunction with furniture it is always *boiled* linseed oil. That doesn't mean that you put raw oil in a pot and brew it yourself. It means you *buy* it boiled. And it's not really "boiled" at all—not anymore—but has had drying agents added in processing. Just be sure that the label says "boiled" instead of "raw," because raw linseed oil is sold side by side for use in paints. Raw oil, like spar varnish, hardly ever dries, which makes it great— again like spar varnish—for exterior use but not so hot for furniture.

Linseed oil is a lovely finish for some antiques. It is, however, the very devil to work with because the job is never done. If you like that feeling of satisfaction that comes when a task is finally finished, stay away from linseed oil.

WORKING WITH LINSEED OIL

Linseed oil is mixed three to two with distilled turpentine. Make sure the surface to be finished is perfectly smooth; wipe with a dry cloth, then a tack rag. Heat the mixture in a double boiler (never directly over heat because of the fire hazard) and apply with a lintless cloth.

Work on the flat surfaces first, then do the carved or grooved parts after the mix has cooled. (If a piece has too much "gingerbread," this finish shouldn't be used at all.) Keep rubbing it into each area for 5 to 20 minutes or until the wood can absorb no more.

After each section has absorbed all the oil it can, wipe away the excess, changing cloths as soon as they become saturated. Remove all traces of oil from crevices or the oil will either harden or become sticky. (That's why it shouldn't be used when there are too many crevices.)

Next, rub thoroughly with a polishing cloth for 10 to 20 minutes. A firmly woven, hard cloth is excellent for developing a nice luster, although flannel can be used, too. Keep rubbing until you can set your hand on the part and it won't pick up oil.

At least four coats are required, with a minimum of a week's drying time in between. Oil cultists disclaim anything less than eight coats, so you'll probably be going at it every week or two for four to six months, maybe a year.

If that isn't enough to discourage all but true believers, you are hereby warned that another coat or two is necessary every six months to a year to keep up that satiny sheen. Furthermore, the undersides of table tops and other unseen surfaces must be continuously oiled, too, to prevent warping.

Unless you have lots of time and an extremely placid disposition, use one of the other finishes. Hurrying ruins the best-intentioned attempts, rendering the surface sticky or gummy. Each and every coat must be completely and thoroughly dry before application of the rest. Be scrupulous with the hand test as described above, and don't skimp on another important lubricant—elbow grease.

DOING IT THE FRENCH WAY

We arrive now, friends, at the ultimate finish—the hallowed, revered, and—I believe—overrated French polish. True, it's beautiful if done right. But that's the problem. It's damned difficult to do right.

French polish is an old finishing technique rather than a "finish" per se.

Some favorite materials—shellac and linseed oil—are used, but applied in a different manner. One of the best things about it is that it can be used for restoring as well as refinishing.

If you are working with an old finish, remove any old wax first with turpentine or mineral spirits. Let the surface dry completely, then dust and wipe with a tack rag. Make a pad about the size of a baseball out of an old shirt or other lint-free cloth, dip it into boiled linseed oil until it is saturated, then squeeze out most of the oil. Dip the pad into a thin cut of shellac (one-pound cut or less) and rub it onto the surface. The *way* you rub it on is vital. The secret of French polish is that you cannot start or stop the wiping process while the rag is on the surface.

Never lay the pad on the surface and then start wiping, but begin your stroke outside and continue it onto the surface. *Don't stop*—ever. Just keep wiping and wiping in a circular or figure-eight pattern until the cloth gets dry or you drop from exhaustion. Always wipe toward the edge and completely off without stopping.

As long as your rag is on the surface, wipe fairly hard, hard enough to force the shellac deep into the pores but not so hard that the pad sticks. When the pad starts to get dry, work over to and off the edge and stop. Apply a few more drops of linseed oil and a teaspoon of shellac to the pad and rub again. Keep at it until the entire surface is coated. Let dry for about a day, then go over it again. Keep going over it until the surface has just the right glow. The more you wipe, the better it will look.

The glow you've produced in this way may look a little *too* glossy. (High gloss is a definite feature of French polish.) If the finish does wind up too shiny, you can dull it by the application of a pumice-oil mix as described above, or by rubbing it down with very fine steel wool. Better yet, don't bother with French polish unless you like a high gloss.

Although French polish doesn't sound too difficult to achieve—and it isn't, really—it does take considerable practice. The novice should try it out on a less-beloved piece before attempting it on Grandma's baby grand. (Pianos are one favorite application, by the way.) One good thing about French polish is that mistakes are easily repaired. If you leave the rag in a spot too long, a little alcohol will wipe off the error. The bad news is that you'll have to start again from scratch.

French polish is really a lovely thing, but wait until you've mastered some of the other finishes first, because it is a tough finish to achieve satisfactorily. Practice with some of the other finishes will give you some expertise and confidence.

OPAQUE (PAINT) FINISHES

An opaque finish is a radical departure from the finishes discussed above. The finishes thus far have been designed to illuminate and heighten the appeal of natural wood. Opaque finishes do just the opposite. They hide the natural color and grain. In some cases, this can be a good thing. Much unfinished furniture, for example, is made of poorer woods, and can benefit from painting. Some woods, like fir and many of the other softwoods, have an unpleasant grain, which is better hidden.

On the other hand, selected painting, such as the techniques discussed briefly in Chapter 5, can enhance the beauty of a piece. The Chinese excelled at this art, and the beauty of some of their lacquers cannot be equaled (mainly because of the scarcity of the materials, which come from rare trees that have to be chopped up to extract the sap).

There are other reasons for using opaque finishes:

- Some furniture was painted originally, and may be in need of repainting. Such styles include variations of Louis XV, Louis XVI, seventeenth- and eighteenth-century Italian, Sheraton fancy chairs, Shaker furniture, Windsor and Hitchcock chairs and rockers.
- The appearance of some furniture may be improved by painting. Examples include Mission and late Victorian pieces, and furniture that has been damaged by stain, wear, etc. Heavy Mediterranean, Moorish, or similar pieces may look better at least partially painted.

APPLYING OPAQUE FINISHES

There are three important steps to be followed in obtaining a successful paint job. First, you must choose a quality paint. Oil-based enamel (pigmented urethane or natural varnish) is best, but semi-gloss may be used if you want a duller finish. Never use latex or other water-soluble paints on surfaces that will hold vases, glasses, etc. Second, the surface must be prepared properly. Third is correct application.

Proper surface preparation depends on the condition of the furniture. Wooden furniture in good condition simply requires a good cleaning to remove oil, wax, or polish. Use paint thinner, then sand lightly. This will dull the gloss and provide tooth. Be sure the furniture is clean and dry before applying the enamel. If the wood furniture is in poor condition, it should be completely stripped of its old finish. Fill any holes or cracks with plastic wood or wood putty and let dry thoroughly. Finally, sand as smooth as possible, apply an enamel undercoat, and allow to dry.

Unfinished furniture is usually factory sanded. It's a good idea to sand it lightly anyway before you apply the enamel undercoat. If a second undercoat is needed, sand lightly between coats.

When repainting wrought iron, aluminum, or other metal furniture, clean thoroughly first. Sand away any traces of rust. Prime the spots of bare metal with a quality metal primer such as zinc chromate. Let the primed areas dry, then apply the enamel, or use spray lacquer in an aerosol can (see below).

(*Minwax.*)

To apply enamel, load your brush generously; flow the enamel onto the surface in long, smooth strokes with the grain. Don't reload the brush or cross-stroke. With your nearly dry brush, go over the surface again with the grain, still using long, smooth strokes. The method provides even coverage and eliminates any excess that might cause runs.

Additional hints:

Remove hardware, drawer pulls, and metal fittings beforehand. Those which can't be removed should be covered with masking tape. If the pulls and handles will also be enameled, it's easier and more efficient to take them off and paint each separately.

Place chairs and small tables upside down on your work platform or on a bench; it's a more convenient height.

Do the undersides first, then put the pieces right side up and finish.

SPRAY PAINTING

Paint for every purpose now comes in aerosol cans. You can buy both enamel and lacquer this way. Bad as the aerosol spray may be for the environment, it is great for painting outdoor furniture and informal indoor pieces. The aerosol is best for small jobs rather than large, as there is ordinarily a great waste of paint. Always spray outdoors if possible. To use any kind of spray paint properly, hold the spray about six inches from the surface, then move your whole arm back and forth in a direction parallel to the surface. Holding your arm steady and just moving the wrist is the cause of most spray-paint failure. It takes a while to get the hang of this technique. Try it on an inconspicuous surface first. Watch out for paint buildups, which cause runs and can ruin an otherwise fine job. Keep your arm moving to avoid this.

One more word about opaque finishes before we leave the topic. Use epoxy paints for anything that will be subject to severe punishment. These finishes are recommended for kids' toys, kitchen use, and outdoor furniture. Check the manufacturer's instructions carefully before use. Most epoxy paints have to be mixed with a hardener before application.

SEALER STAINS AND VARNISH STAINS

These two finishes are discussed last because that's where they belong. No respectable finisher would mention them in the same breath with the other finishes.

Sealer stains are actually all right if you're sure that you like the color. If you don't, once it's on, you can't change it. You can fool around with regular stains a little bit, as described in the preceding chapter, if the shade isn't what you expected it to be, but a sealer stain can't be altered.

Varnish stains are strictly *verboten* if you want your union card as a finisher. They are cheapo for cheapo furniture. They're fast and easy, though, and if you have a piece with an ugly grain or one that's too far gone for legitimate refinishing, it's your business if you want to use a varnish stain.

Other combinations of stain, finish, and filler are available and are steadily becoming more numerous. We old-timers are leery of them all. Give them a try if you like—but not on anything really nice.

A WAX "FINISH"

Wax is commonly (and erroneously) mentioned as a "finish" for wood furniture. But wax should never be applied over bare wood. What is referred to as a wax finish is an extra-heavy wax application over another finish, usually a penetrating sealer.

If you like the waxy look, and many do, first use the sealer, varnish, or shellac, then several coats of wax. Actually, the wax is more a protective coating than a finish. It is discussed as such in Chapter 12 relating to care and maintenance.

11

BASIC UPHOLSTERY

While some jobs are fairly simple, upholstery is a complicated art. Here, we'll deal chiefly with simple upholstery problems related to repair and refinishing.

UPHOLSTERY TOOLS AND MATERIALS

For the type of work under discussion here, the following basics should suffice:

TOOLS

Tack Hammer—The magnetic head holds and starts the tacks, the business end drives them in.

Staple Gun—Often used as a substitute for the tack hammer (and the tacks, or course), but you'll find ample use for both. We like a dual-action gun, with low power for small staples and high power for large staples and harder woods. The office-type stapler is too light for this work.

Upholstery Shears—Any heavy-duty shears will do, but you'll be glad you have a pair of these for cutting thick upholstery fabric.

Webbing Stretcher—There are various types, but all do the same thing—pull webbing (see below) and sometimes fabric so that it is taut for tacking with the other hand.

Upholstery Needles—Regular needles can be used for light materials, but you'll need the thicker, heavy-duty type for thick materials. Some of these large needles are curved, some are straight, for various duties.

Ripping Tools—For removing old upholstery, tacks, etc. A tack puller is one type. Some upholsterers prefer a ripping chisel, which is held along the grain of the wood and whacked with a mallet. Screwdrivers and pliers can also be used to remove staples and other fasteners.

149

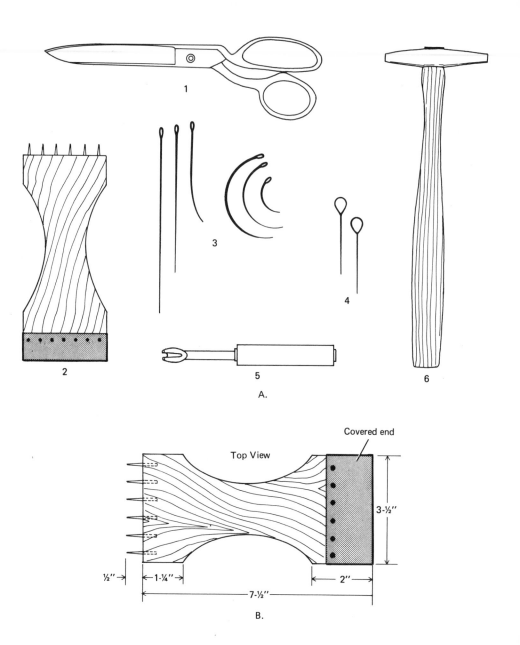

FIGURE 21 (a). The basic upholstery tools: (1) large shears; (2) webbing stretcher; (3) curved and straight needles, assorted sizes; (4) upholstery skewers, for holding material temporarily in place; (5) tack puller; (6) tack hammer with one magnetic head.

FIGURE 21 (b). You can make your own webbing stretcher with a half-inch-thick piece of hardwood sawn as shown. Pre-drill and insert 10d nails in front, with heads cut off and ends filed down to points. Other end is covered with leather, rubber, felt, or similar material.

MATERIALS

Assorted Tacks, Nails, and Staples—How wide an assortment of these you'll need depends on how deeply you get into upholstering. Start off with #8 for tacks for webbing and #4 for most other fabrics.

Webbing—Rolled burlap, rubber, or plastic, usually about 3½ inches wide. Used for reinforcing seats and backs.

Twine—Of flax, hemp, or manila, strong enough to tie and hold springs and do other tying jobs.

Padding and Stuffing—Foam rubber, rubberized hair, felt, cotton, various synthetic materials. Used to soften seats and backs.

Muslin—Casing material to hold stuffing in shape.

Dust Covers—Fine-woven crinoline or cambric or, in newer chairs, continuous monofilament. Used on the undersides of chairs and sofas, and almost always in need of replacement.

Cover Materials (Fabric)—Upholstery materials or fabric, which the pros call "cover" materials to distinguish them from the others mentioned above. There are almost as many types, both natural and synthetic, as you can count.

Springs—Coil springs are used mostly on older furniture, the "zig-zag" type on some newer pieces. If an upholstery supplier doesn't have them, try mail-order houses.

Metal Straps—For attaching some springs, such as the zig-zag type, to wood.

BEFORE YOU DO ANYTHING

The time to think about upholstery is when you're buying a piece of secondhand furniture. Buying somebody else's upholstery is risky. If there isn't a tag or certificate stating that the piece has been deloused, you shouldn't buy it unless you intend to replace all of the upholstery.

Is it necessary to remove all of the old upholstery? In most cases, yes. Even if you're only reamalgamating the finish, you'll probably get some of the chemicals on the fabric, so why take the chance? The only time you don't have to bother is when you're touching up a defect here or there. When completely refinishing, you have no choice but to remove the old fabric.

Do you have to put on new upholstery when you refinish? Not necessarily, but you will certainly want to unless the upholstery is in exceptionally good shape or made of a valuable material like spun gold (a highly unlikely prospect). Whether you do it personally depends on a lot of things. As discussed in Chapter 5, a dining-room chair seat is a simple job. A tufted couch is a job for the professional. There are degrees of difficulty in between.

TAKING OFF THE OLD FABRIC

One of the not-very-secret secrets of upholsterers is to save the old pieces of fabric. Whatever you do, don't throw them away. Whether you do it yourself, or have it done by professionals, the old pieces of fabric serve as handy patterns for the new material. Remove the pieces as carefully as possible, marking them to show where they came from and in what order.

You may find it difficult to figure out where to start with upholstery removal. Check the bottom of the piece for tacks and nails. Remove them first, and with some fabric gone you may reveal more pieces to probe. If the fasteners seem hidden, remove the welting (rolled-up fabric around edges and corners). The tacks may be under that. Or pry off a corner of the fabric with a screwdriver to see exactly how it was applied.

Keep working on the visible fastenings and snooping around until you discover the hidden ones. If necessary, rip the fabric, but don't destroy it completely. Remember that this will be your pattern for the new piece. Store the marked pieces somewhere where you can find them, or take them to the upholsterer if he says he can use them.

THE NAKED TRUTH

With the fabric gone, you'll see what you really have. You'll see what the wood looks like without a stain, and how sturdy the frame and other parts are. Unless you're very fortunate, you're likely to find loose joints, sagging springs, worn webbing, moldy padding, and lots of dirt.

Examine the stuffing. It may be made of cotton batting, animal hair, excelsior, Saran, Tampico, or other fibers. If it isn't too moldy, you can probably use it again, but you may prefer to replace it with foam rubber or another modern material. Foam is considered more comfortable but doesn't always retain the original shape unless expertly installed. Some better manufacturers still prefer animal hair.

Don't worry about the padding now, however. Remove it and set it aside, even if it's in shreds. You can use it to guide you in cutting the new stuff.

At this point, the springs should be exposed. Check to see if any are broken. In a good chair or sofa, the springs should be in good shape, but they may well have slipped their moorings.

Springs in better furniture are tied to the webbing and each other in an intricate pattern which is reproduced in Figures 24 and 25. Each spring is tied to the adjacent frame and to the other springs on all sides, and they are tied diagonally to each other. They are also attached to the webbing below, to metal strips, or to wood cleats, depending on the construction. Underneath the springs is the webbing, which is tacked to the bottom of the frame. In some construction, the webbing may be the *only* thing under the upholstery.

USING A TACK HAMMER

You may have seen pictures of upholsterers working with a mouthful of tacks, spitting one onto the magnetic end of a tack hammer and deftly setting it in exactly the right spot. As with most media portraits, there is some distortion. The modern upholsterer probably uses a high-powered staple gun at least as often as the tack hammer. But there are times when you can't get at something with a stapler, and some materials don't hold too well with staples. For most things that were formerly tacked, though, staples can and should be used instead. To avoid repetitious phrases like "tack or staple" we use "tack" rather than "staple." Just remember that "tack" used here means either way.

An upholstery tack is short and squat with a big head. They're devilishly hard to hold when starting. Sometimes you can push them into soft wood enough to make them hold, but not in very hard woods. A tack hammer has one conventional head (although longer and skinnier than a claw hammer) and one magnetic head. The regular head is for setting tacks that have already been started. The magnetic end holds the tack in position so that you can aim carefully at the spot where it's supposed to go and whack it in right on target.

If the knack eludes you, try practicing on an old board. Mark some targets on it and see how close you can get to bull's-eye. You'll find that at first you'll need the other end to finish driving the tack home, but as your confidence grows, you should be able to drive the tack in with a single blow (at least in softwood).

WEBBING REPAIRS

If the webbing is intact and doesn't look rotted, leave it as is. But if it has even partially deteriorated, replace all of it. Remove the tacks that hold deteriorated webbing with a tack puller or a claw hammer and replace the webbing as described below.

To replace webbing, begin with the center row and work from back to front. Place the chair or sofa upside down on your workbench or platform and lay the roll of webbing over the back of the frame. Allow the edge to hang over about 1½ inches and stagger four #8 tacks into the frame. Fold the end piece over twice, then insert five more tacks in staggered fashion. Run the roll over to the other side and pull taut with the webbing stretcher (press the butt against the side of the frame, then press down with the teeth or holder into the material). Put four more tacks into the webbing at the front of the frame, then cut off the roll about 1½ inches from the edge. Double the excess back over twice and set in five more tacks.

Install webbing from the center to each edge, leaving approximately an inch between strips. Then start the same process from side to side. Start

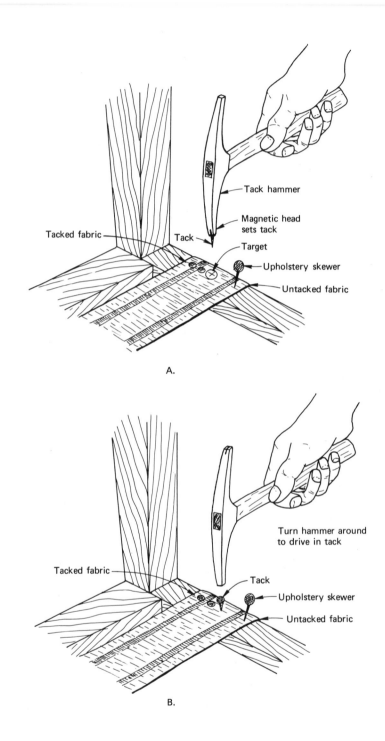

A.

B.

FIGURE 22. Using a tack hammer.

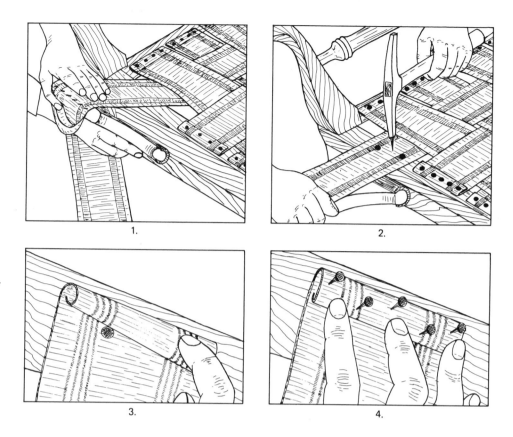

FIGURE 23. Steps in (1) stretching, (2) tacking, (3) folding, and (4) retacking webbing.

at the center again, and weave the strips in and out of the crossing strips. (You'll either have to pre-cut the strips or weave from the roll over to the other side.) Stretch each strip and tack in the same way as the other strips.

The clever reader will have noticed that webbing is applied in a manner that defies logic. The weight of the springs, stuffing, and people's bottoms is in a direction which tends to push out the tacks. This violates all the principles of sound construction, but no way has yet been devised to avoid it. If you use staples, get the coated kind for better holding power.

If not replacing the webbing, check each strip carefully and tighten up any loose strips. Use extra tacks where the old ones have pulled out or loosened, placing the new tacks into fresh spots. If the space between strips is more than two inches, install extra webbing, even if the strips cross over the old ones. Better to err on the side of extra strength.

Most upholstered chair backs also use webbing. In this case, you don't have to worry about tacks being pulled in the wrong direction. The webbing is attached to the *front* side of the chair back using basically the same methods as those used for seats.

FIXING SPRINGS

Springs need not be replaced unless they have lost their "springiness" or are bent out of shape. Clean rusty spots with steel wool, and vacuum out the dust. There should be one coil spring at each webbing intersection. Each spring should be approximately twice the height of the seat frame when untied (5-inch spring for a 2½-inch frame). Better furniture has graduated-size springs. Replace any that are badly rusted or deformed.

If any of the twine holding the springs has rotted or frayed, the rest is sure to follow, so you might as well replace it all. Flax twine is the best. Sew the springs to the webbing first using a 6-inch straight "mattress" needle. If you are tying all the springs, start in one corner with a long strand of twine and make three stitches each at four equally spaced points

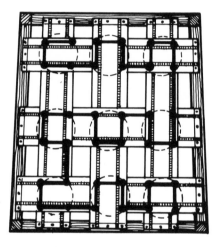

FIGURE 24. Pattern for tying springs to webbing.

around the spring. Stitch continuously from spring to spring to avoid cutting twine (see Figure 24).

If springs are tied to metal or wood instead of webbing, check the attaching devices to make sure they are sound and replace missing parts, nails, staples, etc.

NEW TWINE AND SPRINGS

Each spring is tied eight times, either to the frame or to its neighbors. If the twine is in good condition, simply replace any missing strands with manila or hemp spring-tying twine. The twine is then attached to the frame with #12 tacks. Replace any missing tacks. Tie the twine to the tacks as described below.

Single tacks can be used at each juncture of twine and frame if the

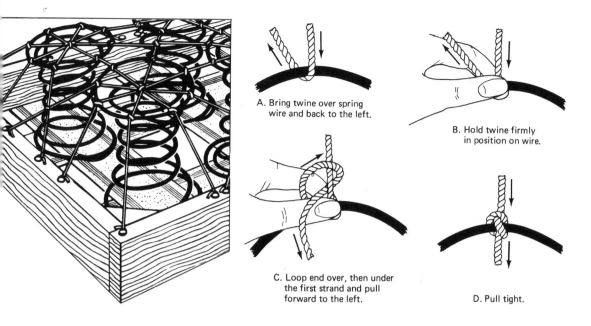

A. Bring twine over spring wire and back to the left.

B. Hold twine firmly in position on wire.

C. Loop end over, then under the first strand and pull forward to the left.

D. Pull tight.

FIGURE 25. Each spring is tied eight times around the edges, and is knotted in the center. Springs are connected by twine either to the frame or the adjacent springs. Tying method is shown at right.

weight isn't too great, but where there is any chance of great strain, double tacks about ⅜ inch apart are much better. To tie twine to single tacks, use a square knot. Use a double half-hitch (Figure 26) for double tacks.

When all the springs need retying, work from back to front, then side to side, and, finally, diagonally across all opposite corners. Start by tying the twine to tacks on top of the rear frame, then run the ball to the front; add an extra 50% per row for knotting, and cut. Starting with the center row, tie twine from the frame to the edge of the nearest spring with a figure-eight knot, then to the opposite side of the same spring. Proceed to the next spring using the same procedures, and continue until you reach the other side. Pull the twine tightly each time. When you get to the other

FIGURE 26. Tying twine to tacks at the beginning (A) and end (B) of the run. It's the same knot (double half-hitch), but you can't use the easier method (A) at the end because one end of the twine is attached.

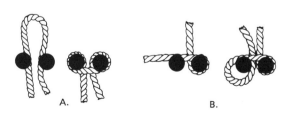

A.

B.

side of the frame, tap tacks in partway on the opposite edge and tie twine tightly to them. When secure, drive tacks in all the way.

Next, proceed to the rows on either side of the center and continue until all "vertical" rows are tied. Start again at the center, this time doing the "horizontal" or side-to-side rows. Then go to the left-hand corner of the back and put some tacks there. Measure a row diagonally to the front right corner and add two-thirds for knotting. Tie to the edge of the first spring, loop around the other crossing cords in the center of the spring, then to the opposite edge of that spring. Continue the same way until finished. Now tie all the diagonal rows in the opposite direction to complete the eight-point tie.

This sounds a lot more difficult than it is, and you can probably get a better idea by studying the accompanying diagrams and the way the old strings were tied. Be sure to realize, though, that the diagram is one-dimensional and does not show how the springs are compressed so that the center of the seat is the highest point and the edge springs are almost down to the level of the frame. This varies according to the chair. A section through the seat of most chairs would look rounded, as shown in Figure 27. Cover springs with burlap as described below.

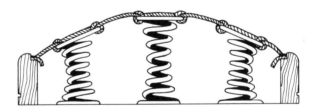

FIGURE 27. The usual configuration of a chair seat.

ZIG-ZAG SPRINGS

Zig-zag, "no-sag" springs are treated a little differently. These are self-supporting, long, thick steel wires which perform the function of both springs and webbing. They are attached from the front to the back of the piece with metal clips made expressly for this purpose (and usually sold in kit form with the springs). If clips aren't available, use clinched (bent-over) nails. Smaller, helical springs are fastened between the zig-zags and to the sides of the chair.

Problems with this type of spring occur when the springs break, or the clips become loose. To repair loose clips, either move the clip over slightly and renail, or fill the old holes with wood dough and renail when it hardens.

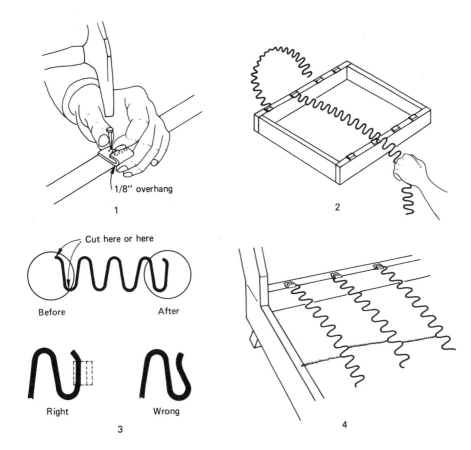

FIGURE 28: Replacing zig-zag springs: (1) Nail a zig-zag spring clip. (2) Stretch spring to a shallow arc, with the center 1 to 2 inches higher than the frame. (3) The proper way of cutting the zig-zag coil (above) and the right and wrong ways of bending ends to fit the clip (below). (4) Helical springs (shown) or strong twine is used to attach zig-zag springs to each other and to the frame.

Remove any broken springs and secure new ones with new clips. Attach the new clips and springs approximately where the old ones were. Ideal spacing is 4½ inches from center to center, if you can't find the old locations or are doing the springs over completely. Clips are positioned on the front and back rails with the curved clip edge even with the inside edges of the rails. Put a nail through the center hole. Don't nail the other holes yet.

This type of spring material comes in coils, which you must measure and cut. To determine the right length, insert the end of the coil into a rear clip and stretch to a shallow arc, between 1 and 2 inches higher in the center than the frame. Hold the coil in place with your hand or insert the nearest loop temporarily into the front clip. Make a mark halfway around the next loop at either of the outside edges.

Cut the coil at the mark with a cold chisel, hacksaw, heavy-duty wire cutters, or similar instrument. Put the cut end in a vise with about ¼ inch protruding. Hammer that part with a ball-peen or mash hammer until it is bent at a rough 45-degree angle. This will prevent the end from slipping out of the clip. Be sure that the loop section at the end is straight and roughly parallel with the direction of the clip to allow free pivoting. If it isn't, bend to the position shown in Figure 28. You can do some of this with pliers, but it's tough. Special tools are available, but are not worth the cost for an occasional job.

Insert each end of the spring into its appropriate clip and double-check the height as directed above. (More than 2 inches will make the cushioning too soft; less than 1 inch will be too hard.) Cut any other springs the same way and attach them. Alternate the direction of the springs so that loops face each other. Nail through the other clip holes, slanting nails toward the center of the rail to prevent splitting.

Helical springs or strong twine should be used to tie the adjacent springs together and to the side rails. Burlap or other strong fabric is laid over the springs loosely to act as an insulator. Tack this to the frame, but not too tightly. Sew to coil springs as shown, but not to zig-zag. Then continue upholstering in the usual way.

FIGURE 29. Sew burlap to coil springs with a curved #4 needle.

STUFFING AND PADDING

If you've sat in a hard, uncomfortable chair for a long time, you know how important proper cushioning is. With any luck, you can use the old materials for this. Check them to see if they smell musty, or are discolored or deteriorated. It is a good idea to treat stuffing you plan to reuse with a moth repellent.

If the stuffing isn't reusable, save it anyway and use it for a pattern to prepare new material. Take some of it to the upholstery shop and ask them to supply you with a similar or better material. The stuffing should be encased in muslin or synthetic material to help it retain its shape.

Reapply the old padding, or buy new felted cotton padding. Tear, don't cut, this material, to avoid hard edges. Use the padding to correct any sags or low sections of the stuffing, and apply it where the sharp edges of the frame will tend to cut the cover fabric. Don't compress the padding by hand. Let the cover material do that. Stitch the padding, where possible, to the stuffing with a sharp, curved needle. Use rubber cement on the frame.

When using foam rubber, apply 3- or 4-inch strips of muslin along the edges for greater smoothness. Glue the muslin to the foam and tack down the other edges to the frame. Snip the strips around corners so that the padding will lie flat.

SELECTING A COVER FABRIC

Cover materials are difficult to find in many areas, and where they are stocked, the selection is likely to be limited. Sometimes you can find a larger stock of interesting and relatively inexpensive fabrics in discount fabric stores. This type of place is not for the fainthearted, but if you're persistent and can haggle, you'll probably find what you want there at a reasonable price.

No matter where you shop, the key is to get the best fabric you can afford. How do you tell the best? That's a difficult question. Here are some guidelines as gathered from experience, consumer groups, and the Cornell University Extension Service.

CHECKING THE APPEARANCE

Color—Analyze the colors you have in the room where the piece will go. If you want the room to look spacious and restful and the chair inconspicuous, choose a fabric related in color to that of the wall. If you wish to feature the chair itself, use a contrasting color or a printed fabric.

The most practical colors are those between very dark and very light. They do not soil readily, do not show lint or animal hairs, and are immune to sun-fading.

Pattern—Plain fabrics look good in most rooms and on most chairs, and are less expensive than patterned fabrics, which require matching. Patterned fabrics usually show wrinkles and soil less quickly than do plain ones. Be sure to test the fabric on the chair before you cut it. The effect may be quite different from what you envisioned. Most stores will accept returns, although there may be a handling charge.

Texture—Shiny, smooth, sleek textures or tweedy fabrics usually look good with modern and new furnishings; dull, soft textures often complement fine old woods and furnishings that have begun to show wear.

LABELING

Proper labeling of all fabrics, which helps identify fibers, became mandatory when the Textile Fiber Products Identification Act was passed on March 1, 1960. The label must give:

- The generic (family) name. Fibers with similar characteristics are grouped together in 20 different groupings. For example, "natural fibers" include cotton and linen; "man-made fibers, not sensitive to heat," include rayon and metallics; "man-made fibers, sensitive to heat," include acetates and acrylics.
- The percentage, using the generic name, of all fibers 5% or over in order of predominance by weight. For example—cotton, 75%; rayon, 25%.
- The country of origin, if foreign made.
- The registered identification number, house mark, or name under which business is conducted.

Read and interpret labels accurately; for example, a small percentage of a certain fiber may add glamor but little to quality and may increase cost. Some fiber characteristics important in the selection of cover fabrics are as follows:

Cotton—The fiber from which many chair cover fabrics are made, is strong, durable, and easily laundered, but should be treated for shrink resistance. Special chemical *finishes,* mainly resins, can give added protection not inherent in the fiber itself. They can make the fabric crease- or wrinkle-resistant and less likely to absorb soil, spots, or stains. Some finishes render cotton water-repellent, easy to care for, or mildew- and flame-resistant. Good-quality finishes should last as long as the fabric, and in most instances are best applied by the manufacturer, but a few can be sprayed on at home (Scotchgard is one well-known brand). Some add considerably to the cost. They can also make the fabric less pliable and more difficult to handle.

Man-made Fibers—Nylon, dacron, acrylics, acetates and rayon in cover fabrics are usually used in blends (two or more fibers blended together to make the yarn), in combinations (different fibers for lengthwise and for crosswise yarns), or in blend combinations (a blended fiber yarn for one direction and a single fiber yarn for the other). These man-made fibers add characteristics such as crease resistance, stability, and easy care. However, special treatment is needed for rayon acetates to prevent shrinkage.

COLORFASTNESS AND WEAVE

Labels should indicate colorfastness and specify whether the fabric is fast to light, laundering, dry cleaning and/or gas fumes. Labels usually indicate "resistance" rather than "proof" (light-resistant rather than light-proof). The term "vat" in the label indicates good colorfastness.

How the fabric will wear depends on the fiber or fibers used, the yarns from which the cloth is woven, and how the cloth is woven. Tightly twisted yarns usually wear better than those loosely twisted; a two-ply strand usually is stronger than a one-ply. Pull out and untwist a lengthwise and a crosswise yarn to see how they are made.

A firm, compact weave holds its shape better than a loosely woven fabric of similar texture and weight, and dust does not sift through easily. However, the fabric should be pliable enough to handle and shape to the frame. Smooth fibers, bulky heavy yarns, and loose weaves often fray with wear and cleaning.

Balanced weaves, with about the same number of yarns both ways and with all yarns of about the same size and strength, wear better than those with thick filling yarns and thin warp yarns, for example. A twill weave (diagonal ridges) may resist wear and soil better than a plain weave of comparable quality. A satin weave may have long surface yarn to catch and be pulled by buttons, sharp edges, and claws. (A satin pillow on a satin couch tends to be very slippery.)

BUYING TIPS

If the design is printed on the surface only instead of woven the same on both sides of the material, draw a yarn or follow the weave partway across the width at the cut end. If not printed true, you usually have to cut with the design rather than with the grain. Fabrics cut this way neither wear nor clean well, unless given special finishes to help them keep their original shape; these finishes should be guaranteed to last the life of the fabric.

Materials come in 48- and 54-inch widths (rarely in 60-inch). Estimate yardage for different widths. Wide fabrics are more economical if back and arm pieces can be cut from half the width; if not, a narrower fabric might be a better buy.

From 4 to 8 yards of fabric are required for the average stuffed chair. A couch uses 12 yards and up, depending on its length. If you want to get a good estimate the easiest way, line up all the old pieces in a more or less tight pattern about 3 feet wide. Find out how long a line you have, and that's about how much you'll need of the new fabric (but see below regarding "grain").

CUTTING THE FABRIC

The intelligent way to cut fabric is to do the same thing you did when you measured it. However, a problem arises when the cover material has a definite "grain" or pattern. Be sure to measure and cut with the pattern going in the right direction if using that type of fabric. It's best, even with plain materials or patterns which go on in any direction, that the vertical dimension be parallel to the selvage, since the fabric will be more workable that way. Lay out all the old pieces on the material and move them around until you determine the most economical way to cut the material without waste (or without being too skimpy).

Cut out all the pieces at the same time, using the old pieces as patterns, and marking the new pieces as to their location just as you did the old ones. Attach the pieces in the same sequence as you took them off, and you should be able to manage the job all right. If some of the old pieces were sewn together, sew the new pieces together in the same way. What is hard for the novice is to find ways to hide the tacks. Make welting out of the same material or have an upholstery store make some for you. Like molding in woodwork, welting covers a multitude of sins.

You can finish off the back and sides with ornamental tacks if you find that you lack the skill with a curved upholstery needle needed to attach the last few pieces.

12

DEPARTMENT OF TLC

Now that you've expended all that energy, time, and money turning a broken-down piece of furniture into a showpiece, you have another problem. Unlike other masterpieces of art, your pride and joy is not only a *pièce de résistance,* it's also a utilitarian object.

You know all those springs you so carefully tied together? Well, there will come a day when Number One son will plop his heavy frame onto them. That finish you so lovingly and carefully applied? Number Two daughter is going to remove her nail polish over it one of these days. And the little one? He'll be crashing his riding horse into those legs you so painstakingly glued back on.

Presumably, you've prepared for all of this by giving your work of art the strongest repair and the toughest finish you could. But, to *keep* it in the best shape possible, there are certain things you should do. This is the TLC (tender, loving care) department. It is the best defense against greasy fingers and spilled martinis.

CARING FOR WOOD

All the many types and brands of furniture-care products claim to be the best, and to do whatever it is they do in a different way. Old-time furniture experts have their favorites, and they're all different, too.

The truth of the matter is that it doesn't matter much *what* you use, but how often. Most of the polishes are usually mineral oil emulsions, with a little lemon, wax, or some other "magic" ingredient mixed in. They do a good job of getting rid of the grime that might eventually be rubbed into the finish and ruin it. They also offer a thin protective film, which doesn't last too long. If you use the polish on a regular basis, it will adequately protect the finish. *Regular* is the key word—not once a year, nor every week necessarily, but every month or so, as recommended by the manufacturer.

No polish made, however, is as good as a coat of tough paste wax. Liquid

165

or spray wax is a step in the right direction, but still not as good as the paste variety. Not that any of these products does a poor job. They just aren't very durable. And paste wax isn't anything miraculous, either. It simply lasts longer than anything else. With a good coat of paste wax, an occasional light dusting is all the surface needs for months at a time.

Most wax products don't say what type of wax is contained inside. If they do, however, look for the one that contains a high proportion of carnauba or candelilla. Butcher's is one company that makes a paste wax with a healthy portion of carnauba. If you can't find a furniture wax that contains it, you can use an automotive wax like Simoniz.

APPLYING WAX

Apply the wax as thinly as possible. This doesn't mean to skimp, but don't put it on too thickly. Spread it on thoroughly and evenly, and don't let it build up in any one spot.

Next, buff it well. That's why thick buildups are bad. The thicker it is, the harder it is to buff. The old-timers will tell you to buff with a chamois cloth, and this does do a great job, but it's hard work. The modern way is to attach a lamb's wool applicator to your electric drill.

The amount of wax to use depends on what is under it. You don't really need wax at all if your furniture has a new factory-sprayed lacquer finish. Occasional polishing with a lint-free cloth is all new lacquer needs. At the other end of the spectrum are penetrating sealers. They require several coats of wax—always very thin, regardless of the number of coats. Varnish, shellac, and other finishes will benefit from one or two thin coats of wax.

A good wax coating should last at least six months. If it starts to fade before then, the sheen can be revived by rebuffing with a soft, lintless cloth. When this fails, another coat of wax is in order. Don't overdo it, though. Only so many coats can be applied before the surface starts to look too shiny. When the humidity is high, the wax may become sticky and pick up dirt more easily.

If the wax gets to this stage, remove all of it with liberal doses of mineral spirits or turpentine and start over.

PERFECT POLISHING

There are right and wrong ways to apply furniture polish. You get better results when you apply it with a damp rag to help clean off dirt, and keep folding the cloth over to use a clean surface. It also works better if you polish with the grain. No matter what you use, rub hard.

Tung oil can be used as a protective coating and looks rather rich. You can also make your own polish by mixing one part turpentine to one part boiled linseed oil. This mixture is good for lacquered or other finishes that are already highly polished and durable. The turpentine digs out the dirt and helps the oil to penetrate. The oil brightens and feeds the hungry fibers of the wood.

HOW TO MAKE UPHOLSTERY LAST LONGER

Regardless of whether the cover material is good, bad, or somewhere in between, it makes sense to give it a protective film. Though there are other brands on the market, this process is usually referred to as "Scotch-garding" (a 3M trademark). This film is better and cheaper when factory-applied, but you can do it yourself with aerosol varieties of the same ingredient.

Doing an entire couch takes a lot of spray, but it's a worthwhile investment. It doesn't show on the material, and it helps repel dirt, stains, liquids, and other fabric-ruiners. When spills do occur, they can be wiped up before they soak into the cover material, the padding, and the stuffing.

One helpful but commonly overlooked Rx for upholstery is the vacuum cleaner. If you believed the salesman when he sold you all those fancy attachments, you should believe him now. Surface dirt doesn't hurt, but it has a way of working down into the fabric if it stays too long. If you vacuum the furniture at the same time you do the rugs—at least every other time—you'll prevent the dirt from doing its dirty work. Those who don't have the appropriate attachments or lack a vacuum cleaner should use a whisk broom to brush out accumulated dirt and debris. (If you possess down pillows, you *have* to use the whisk broom. A vacuum cleaner pulls out the tiny feathers.)

Since furniture is made for people, and people are inclined to perspire, smoke, or do other things which offend the nose, upholstered pieces benefit from an occasional dose of fresh air. Take the cushions outside on nice days, or the whole piece, if you or someone else can supply the necessary muscle. It also helps to turn the cushions over once in a while.

SPOT AND STAIN REMOVAL

As with all fabrics, the time to remove spots and stains is as soon as they happen. It's good to have a can of cleaning fluid around for such emergencies. While it won't remove everything, it will help with most.

More difficult stains can usually be eradicated by absorbent powders such as fuller's earth, cornstarch, French chalk, or talcum. Make a paste out of the powder, mixing it with cleaning fluid or some form of naphtha like lighter fluid. Carbon tetrachloride also makes a good vehicle. The powders themselves are harmless, but the fluid might damage some cover materials. Always test for colorfastness with any cleaner, including commercial cleaning fluid, on an inconspicuous part of the fabric.

It's a good idea to keep a corner of one of your closets stocked with some of the cleaning agents mentioned above. Most of them can also be used on clothes and other fabrics, too. Keep them together with your paste wax and furniture polish. A good book on removing the various types of stains is Alma Chestnut Moore's *How to Clean Everything* (Pocket Books).

Upholstery which is just plain dirty should be shampooed, using a shampoo made specifically for upholstery fabrics. This type makes a thick, soapless lather. Apply the shampoo, let stand for a few minutes as directed by the manufacturer, then whip it into a good lather. Rub the fabric down with a clean, stiff-bristle brush, then wipe clean with a cloth or sponge. Keep pets and people off until the cover material is completely dry.

A decent homemade shampoo can be brewed by dissolving six tablespoons of white soap flakes in a pint of boiling water. A dash of ammonia, or a few tablespoons of borax will aid in softening the soap flakes. This won't lather up like commercial shampoo without some extra rubbing, but it's cheaper and doesn't require shopping around. As with all shampoos, let the foam, not the liquid, do the work.

If you can't cope with all of this, and you can afford it, you can have a professional cleaning service come to your home. You wouldn't hire them just to clean a couch or chair, but you may want to have them do your upholstered furniture while they are there to clean rugs, windows, etc.

PLASTICS

The plastics used most in furniture are vinyl fabrics and laminated tops. Both are highly resistant to stains, water damage, etc. Be careful with cigarettes, however, since plastics can be scorched. Chlorine bleach is one chemical that can damage furniture plastics. Laminated plastic table tops are about as tough a surface as you can get, but don't cut apples, cheese, or anything else on them with a sharp knife. The surface can be scratched by a sharp instrument. The same applies to abrasive powders and other rough objects.

Worn laminated plastic can do with an occasional coat of wax to renew the original sheen, and vinyl benefits from a liquid wax cleaner when it starts to look a little dull. Wash plastics off with soap or detergent and rinse. A damp cloth is enough for most cleaning jobs. Always dry the surface afterward.

LEATHER

One of the worst things for leather is water. Use as little of it as possible when cleaning. Clean and renew leather with saddle or other mild soap and follow directions, using only as much water as you need. Wipe off with a minimally damp rag and dry quickly with a soft cloth.

MAINTAINING MARBLE

Strong and durable as marble is, it needs a lot more care and maintenance than people realize. It should be covered with a light coat of paste wax or a suitable sealer. Make sure that any sealer you use is recommended for use on marble. You can put wax over the sealer for double protection.

Scratches and gouges are difficult to remove. The best bet is to get fine-grit wet-or-dry abrasive paper and keep rubbing with oil (see p. 109). Polish the abraded spot afterward with jeweler's rouge or tin oxide, followed by a good buffing with wax.

Stains should be removed promptly by rubbing lightly with a non-abrasive detergent. If the stain has set awhile, try some laundry bleach or hydrogen peroxide with a drop of ammonia. Naphtha, alcohol, or acetone may also remove the stain, depending on what caused it. Tea and coffee are eradicated with bleach. Use naphtha (cleaning fluid) on grease and oil stains. Let the naphtha soak into a white blotter, put the blotter over the stain and cover with cardboard and a big book or other heavy object. You can also make a poultice out of naphtha and fuller's earth. Cover the mixture with a damp cloth to retard drying.

GLASS AND METAL

Neither of these materials needs much in the line of routine care. When cleaning them, a wax-base cleaner will make dusting easier and future spills easier to wipe up.

Metal used indoors shouldn't get rusty unless it was poorly finished. Rust could be a problem, however, in damp basements and especially on outdoor metal furniture. Touch-ups are possible if you can find a matching paint. Be sure to sand or steel away all traces of rust first, then apply a corrosion-resistant primer before the final coat. When the entire surface gets pitted or rusty, you may as well do over the whole piece. Spray paints are handy for this.

ROUTINE DUSTING

All furniture needs a weekly dusting for the same reasons that you vacuum upholstery at less frequent intervals. Dust particles build up and work their way into wax and finishes. Besides, dusty furniture looks bad. In spite of the wondrous claims made for some products on TV and elsewhere, you don't need anything other than a clean, dry, hemmed cloth. Old handkerchiefs, diapers, or other cotton cloths are ideal. None of those wonder products will harm the finish, however, and may even do it a bit of good. More important, though, is the right type of cloth and that old-fashioned product, elbow grease. Don't be afraid to rub hard. It won't hurt you or the finish.

For waxed finishes, avoid the use of treated or oily cloths. They only gum up the wax. You can use a polish which contains wax, but not oils. The best treatment for wax is to give it a really tough rubdown every month or so to bring back the original sheen.

ATTENTION

It doesn't matter whether you remember all of the tips and technical advice about stains, etc., if your heart is in the right place. That's because if you truly love your furniture, which is what this book is all about, you will give it the attention you need. Like all of us, furniture needs to be loved and cared for. All the chemicals, waxes, and polishes in the world mean nothing compared to TLC. If you keep that in mind, you'll do the right thing automatically. It may take a little time and effort, but you will be rewarded by loyal and good friends in every room of the house.

NINE NO-NO'S

If you want your furniture to wind up in the junk heap, here is a list of things that will speed its journey:

1. Set vases of flowers on table and bureau tops without any barrier underneath. Vases of flowers contain water, and the vase will "sweat," causing puddles on the bottom. This will do a job right away on shellac, and eventually ruin any finish. Dripping glasses are also good for this.

2. Move your furniture around from warm rooms to cold attics, damp basements, and even outside in the winter air. Keep the room as hot as you can. Exposing wood to extremes of heat and cold not only ruins finishes, but glues, wood, and almost anything else. This way you can destroy the whole piece in no time at all.

3. Ignore dust, dirt, and grime until it builds up a nice abrasive surface. This is effective not only on finishes, but on upholstery fabrics.

4. Spill martinis, grease, and other kinds of material- and finish-destroyers as often as possible.

5. Ignore the above until they soak in well.

6. Use water-based waxes meant for resilient floors on your wood surfaces.

7. Don't use any wax at all on shellacked surfaces.

8. Apply wax in thick, heavy coats and don't bother rubbing it.

9. Encourage kids and pets to jump on, lounge on, and generally beat up your most treasured pieces.

13

MAKING YOUR OWN

This chapter is for beginners only. The projects are simple, with uncomplicated joints. They are, frankly, the type of furniture that we told you not to buy. They're held together with nails, screws, and glue, and they should be made out of inexpensive wood like white pine and fir plywood. Most of the surfaces are painted, or covered over with some other material.

But they're fun to make, and admirably serve the purposes for which they were intended. This type of project will get you used to working with wood and other materials and prepare you for the more advanced projects in the next chapter.

DRESSING UP AN UNPAINTED CHEST

This is an easy one. You start with most of the work already done for you. Buy an unfinished chest of some sort and the moldings to dress it up in Traditional, Spanish, or Contemporary style.

The Materials Lists (p. 176) specify the moldings needed for a four-drawer chest (two small drawers at the top) about 3 feet wide, allowing

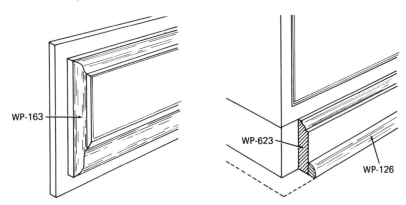

FIGURE 30. Assembling the moldings for your Traditional-style dresser.

171

Dressing up an unfinished chest with moldings in the Traditional style. Other styles are illustrated in the drawings. (*Western Wood Moulding and Woodwork Producers*)

for waste. Measure your own piece and plan accordingly. Moldings are usually available in sizes from 3 feet to 16 feet. Add up all the dimensions, and buy pieces as large as you can handle. You should always plan on extras when buying wood, but add even more for moldings, because they are usually mitered (see below).

Mitering wastes more wood than other types of cuts. The beginner often thinks he can turn the cut piece over and use the other side, but you can't unless you have perfectly symmetrical moldings and are using both inside and outside corners. Always add the width of the molding for each cut when buying. In other words, if the molding is 3 inches wide, and you plan on getting three miters out of the piece, add 9 inches to the dimensions, then round out to the next highest foot.

You must have a miter box for this type of work. Even if you have a try square that measures a 45-degree angle, you'll have lots of trouble cutting it to exactly that angle. You may have trouble cutting even with a miter box. A hardwood miter box will do, but the steel type is preferable. And a backsaw or miter-box saw is almost a necessity, although it *can* be done with a crosscut saw.

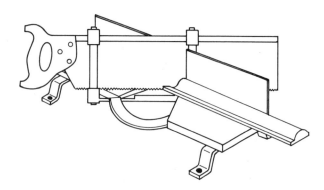

FIGURE 31. A good miter box and saw are essential for accurate cutting of moldings.

Using Moldings—Start with the base first. Miter the base molding and attach it to the front and two sides with #5 finishing nails. Then do the same for the base shoe and nail it into the base.

Cut the cap molding and attach that with white glue and brads. The moldings should be located about 1½ inches from the edges of the drawers. Set all the nails and brads, fill with wood putty, and finish as you would any other piece of furniture. Use an opaque finish if the grain is unattractive. Remember that the unfinished piece may require a heavier sanding than one which has been stripped of an old finish. Since the "hardware" on the unfinished piece will probably be wooden knobs, you may want to replace that, too.

You will see in the diagrams that some of the moldings on the Spanish and Contemporary pieces are screwed on from the inside of the drawers. The screws should be long enough to penetrate about halfway into the

FIGURE 32.

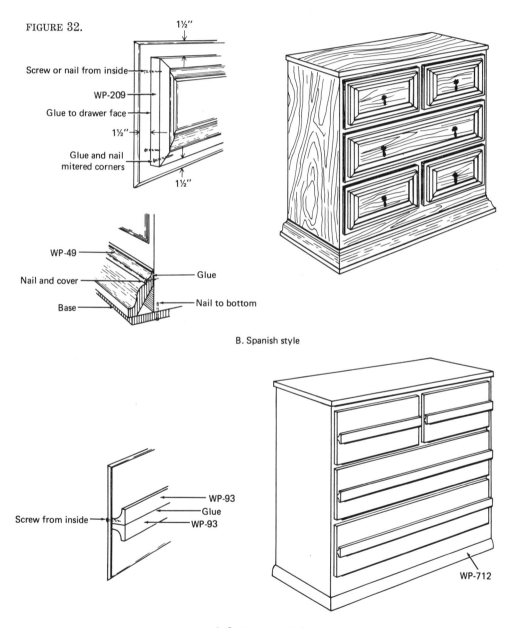

B. Spanish style

A. Contemporary style

moldings without breaking through. The Contemporary piece abandons the use of drawer pulls altogether. The molding serves as its own drawer pull.

MATERIALS LIST—Traditional-Style Chest

Wood

NO.	SIZE	DESCRIPTION
1 piece	36 inches long	WP-623 base molding
2 pieces	18 ″ ″	WP-623 base molding
1 piece	36 ″ ″	WP-126 base shoe
2 pieces	18 ″ ″	WP-126 base shoe
4 pieces	32 ″ ″	WP-163 cap molding
8 pieces	10 ″ ″	WP-163 cap molding

Hardware

½ pound #5 finishing nails
½ pound ¼ × 18 brads

MATERIALS LIST—Spanish-Style Chest

Wood

NO.	SIZE	DESCRIPTION
1 piece	36 inches long	WP-49 crown molding
2 pieces	18 ″ ″	WP-49 crown molding
2 pieces	36 ″ ″	1 × 3 stock lumber
2 pieces	18 ″ ″	½ × 3 stock lumber
4 pieces	32 ″ ″	WP-209 shingle molding
8 pieces	10 ″ ″	WP-209 shingle molding
4 pieces	15 ″ ″	WP-209 shingle molding

Hardware

(same as above)

MATERIALS LIST—Contemporary-Style Chest

Wood

NO.	SIZE	DESCRIPTION
1 piece	36 inches long	WP-712 base molding
2 pieces	18 ″ ″	WP-712 base molding
4 pieces	36 ″ ″	WP-93 cove molding
4 pieces	18 ″ ″	WP-93 cove molding

Hardware

10 screws to fit

USING PRE-CUT PARTS

The tables shown here are even easier than the molding project. They just look harder. Several companies make these pre-cut, pre-turned parts which are used to create interesting pieces such as the cocktail table and desk shown here. Tops and shelves are made entirely out of plywood. The hardwood parts are from Spindleflex.

The cocktail table is made from fir plywood and is shown unfinished. The desk is made from birch plywood and is stained to a dark shade. Holes are drilled through the plywood and the parts are twisted together using screw-like wood connectors. To make smooth surfaces, such as the desk top, threaded dowels are inserted and glued halfway into the plywood. All plywood edges should be finished by using wood tape to match the finish. Moldings can also be attached and stained to match.

Companies that make the hardwood parts usually have a wide variety of leg styles available. The brand shown here comes in 12 different sizes. There are several different parts and connectors for various uses. Plans for furniture and built-ins are generally available from dealers. If not, write Russ Stonier, Inc., 1375 Merchandise Mart, Chicago, Ill. 60654.

(Russ Stonier, Inc.)

"UPHOLSTERED" PARSONS TABLE

We've called this an upholstered Parsons table because it's covered with fabric, but that's really the only way it differs from an ordinary wood Parsons table. No padding, springs, or stuffing is used. The cover material, however, does give it added interest and individuality which you can't achieve with just the wood.

The table shown here has a rather striking pattern. Yours can be more subdued if you prefer. Or your table can be covered with a fabric to match your draperies, couch, or wallpaper. The fabric should have a reasonable amount of "body," not too thick or thin. Edges must be turned over and overlapped. A thin cloth will show the overlaps. A thick one won't make the bends.

This table, with its characteristic simple flat lines, is especially well suited for a cloth lamination. You can start from scratch constructing a table for the purpose. Or you may have an old table needing a facelift. If the latter is your choice, then you'll need only to remove the old finish down to bare wood before you start.

This project uses a spray adhesive like Spra-Ment. It makes a strong permanent bond almost immediately. This "almost" factor is quite important; it allows time to make slight adjustments, if necessary, to obtain accurate fitting. In the event a gross error is made in positioning the fabric, there is a leeway of several minutes during which time the material can be removed for an additional try. Once the adhesive has set, however, the bond will be absolutely permanent.

The table shown is $18 \times 48 \times 30$ inches high with $2\frac{3}{4}$-inch-thick sides and legs. You can alter the dimensions any way you like, but the sides

(3M Corp.)

and legs should measure equal. We used 1⅜-inch poplar, doubled up to make the squares for the legs. Cost for lumber was approximately $20. Inasmuch as none of the wood remains exposed, you have the option of cutting costs by using less expensive lumber such as fir plywood for the top (it simplifies the job, too) and pine 2 × 4s for the legs.

To make a solid lumber top, join several boards with butted dowel joints. Square the ends of the legs accurately, then temporarily tack-nail the top onto the legs to facilitate drilling holes for a ⅜ × 3-inch hex-head lag screw. Counterbore a hole large enough to receive a socket wrench for driving

Square legs are made by gluing and clamping two pieces of lumber, in this case 1½-inch poplar. (*3M Corp.*)

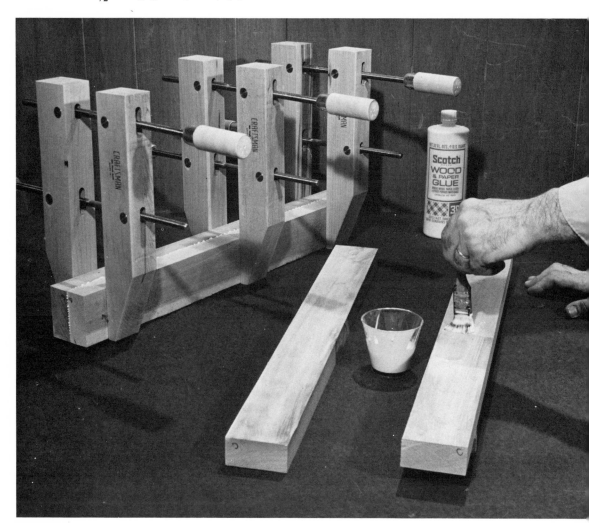

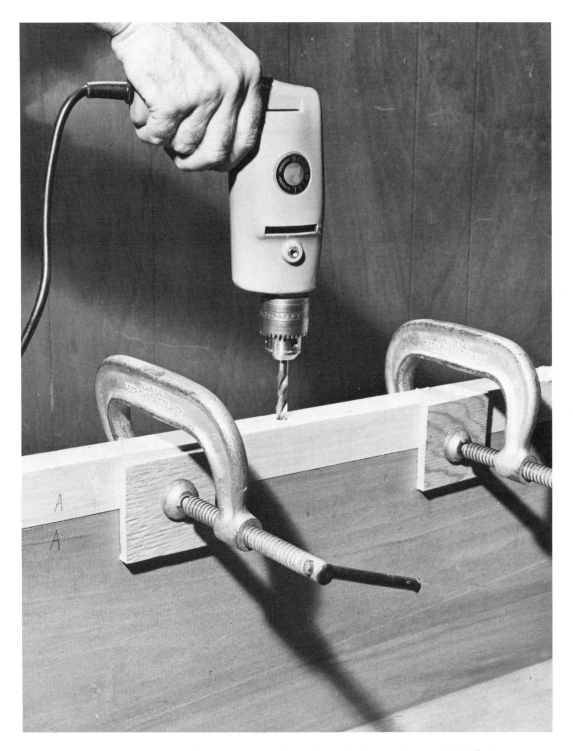

When gluing top boards together edge to edge, clamp both together and drill through narrow into larger one. This ensures exact dowel alignment. Outside hole is later plugged as shown below. (*3M Corp.*)

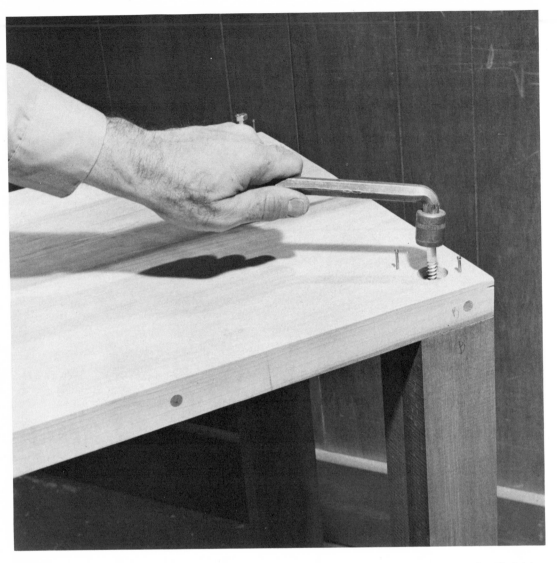

Lag screw is turned down through top into leg with a socket wrench. Finishing nails give leg stability until glue sets and lag is in place. Nails are removed later. (*3M Corp.*)

the screw. Bore just deep enough so the head with washer rests a bit below the surface. Later the hole can be filled with wood putty or spackle.

Temporarily attach the legs while custom-fitting the built-up sides. Use nails and glue to secure the side pieces. Apply glue to all contact points of legs, sides, and top for a lasting joint. Insert the lag screws to draw the legs up tightly. The lag negates the need for clamps. Fill in the screw head holes on top. Sand the top and legs if necessary to true up. Don't apply any finish coat if you are using fabric.

Laminating the Fabric

For a neat, finished look, all raw edges of the fabric should be turned under at least 1 inch. Sewing is not necessary; simply spray a band of adhesive 2 inches wide along an edge, allow it to get tacky, about one minute, then fold over 1 inch of material and press down. Although the instructions on the adhesive container seem to indicate that only one surface need be coated, you will find that both surfaces must be treated for this project.

The table is covered in two phases, the top in one piece and the legs separately. Work on the top first. Measure the width and both side thicknesses of the table and add to this the extra 2 inches for turning under. To determine the long dimension of the cloth, add both side thicknesses (5½ inches in the example) to the length plus an additional 10 or 12 inches. This

FIGURE 33. How to cover the table with upholstery cover material.

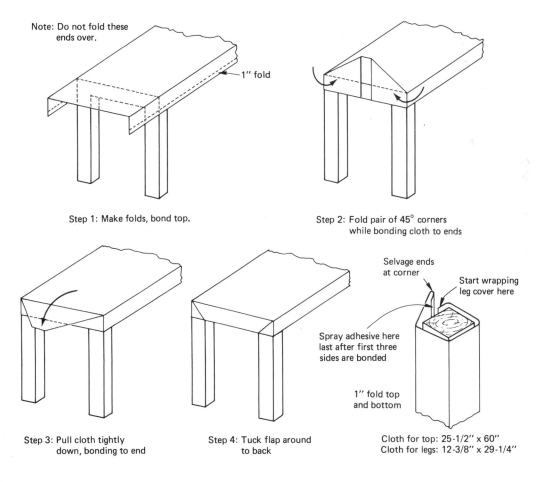

Note: Do not fold these ends over.

1" fold

Step 1: Make folds, bond top.

Step 2: Fold pair of 45° corners while bonding cloth to ends

Step 3: Pull cloth tightly down, bonding to end

Step 4: Tuck flap around to back

Selvage ends at corner

Start wrapping leg cover here

Spray adhesive here last after first three sides are bonded

1" fold top and bottom

Cloth for top: 25-1/2" x 60"
Cloth for legs: 12-3/8" x 29-1/4"

is to allow the ends to reach down and around to the inside surface of the table ends.

Fit the cloth so that the end of the fold meets flush with the bottom edge of the wood. The ends get a "hospital corner" treatment. Don't try to cover the top in one operation, work instead in sections. Apply a coating of adhesive to half of the table top, lengthwise, and to one of the sides. Coat the same portions of the fabric. Wait about one minute to allow the adhesive to become tacky, then join. Repeat the procedure with the other half. You can tackle smaller portions if you prefer, until you get the hang of it. Tape single sheets of newspaper to sections where adhesive is unwanted.

The ends are next. Make a pair of 45-degree folds at both corners, coating with adhesive as you go along. Due to the buildup of cloth layers at the ends, you may want to build up the center portions, which may be slightly depressed. Make up a filler with scrap cloth and insert where needed to relieve the depression. Do this before finalizing the hospital corner.

If possible, the fabric for the legs should be cut so that the selvage can be utilized as a finished, exposed edge. Cut each leg piece 2 inches extra in length and turn over 1 inch top and bottom. The width should be equal to $4\frac{1}{2}$ thicknesses of the leg to allow ample overlap. Mask off the finished top areas with paper and apply adhesive. Apply the fabric butting the top edge firmly to close the joint between leg and sides. An additional spray of adhesive will be necessary at the overlap portion of the leg. Determine how far the selvage will reach, mask off the area beyond, then spray. Be sure to get adhesive onto the selvage.

MATERIALS LIST—Parsons Table

Wood

NO.	SIZE (INCHES)	DESCRIPTION
8 pieces	$1\frac{3}{8} \times 2\frac{3}{4} \times 28\frac{1}{2}$ poplar	Legs
2 pieces	$1\frac{1}{4} \times 1\frac{1}{4} \times 42\frac{1}{2}$ poplar	Side blocks
2 pieces	$1\frac{1}{4} \times 1\frac{1}{4} \times 12\frac{1}{2}$ poplar	End blocks
6 pieces	$\frac{6}{4} \times 3 \times 48$ poplar (or enough to make 18" width)	Top

enough spiral dowels to join $\frac{6}{4}$ poplar top

Hardware
$4\frac{3}{8}'' \times 3''$ lag screws
1 lb. 8d finishing nails

Miscellaneous
1 piece of fabric $23\frac{1}{2}'' \times 65''$
4 pieces of fabric $12\frac{1}{2}'' \times 25\frac{3}{4}''$
white glue
Spra-Ment spray adhesive

SHEPHERD'S CHAIR

Here is a simple but very different chair in the Colonial mode. Cherry is recommended for an authentic look, but any other hardwood is suitable. The seat is made from a piece of 14 × 14-inch stock, 1¾ inches thick. The back is a piece 5 × 30 inches, 1 inch thick, and the legs are made from four pieces 1½ × 1½ × 17 inches long.

Begin with the seat, drawing a circle with a string compass (a pencil at the end of a piece of string and tacked to the center of the board). Cut out a rectangular slot in the rear for the seat, 3½ inches long by 1 inch deep. Make another circle on the bottom of the seat with a 4½-inch radius as a guide for the leg joints. Drill holes about 1 inch deep all the way through the seat in the pattern shown. Holes should be offset 8 degrees. Use a lathe or hand tools to round out the leg stock. Cut a wide saw kerf in the top of each. Insert the glued tops of the legs into the drilled holes. Drive a piece of glued wood into the saw kerfs from the top for a really solid joint. Sand leg tops level with the seat.

Shape the back into the pattern shown, making a 2½-inch hole in the top for easy carrying. See the detail drawing for shaping the back and establishing screw centers. Attach the back with 2½-inch #10 flathead screws. For a better-looking back, countersink screws and fill holes with plugs or wood putty. Finish as for any other wood. (Plans for similar Colonial and other pieces are available from the Stanley Tools Educational Department, New Britain, Ct. 06050.)

MATERIALS LIST—Shepherd's Chair

Wood

NO.	SIZE (INCHES)	DESCRIPTION
1 piece	14 × 14 × 1¾ cherry	Seat
1 piece	5 × 30 × 1¾ cherry	Back
4 pieces	1½ × 1½ × 17 cherry	Legs
4 pieces	thin scrap wood	Wedges

Hardware

2 #10 2½" flathead screws

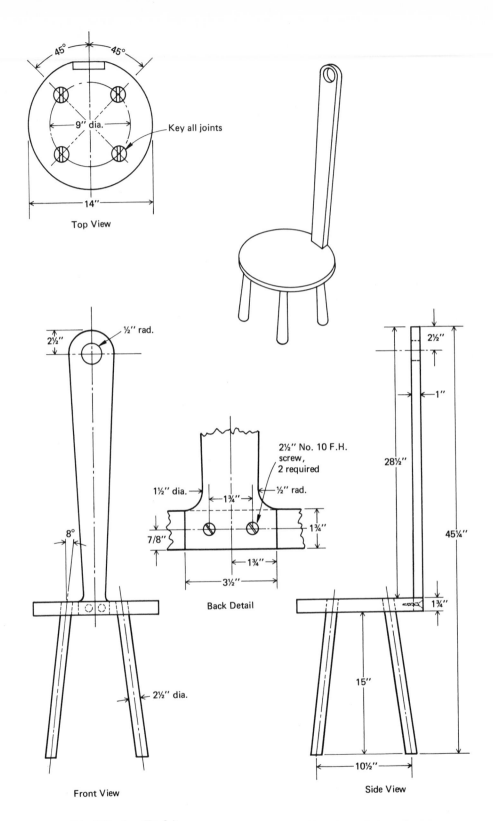

45°   45°

9″ dia.

Key all joints

14″

Top View

½″ rad.

2½″

8°

2½″ dia.

Front View

1½″ dia.

2½″ No. 10 F.H.
screw,
2 required

½″ rad.

1¾″

1¾″

7/8″

1¾″

3½″

Back Detail

2½″

1″

28½″

45¼″

1¾″

15″

10½″

Side View

FIGURE 34. (*Stanley Tools*)

TAKE-APART TRESTLE TABLE

This project in the Early American style can be used as a dining table for six people, or as a writing desk. One of the nice things about it is that it is put together with pegs for easy assembly and disassembly in five minutes. It's also ideal for outside use, and winter storage. Use exterior plywood, preservatives, and resorcinal glues for outdoor use.

The larger sections are made of one sheet of 4 × 8 plywood. Get lumber of the same species for the other parts, or a type with similar grain patterns if planning a natural or stained finish. With fir plywood, apply a wash coat of one part finishing product to six parts of its solvent. This will tame down the grain.

Although the job can be done with hand tools, large sheets like these are much more easily worked with power equipment. See the Materials List for plywood, lumber, and hardware needed.

Lay out the plywood panels for cutting as shown in the diagram (Figure 35). Use a straight edge and square for accuracy, and be sure to allow for saw kerfs when plotting dimensions. (Check the width of your saw for the exact kerf.) Cut out each piece and true the edges with a sanding block. All exposed plywood edges (legs, brace, and supports) should be filled with wood putty or covered with wood tape. Saw lumber to size and make cutouts where indicated. Make the pegs (eight are needed) from the dowel stock. Six pegs are 3 inches long, and two are 2¼ inches.

Assemble the top first. Use #8 1¼-inch flathead screws through the lumber into the plywood. Pre-drill if using hardwood and countersink the holes. Fill them with plugs or wood putty. Glue and nail the supports through the top. Set nails and fill. Then try all parts to see if they fit and sand down where necessary. Parts should not fit too tightly, since they will all be finished before final assembly.

When each part is properly snug, disassemble and finish as desired. After all parts are finished and completely dry, put them together again with the pegs and enjoy.

MATERIALS LIST—Trestle Table

Wood

NO.	SIZE	USE
1 sheet	4 × 8 ¾-inch plywood, #1 Hardwood or A-A DFPA (Int.)	Basic parts
7 feet	2 × 8 select lumber	Top frame
7 feet	2 ×2 select lumber	Top frame
2 feet	¾-inch diameter hardwood dowel	Pegs

Hardware

3 dozen #8 flathead screws
½ pound 6d finishing nails

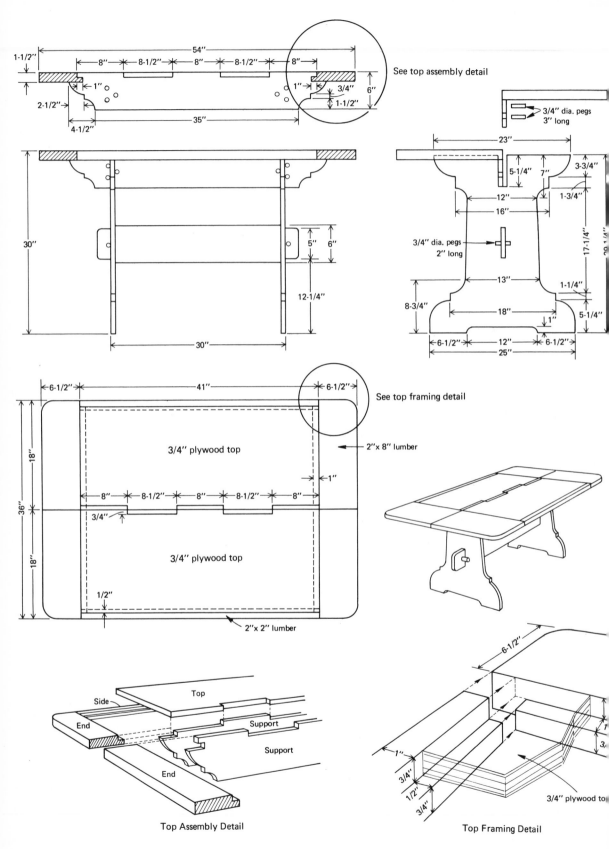

FIGURE 35. (*American Plywood Association*)

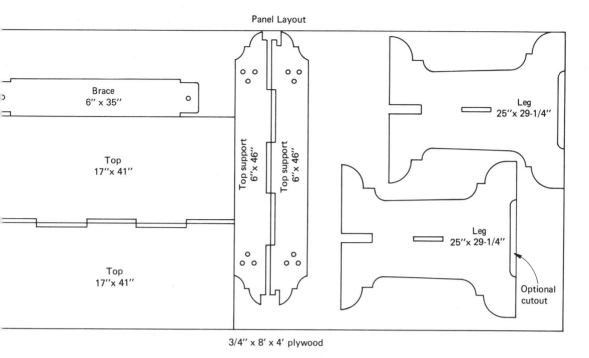

FIGURE 35. (*American Plywood Association*)

SOFA BED WITH BUILT-IN STORAGE CHEST

This project is a sofa, guest bed, and storage chest all in one, and can be built for about $100. Such a three-way unit provides comfortable seating atop a spacious cedar-lined storage chest and, with the back cushion removed, it converts into an extra bed.

On a frame of 2 × 4s attach a standard 3-foot wide × 6-foot 8-inch hollow-core door. The door, forming the bottom of the bed and the top of the chest, is placed flush along the back with a 6-inch overhang in front and at both ends.

Nailed to the 2 × 4 chest framing are 3½-inch-wide pieces of tongue-and-grooved aromatic red cedar. The cedar on the inside of the chest is left in its natural state for moth-repellency; the outside is sealed and varnished.

A drop-down hinged door consists of the same cedar lining material glued and tacked to both sides of a ¼-inch piece of hardboard. A setback along the four edges of the door permits the door to close tightly and retain the cedar fragrance. A section of chain at each end of the door lets the door open a maximum of 180 degrees, stopping it an inch or two off the floor and providing an access platform for transferring articles in and out of the storage chest.

A 4-inch-thick piece of foam rubber padding covered with green felt (any heavy fabric can be used) forms the seat cushion. Back cushions also are made of upholstered foam rubber.

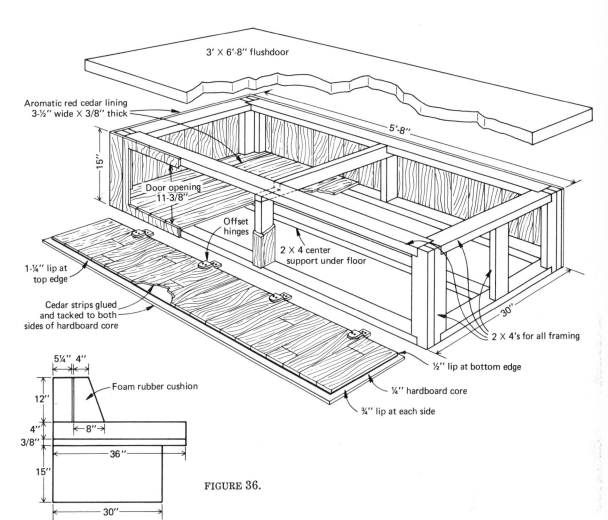

3' × 6'-8" flushdoor

Aromatic red cedar lining
3-½" wide × 3/8" thick

5'-8"

15"

Door opening
11-3/8"

Offset
hinges

2 × 4 center
support under floor

1-¼" lip at
top edge

Cedar strips glued
and tacked to both
sides of hardboard core

30"

2 × 4's for all framing

½" lip at bottom edge

¼" hardboard core

¾" lip at each side

5¼" 4"

Foam rubber cushion

12"

4"
3/8"

8"

36"

15"

30"

FIGURE 36.

The bolsters rest against two rectangular storage compartments which are built on a light wood frame covered with ¼-inch hardboard and upholstered to match the bolsters and seat cushion. The compartments act as spacers to narrow the width of the bed when it's used as a sofa and provide storage for pillows and bedding.

MATERIALS LIST—Sofa Bed

Wood

NO.	SIZE	DESCRIPTION
1	36″ × 80″ flush door	Top
54	linear ft of 2 × 4s	Framing
72	linear ft. 3½″ × ⅜″ aromatic red cedar	Lining

1 piece	15″ × 68″ × ¼″ hardboard	Door
40	linear ft. of 2 × 2s	Storage box framing
2 pieces	12″ × 34″ × ¼″ hardboard	Storage box fronts
4 pieces	5¼″ × 34″ × ¼″ hardboard	Storage box tops and bottoms
4 pieces	5¼″ × 12″ × ¼″ hardboard	Storage box sides

Hardware

4 offset hinges
2 lb. 8d common nails
2 lb. 16d common nails
5 lbs. 4d finishing nails

Miscellaneous

1 piece 36″ × 80″ × 4″ foam rubber
2 pieces 12″ × 34″ × 8″ foam rubber (precut bolster shape)
approx. 10 yards upholstery cover fabric

A HANDSOME STORAGE CHEST

This good-looking storage chest (opposite) is a little harder to make, but it still doesn't require any involved joinery. Nor does it require the more advanced power equipment of the projects in the next chapter.

The chest can be used and finished in a number of ways. In the bedroom, use the upper compartment with dividers to store linens, shirts, sweaters, or socks. The lower compartment can be used for blankets, bedspreads, or shoes. With the top down, the chest is a convenient bench while you're dressing.

Choose the wood to be used according to the finishing technique. With an opaque finish, the grain is irrelevant, but if you use a clear finish with fir plywood, select the piece yourself for a pleasing grain, and apply a wash coat before staining, as described on p. 187. The lumber should be of the same wood or a similar species.

Lay out the pieces of plywood as shown in the cutting diagrams, and allow for saw kerfs. Cut and rabbet the wood framing. There are no exposed plywood edges, so you don't have to worry about that. Layout and cutting are a little complex, but after that it's easy.

Begin your assembly by gluing and nailing bottom, sides, back, shelf, and front together. Assemble top framing around the plywood top by gluing and screwing through the lumber into the plywood top. Glue and nail the divider supports in place (see Top View). Do the same for the leg molding and the trim. You can buy molding for the trim, but you may as well use the plywood scraps as shown.

Countersink screws and set nails, fill with plugs and/or wood putty. Finish as desired, then apply the hardware.

Panel Layout

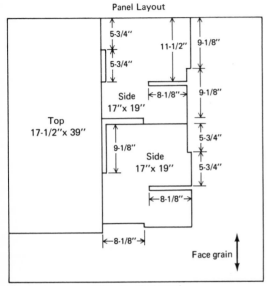

5-3/4″
11-1/2″
9-1/8″
5-3/4″

Side
17″ x 19″

8-1/8″

9-1/8″

Top
17-1/2″ x 39″

9-1/8″

5-3/4″

Side
17″ x 19″

5-3/4″

8-1/8″

8-1/8″

Face grain

3/4″ x 4′ x 4′ plywood

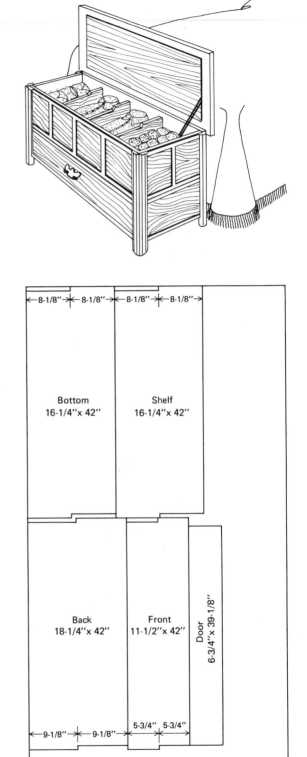

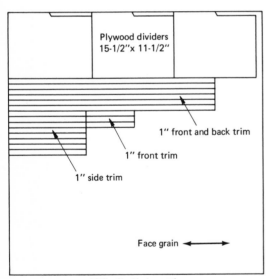

Plywood dividers
15-1/2″ x 11-1/2″

1″ front and back trim

1″ front trim

1″ side trim

Face grain

1/4″ x 4′ x 4′ plywood

FIGURE 37.
(*American Plywood Association*)

8-1/8″ 8-1/8″ 8-1/8″ 8-1/8″

Bottom
16-1/4″ x 42″

Shelf
16-1/4″ x 42″

Back
18-1/4″ x 42″

Front
11-1/2″ x 42″

Door
6-3/4″ x 39-1/8″

9-1/8″ 9-1/8″ 5-3/4″ 5-3/4″

3/4″ x 4′ x 8′ plywood

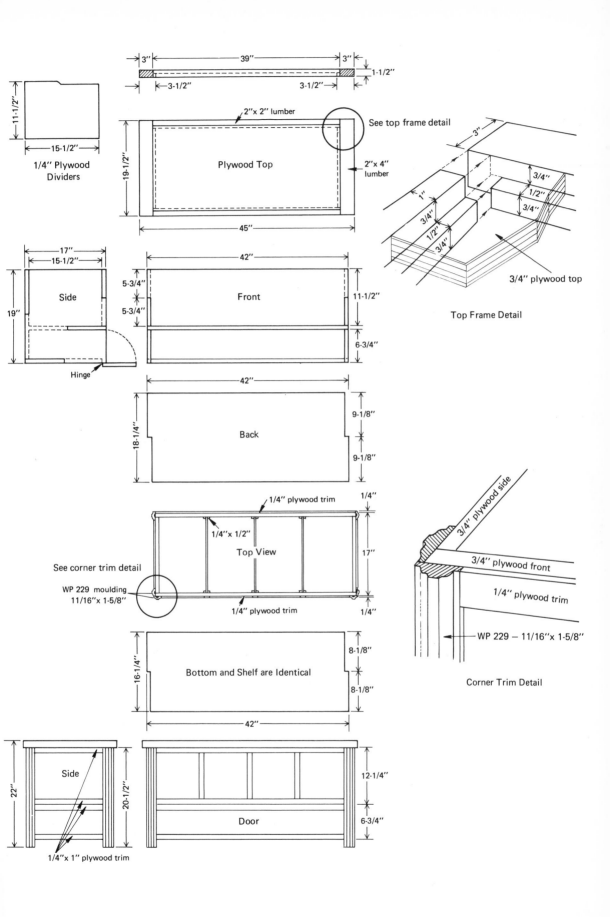

1/4" Plywood Dividers

11-1/2"
15-1/2"

3"
39"
3"
1-1/2"
3-1/2"
3-1/2"

2"x 2" lumber
Plywood Top
See top frame detail
2"x 4" lumber
19-1/2"
45"

See top frame detail

Top Frame Detail

3"
3/4"
1/2"
3/4"
1"
3/4"
1/2"
3/4"
3/4" plywood top

Side
17"
15-1/2"
19"
Hinge

Front
42"
5-3/4"
11-1/2"
5-3/4"
6-3/4"

Back
42"
18-1/4"
9-1/8"
9-1/8"

3/4" plywood side
3/4" plywood front
1/4" plywood trim
WP 229 — 11/16"x 1-5/8"

Corner Trim Detail

Top View
1/4" plywood trim
1/4"x 1/2"
1/4"
See corner trim detail
WP 229 moulding
11/16"x 1-5/8"
1/4" plywood trim
17"
1/4"

Bottom and Shelf are Identical
16-1/4"
42"
8-1/8"
8-1/8"

Side
22"
20-1/2"
1/4"x 1" plywood trim

Door
42"
12-1/4"
6-3/4"

MATERIALS LIST—Storage Chest

Wood

NO.	SIZE	USE
1½ panels	4 × 8 ¾-inch plywood, #1 Hardwood or A-B DFPA (Int.)	Box parts
½ panel	4 × 4 ¼-inch A-A DFPA (Int.)	Dividers, trim
4 feet	2 × 4 select pine	Top frame
7 feet	2 × 2 select pine	Top frame
7 feet	WP-229 molding, $\frac{11}{16} \times 1\frac{5}{8}$ inches	Legs

Hardware

3 dozen # 10—1¼″ flathead screws
½ pound 6d finishing nails
½ pound 3d finishing nails
½ pound ¾-inch brads
4—2-inch hinges
1 magnetic catch
1 lid support

14

NOT FOR BEGINNERS

The projects here are not for beginners. All of the pieces in this chapter require a fairly large arsenal of power equipment, which the average handyperson just doesn't have. Although you *could* make them with hand tools, trying these projects without a router, a lathe, and a power saw is like trying to pound in a nail with a rock. Eventually, you'll get the job done, but there are easier ways.

It is assumed here that anyone who tries these projects has a good command of basic woodworking, and the patience to interpret the plans without elaborate instructions. We'll point out some of the prospective problems and give a few tips here and there. After that, you're on your own.

AN OLD-FASHIONED PINE CABINET

Here's a true antique lover's delight. Its styling will fit in with any eclectic or Early American room and it is a practical storage area for almost anything. Solid ¾-inch white pine is used for the sides, top, doors, and front trim as well as the drawer front. If you prefer, you can use pine paneling, good one side, instead.

All pieces should be cut out first, following the Materials List, from pine stock or plywood. The V notches can be formed with a router or circular saw using Rockwell molding cutter #35–106 with a #265 cutterhead. The bottom cutout of the side pieces follows the same radius as that on the bottom rail of the front.

Rabbet out the inside edge of the side pieces to take the ¼-inch back panel. Two ¼-inch-deep dadoes are made in the side pieces, one to take the cabinet bottom and the other for the drawer slide frame. See drawings for details.

The drawer slide frame is made up of ¾ × 2-inch stock, using ⁵⁄₁₆-inch shallow mortise and tenon joints. Glue and nail the sides to the bottom and the drawer slide frame, then glue the back panel and the two front uprights

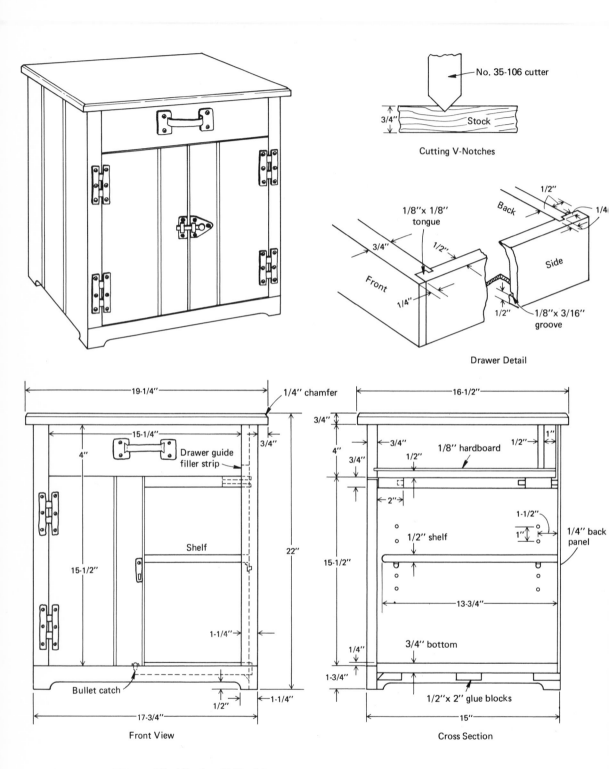

No. 35-106 cutter

Stock

3/4"

Cutting V-Notches

1/8"x 1/8" tongue

Back

1/2"

1/4"

3/4"

1/2"

Front

Side

1/4"

1/2"

1/8"x 3/16" groove

Drawer Detail

19-1/4"

1/4" chamfer

15-1/4"

3/4"

4"

Drawer guide filler strip

Shelf

22"

15-1/2"

1-1/4"

Bullet catch

17-3/4"

1-1/4"

1/2"

Front View

16-1/2"

3/4"

3/4"

1/8" hardboard

1/2"

1"

4"

1/2"

3/4"

2"

1-1/2"

1/2" shelf

1"

1/4" back panel

15-1/2"

13-3/4"

1/4"

3/4" bottom

1-3/4"

1/2"x 2" glue blocks

15"

Cross Section

FIGURE 38. (*Rockwell Tools*)

and base rail. Nail the top piece to the assembled base, leaving a ¾-inch overlap on all sides.

Next glue two ½ × ¾-inch drawer filler guide pieces to the sides, and the drawer slide frame, as shown in Figure 38. Drawers are constructed of a ¾-inch pine front, a ½-inch pine back and sides, with the bottom of ⅛-inch hardboard. Dado a ⅛ × ⅛-inch groove in the front and a ¼ × ¼-inch groove in the back to hold the drawer bottom. See the drawer detail in Figure 38.

Shelves can be permanently attached, if desired, for a more authentic look, but since no one will see the inside, metal shelf standards can be used. A good compromise is to drill ¼-inch holes in the sides at 1-inch intervals as shown, and set the shelves on metal supports.

Fit the doors to the opening, and notch if necessary, as for the sides. Finish as desired—orange shellac may look good here—and apply the hardware. Hammered Colonial "wrought iron" looks best.

MATERIALS LIST—Pine Cabinet

Wood

NO.	SIZE (INCHES)	USE
2 pieces	¾ × 14½ × 21½	Sides
1 piece	¾ × 14 × 16¾	Bottom
2 pieces	¾ × 1¼ × 15½	Front upright
1 piece	¾ × 1¾ × 17¾	Front base
2 pieces	¾ × 17¼ × 20	Doors
1 piece	¾ × 2 × 16¾	Front drawer slide frame
2 pieces	¾ × 2 × 14⅜	Side drawer slide frame
1 piece	¾ × 2 × 13½	Back drawer slide frame
1 piece	¾ × 16½ × 19¼	Cabinet top
1 piece	¾ × 4 × 15¼	Drawer front
2 pieces	½ × 4 × 14¼	Drawer sides
1 piece	½ × 13¾ × 16¼	Shelf
10 pieces	½ × ½ × 2	Glue blocks
1 piece	¼ × 17¼ × 20	Back panel
1 piece	⅛ × 14⅝ × 14¼	Drawer bottom (hardboard)

Hardware

4	Metal shelf supports
2 pairs	Colonial "H" hinges, 3 inches long
1	Colonial door catch
1	Colonial drawer handle

A PENDULUM CRADLE

If the little one doesn't appreciate this now, he or she will when he gets old enough to have one of his own. And so will your granchild's grandchild, if you make this out of a long-lasting wood like maple or cherry. It's not only sturdy, but attractive, too, in the Colonial tradition.

Use straight-grained stock for the whole project. Start by cutting all the parts needed to make turnings. The four corner posts are made of 1⅜-inch square stock turned as shown in Figure 39. Mortises are cut on the end faces of the square tops and bottoms of each corner post. They are ⅜ × 2 inches and 1 inch deep. These are the only complicated joints in the piece.

You'll need 28 spindles in all for the cradle section, and a lot of time can be saved by making a template from hardboard. Then all of them can be accurately turned on the lathe with a device such as Rockwell's Wood Turning Duplicator. Otherwise, you'll have to do each one individually and check with calipers. Holes are drilled into the rails ½ inch deep to hold the spindles. There are 9 spindles on each side and 5 at each end.

Cleats, ¾ × ¾ inch, are glued and nailed to each side. The cleats are recessed ¼ × 2 inches at each spindle to hold the 9 slats (see Figure 39). Bottom and top side rails are attached to the corner posts with one #8 3-inch roundhead wood screw each.

The cradle support parts are sawed to the dimensions shown. Fasten the leg stretchers to the basket supports with #8 1¼-inch flathead wood screws. Assemble the two ends to the cross stretcher with four #8 2-inch roundhead screws.

Use ⅜-inch diameter commercial carbon drill rods for the cradle hanging rods, rod hooks, and rocker stop. These should be available at an industrial steel supply house or a large hardware store. Fabricate to the shape shown and drill $\frac{7}{32}$-inch holes in the steel at the points indicated. Attach the steel with $\frac{3}{16}$ × 1¼-inch machine screws. Insert cradle stop where you think it's safe, and cap with a wooden ball ⅞ inch in diameter. Finish as desired.

MATERIALS LIST—Pendulum Cradle

Wood

NO.	SIZE (INCHES)	USE
4 pieces	1⅜ × 1⅜ × 13⅞	Cradle posts
4 pieces	¾ × 2½ × 32	Side stretchers (cradle)
2 pieces	¾ × 4 × 20	End stretchers (cradle top) (including tenons)
2 pieces	¾ × 2½ × 19	End stretchers (cradle bottom) (including tenons)
28 pieces	⅞ × ⅞ × 7	Cradle spindles
2 pieces	¾ × ¾ × 36	Slat cleats

(Continued on page 203)

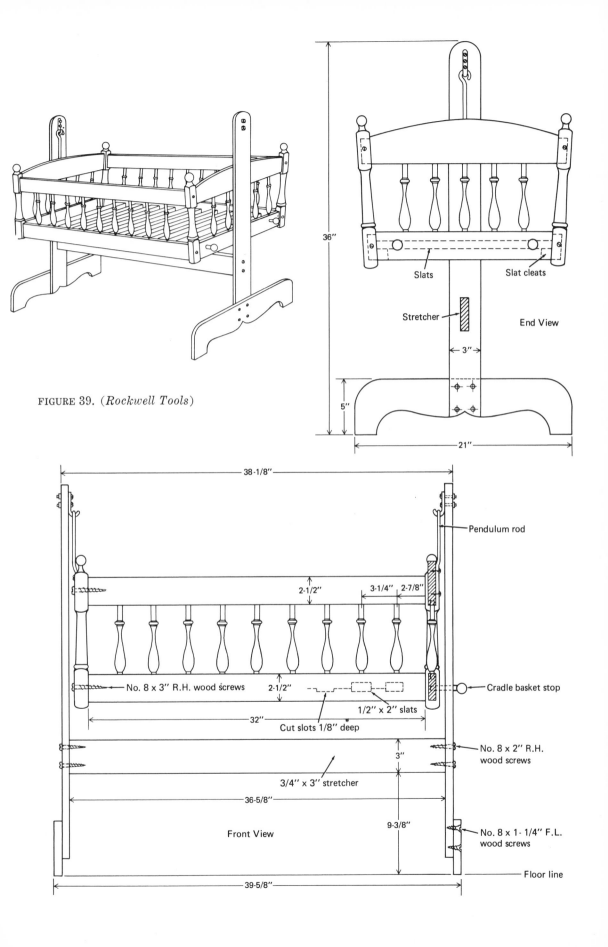

FIGURE 39. (*Rockwell Tools*)

36″

Slats

Slat cleats

Stretcher

End View

3″

5″

21″

38-1/8″

Pendulum rod

2-1/2″

3-1/4″   2-7/8″

No. 8 x 3″ R.H. wood screws

Cradle basket stop

2-1/2″

1/2″ x 2″ slats

32″

Cut slots 1/8″ deep

No. 8 x 2″ R.H.
wood screws

3″

3/4″ x 3″ stretcher

36-5/8″

9-3/8″

Front View

No. 8 x 1- 1/4″ F.L.
wood screws

Floor line

39-5/8″

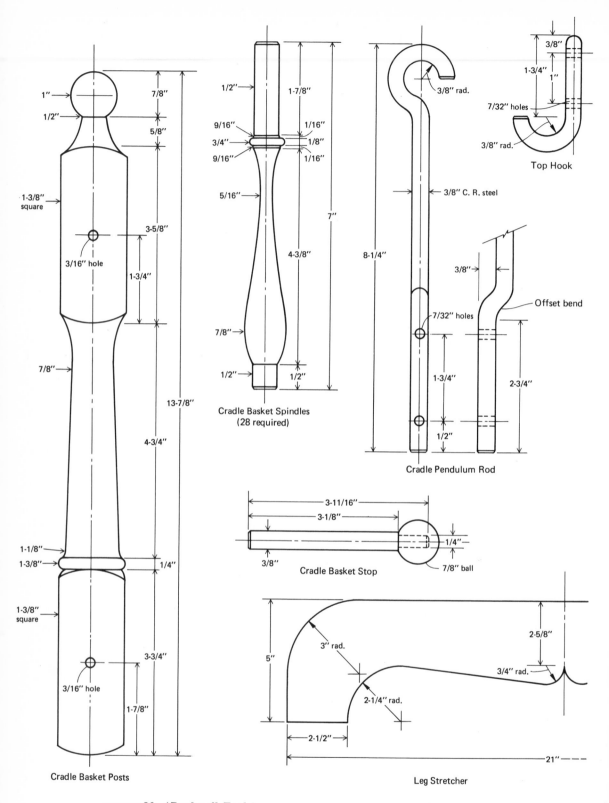

FIGURE 39. (*Rockwell Tools*)

Materials List, Pendulum Cradle (*continued*)

9 pieces	$\frac{1}{2} \times 2 \times 16\frac{7}{8}$	Mattress slats
2 pieces	$\frac{3}{4} \times 3 \times 34\frac{1}{2}$	Cradle holder uprights
2 pieces	$\frac{3}{4} \times 5 \times 21$	Bottom stretchers
1 piece	$\frac{3}{4} \times 3 \times 36\frac{5}{8}$	Bottom cross-stretcher
2 pieces	$\frac{3}{8}$ diameter $\times 10\frac{1}{4}$	Pendulum rods
2 pieces	$\frac{3}{8}$ diameter $\times 4$	Pendulum hooks
1 piece	$\frac{3}{8}$ diameter $\times 3\frac{11}{16}$	Cradle basket stop rod
1 piece	$\frac{7}{8}$ diameter	Cradle basket stop rod ball

Hardware

8	#8 $\times 1\frac{1}{4}$ flathead wood screws
4	#8 $\times 2$ roundhead wood screws
8	#8 $\times 3$ roundhead wood screws
8	$\frac{3}{16} \times 1\frac{1}{4}$ roundhead machine screws

A DRESSER CADDY

This can be used on top of a dresser by both men and women. The tilting mirror can be used for shaving or applying makeup. The depressed slots on top can be used for keys, small change, a wristwatch, cuff links, jewelry, or what-have-you. The design shown is Early American, but simple revisions can make it any style. Change the pulls and mirror frame supports to give it a Spanish or Provincial look, or square off the mirror itself and get streamlined pulls for a modern look.

Since it's a small item, you can afford to use expensive woods like walnut, mahogany, or cherry. Go over the Materials List to see what you need.

Mirror frame supports are made of $\frac{3}{4}$-inch-square stock and turned on a lathe to the dimensions given in Figure 40. Turn the frame spacers and lock knobs at the same time as shown in the photo. Cut them apart later with a band or other saw. Swivel posts can also be made in one piece with the lock knobs, if desired.

The mirror frame can be made with a straight top or molded with a slight curve as shown in the plans. The first cutting of the curved top is made by fitting the curved top piece in a cut-out jig. The first cut is made with Rockwell cutter D-253 and D-147 collar used as a depth guide. With the curved piece still in the jig, the rabbet can be made with a $\frac{3}{8}$-inch-wide straight cutter set to make a $\frac{1}{4}$-inch-deep rabbet. The rabbet can also be cut before you finish cutting the curved piece using a D-107 straight cutter and D-147 collar.

Sides, back, top, and bottom of the drawer case are made of $\frac{3}{8}$-inch stock. Parts are held together with glue. To make the well slots on the top piece of the caddy assembly, cut a template from $\frac{1}{2}$-inch plywood. The openings in the template are $\frac{3}{16}$ inch larger than the actual well slots. This allows for

the wall stem on the B-103 template guide. The stem of the template guide must be cut to ⅜ inch long so that it will clear the stock being routed. All four wells are made with the C-420 core box cutter.

The drawer is made in the conventional manner. Front and back are ⅜ inch thick, sides are ¼ inch. The drawer bottom is made of ⅛-inch-thick-hardboard. Dovetailed joints aren't necessary for a small drawer like this. Tongue-and-groove joints can be used on the drawer front and back piece or simply butt them as shown. Finish to taste.

The inside of the drawer is lined with green or brown felt. Miniature brass drawer pulls shown are in Chippendale design, with a 1¹³⁄₁₆-inch bore. These are available from several sources, most of them listed in Appendix D. Those most likely to carry the hardware are Constantine, Craftsman, and Real Wood.

The two frame spacers and lock knobs are turned at one time on the lathe and later cut apart with a band or other saw.

Make a template for the well slots, then rout the slots using a core box cutter. (*Rockwell Tools*)

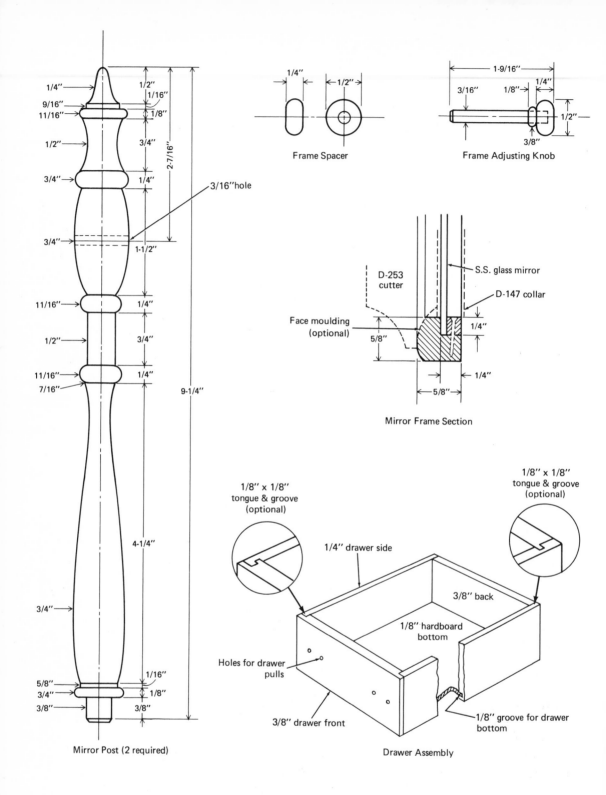

Frame Spacer

Frame Adjusting Knob

3/16"hole

S.S. glass mirror

D-253 cutter

D-147 collar

Face moulding (optional)

Mirror Frame Section

1/8" x 1/8" tongue & groove (optional)

1/8" x 1/8" tongue & groove (optional)

1/4" drawer side

3/8" back

1/8" hardboard bottom

Holes for drawer pulls

3/8" drawer front

1/8" groove for drawer bottom

Mirror Post (2 required)

Drawer Assembly

FIGURE 40. (*Rockwell Tools*)

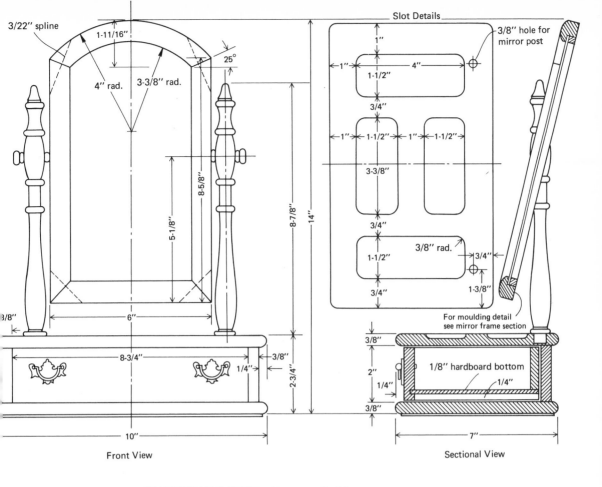

Front View

Sectional View

MATERIALS LIST—Dresser Caddy

Wood

NO.	SIZE (INCHES)	USE
2 pieces	$\frac{3}{4} \times \frac{3}{4} \times 9\frac{1}{4}$	Frame support posts
2 pieces	$\frac{3}{4} \times \frac{1}{2} \times \frac{1}{2}$	Frame spacers
2 pieces	$\frac{1}{2} \times \frac{1}{2} \times 1\frac{9}{16}$	Frame swivel knobs
2 pieces	$\frac{5}{8} \times \frac{5}{8} \times 8\frac{5}{8}$	Frame sides
1 piece	$\frac{5}{8} \times \frac{5}{8} \times 6$	Frame bottom
1 piece	$\frac{5}{8} \times 1\frac{11}{16} \times 6\frac{1}{2}$	Frame top
2 pieces	$\frac{3}{8} \times 7 \times 10$	Top and bottom (base compartment)
2 pieces	$\frac{3}{8} \times 2 \times 6\frac{1}{2}$	Sides (base compartment)
1 piece	$\frac{3}{8} \times 2 \times 8\frac{1}{4}$	Back (base compartment)
1 piece	$\frac{3}{8} \times 2 \times 8\frac{3}{4}$	Drawer front
2 pieces	$\frac{1}{4} \times 2 \times 6$	Drawer sides
1 piece	$\frac{3}{8} \times 1\frac{5}{8} \times 8\frac{1}{4}$	Drawer back
1 piece	$\frac{1}{8} \times 5\frac{7}{8} \times 8\frac{1}{2}$	Drawer bottom (hardboard)

Hardware

2 drawer pulls

1 piece $6\frac{3}{4} \times 9\frac{3}{4}$ felt, green or brown, medium weight

A SEVENTEENTH-CENTURY COLONIAL BENCH

This is an authentic reproduction of a seventeenth-century American-made bench on display at the Carnegie Institute, Pittsburgh, Pa., on loan from Baroness Cassel Van Doorn. It was measured and the plans were drawn by Al Warkaske, editor of *Flying Chips* magazine. It is reproduced here with the kind permission of the Institute and Rockwell Tools, publisher of the magazine.

The original bench was made of both oak and walnut, but it is suggested that you stick to one or the other to avoid finishing difficulties. A dark finish is also recommended for authenticity.

The back legs are cut from stock $2\frac{1}{4}$ inches thick and $4\frac{1}{4}$ inches wide, and shaped as shown in Figure 41. A band saw is the best tool for cutting the tapers on the legs. Mortises for the side stretchers are marked and carved or cut out with a hollow chisel on the drill press. The mortise is $\frac{3}{4}$ inch wide and requires two passes with a $\frac{3}{8}$-inch hollow chisel. Four dowel holes, $\frac{1}{2}$ inch in diameter, are drilled in the inside faces of the back legs to accommodate both back rails. See drawings for location.

The top side stretchers have a $\frac{3}{4}$-inch mortise at the front and a $\frac{3}{4}$-inch tenon at the rear end. The top of the top side stretcher is notched dovetail-fashion at a 45-degree angle, $\frac{3}{8} \times \frac{3}{8}$ inch (see Figure 41). Note that the front mortise is cut at a 6-degree angle, and that the same angle is used for the mortise at the lower end of the leg for the bottom side stretcher. The bottom side stretcher has tenons at both ends, with the tenon at the front also cut off in front at a 6-degree angle to fit the angled mortise. Since these are through mortises (the tenon goes through to the front), the tenon can be made as usual, then sawn off after insertion, if you prefer.

The seat is grooved $\frac{3}{8}$ inch deep at the same 45-degree angle as at the top of the front legs. The top of the groove is $2\frac{1}{4}$ inches wide, as shown in Figure 41. These mating angles are most easily made with a dovetail cutter in a router. The legs are then slid into the grooves of the top for a strong, if unusual, joint.

The edges of the seat are routed to the pattern shown in the detail drawing. For an exact reproduction, use Rockwell cutters #35–221 for the top, and #35–102 for the bottom. Five different cutters are used to mold the top rail, as shown and named in Figure 41. The very tops of the back legs are also molded to match the top rail with just two cutters, #35–245 and #35–103.

Though it is difficult to tell from the drawing, the bottom ends of the braces are notched in a slightly off-center V shape. This is best accomplished on a bench saw with the blade tilted 42 degrees. The notched end is attached to the leg stretcher with $\frac{3}{8}$-inch diameter dowels. The top is screwed into the seat with #8 $2\frac{1}{4}$-inch flathead screws.

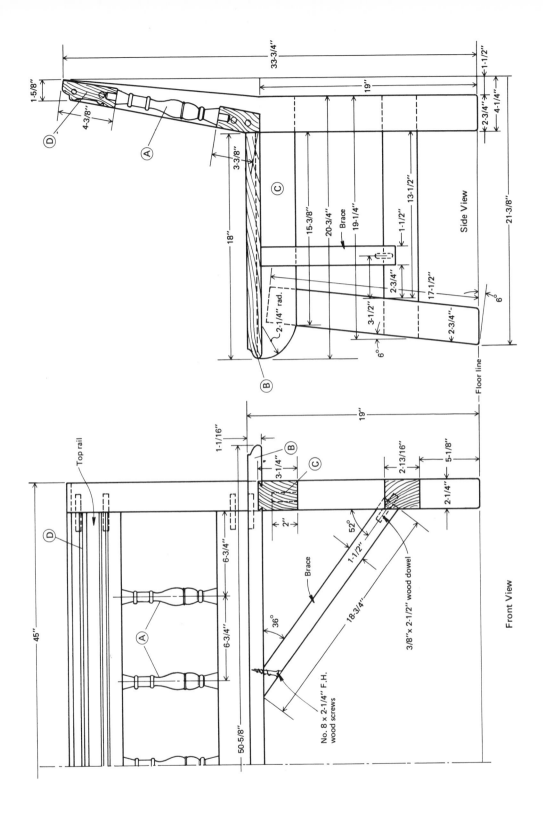

FIGURE 41. (*Rockwell Tools*)

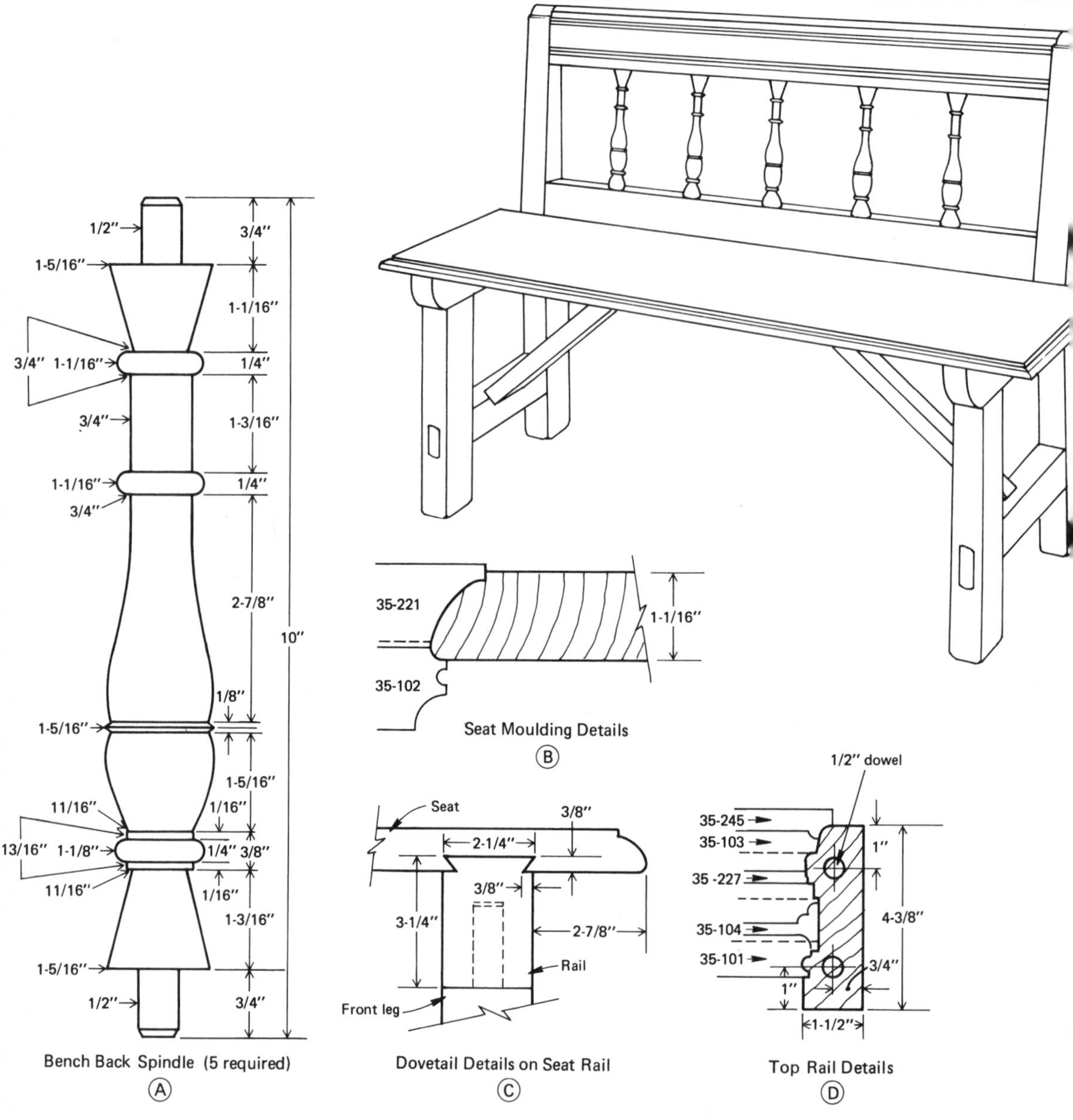

1/2"
3/4"
1-5/16"
1-1/16"
3/4" 1-1/16"
1/4"
3/4"
1-3/16"
1-1/16"
1/4"
3/4"
2-7/8"
10"
1/8"
1-5/16"
1-5/16"
11/16"
1/16"
13/16" 1-1/8"
1/4" 3/8"
11/16"
1/16"
1-3/16"
1-5/16"
1/2"
3/4"
Bench Back Spindle (5 required)
A
35-221
1-1/16"
35-102
Seat Moulding Details
B
Seat
3/8"
2-1/4"
3/8"
3-1/4"
2-7/8"
Rail
Front leg
Dovetail Details on Seat Rail
C
1/2" dowel
35-245
35-103
1"
35-227
4-3/8"
35-104
35-101
3/4"
1"
1-1/2"
Top Rail Details
D

FIGURE 41. (*Rockwell Tools*)

Five spindles are required, and are turned on a lathe to the pattern shown in Figure 41. Put the finishing touches on the spindles with a ¼-inch tungsten carbide chisel. Assemble the pieces and finish. Mr. Warkaske recommends a dark stain and filler, followed by two coats of thin white shellac and a topping of satin-finish varnish for an authentic rubbed look.

MATERIALS LIST—Colonial Bench

Wood

KEY	NO.	SIZE	USE
A	2 pieces	$2\frac{1}{4} \times 4\frac{1}{4} \times 33\frac{3}{4}$	Rear legs
B	2 pieces	$2\frac{1}{4} \times 2\frac{3}{4} \times 17\frac{1}{2}$	Front legs
C	2 pieces	$2\frac{1}{4} \times 3\frac{1}{4} \times 20\frac{3}{4}$	Top side stretchers
D	2 pieces	$2\frac{1}{4} \times 2\frac{13}{16} \times 19\frac{1}{4}$	Bottom side stretchers
E	1 piece	$1\frac{1}{2} \times 4\frac{3}{8} \times 40\frac{1}{2}$	Top back rail
F	1 piece	$1\frac{1}{2} \times 3\frac{3}{8} \times 40\frac{1}{2}$	Bottom back rail
G	1 piece	$10\frac{1}{16} \times 18\frac{1}{2} \times 50\frac{5}{8}$	Bench seat
H	2 pieces	$1\frac{1}{2} \times 1\frac{1}{2} \times 18\frac{3}{4}$	Braces
I	5 pieces	$1\frac{5}{16} \times 1\frac{5}{16} \times 10$	Back spindles

Hardware

2		#8 $2\frac{1}{4}$-inch flathead screws

Appendix A
POPULAR FURNITURE WOODS

ALDER, RED (*Alnus rubra*)—Alder, Western Alder
  Source: Pacific Coast (California and north).
  Color: Pale pinkish-brown to almost white.
  Pattern: Not distinct.
  Characteristics: Good working properties; strength between Red Gum and Yellow Poplar.
  Uses: Unexposed structural parts for furniture: core stock.
  Availability: Scarce as veneer; plentiful as lumber.
  Price Range: Low.

ASH, BLACK (*Fraxinus nigra*)—Brown Ash, Hoop Ash, Swamp Ash.
  Source: Principally the Great Lakes States.
  Color: Warm brown heartwood with a thin white or light brown sapwood.
  Pattern: Clusters of eyes occasionally scattered over plain wood.
  Characteristics: Extremely stable; heavy; rather soft; tough.
  Uses: General furniture.
  Availability: Plentiful, rarely as burls.
  Price Range: Medium.

ASH, WHITE (*Fraxinus americana*)
  Source: Principally Great Lakes States, also New England and Central States.
  Color: Cream to very light brown heartwood with thick, lighter-colored sapwood.
  Pattern: Both flat cut and quartered. Moderately open grain.
  Characteristics: Heavy; hard; strong; medium-grained; tough.
  Uses: Interiors, furniture, handles of tools and implements.
  Availability: Veneer—plentiful; lumber—plentiful.
  Price Range: Medium.

ASPEN (*Populus alba*)—English Poplar, Silver Poplar, White Poplar.
  Source: Europe and Western Asia; transplanted to United States, principally in Middle Atlantic States.
  Color: Pure white to whitish-yellow or gray sapwood similar to Rock Maple with light tan, sometimes brown-streaked, heartwood.

213

Pattern: Most widely known for its crotches and swirls.

Characteristics: Soft; light; easy to work; close-grained; tough texture; natural sheen; tools very smoothly.

Uses: Furniture, interiors, inlays.

Availability: Veneer—scarce. Principally produced as crotches.

Price Range: Moderate to costly.

BASSWOOD (*Tilia americana*)—Linden, American Whitewood.

Source: Northern United States and Canada. Called Linden in Europe.

Color: Creamy white.

Pattern: Fine grain; little or no grain character.

Characteristics: Very light; fairly soft; glues well.

Uses: Largely as core stock and cross-banding.

Availability: Plentiful.

Price Range: Low.

BEECH, AMERICAN (*Fagus grandifolia*)—Sweet Beech.

Source: United States—Great Lakes States and Appalachian region.

Color: Reddish-brown heartwood; thin white sapwood.

Pattern: Straight grain.

Characteristics: Hard; strong; stiff; very close-grained.

Uses: Flooring, chairs, tool handles.

Availability: Plentiful.

Price Range: Inexpensive.

BIRCH, SWEET (*Betula lenta*)—Black Birch, Cherry Birch

Source: Mainly produced in Adirondack and the eastern Appalachian areas, although it occurs as far south as northern part of Gulf States.

Color: Brown tinged with red, with thin, light brown or yellow sapwood.

Pattern: Mostly rotary as well as sliced; grain distinct but not prominent.

Characteristics: Heavy; very strong and hard; close-grained.

Uses: All cabinetwork where strength and hardness are desired.

Availability: Abundant.

Price Range: Medium.

BIRCH, YELLOW (*Betula alleghaniensis*)—Gray Birch, Silver Birch, Swamp Birch.

Source: Canada and the Great Lakes States and New England to North Carolina in the United States.

Color: Cream or light brown tinged with red, with thin, nearly white, sapwood.

Pattern: Both rotary and sliced, plain and often curly or wavy.

Characteristics: Heavy; very strong; hard; close-grained; even-textured.

Uses: Furniture; interiors; interior and exterior doors; etc.

Availability: Abundant. As veneers and sapwood of rotary birch is sold as "selected white" and the heartwood as "selected red." The greater volume produced is "natural birch" and contains a normal combination of color tones.

Price Range: Medium.

BUTTERNUT (*Juglans cinerea*)—White Walnut.

Source: North Central States and Southern Canada.

Color: Pale brown.

Pattern: Satiny wood with leafy grain.

Characteristics: Soft to medium textured, with occasional dark spots or streaks.

Uses: Interior finish of houses; furniture.

Availability: Somewhat more than "rare."

Price Range: Medium.

CATIVO (*Prioria copaifera*)—Florisa, Tabasara.

Source: Tropical America.

Color: Heartwood—brown; thick sapwood—dingy white color.

Pattern: Dull in appearance, straight-grained.

Characteristics: Medium-textured and rather stringy; contains considerable deep brown gum.

Uses: Cross-banding, center ply, etc.

Availability: Plentiful as veneers.

Price Range: Low.

CHERRY, BLACK (*Prunus serotina*)—Rum Cherry, Wild Black Cherry.

Source: Maine to Dakotas and Appalachians; production largely Pennsylvania to West Virginia.

Color: Light reddish-brown.

Pattern: Straight-grained; satiny; some figured. Small gum pockets are normal markings.

Characteristics: Light; strong; rather hard; fine-grained.

Uses: Fine furniture; woodwork and engravers blocks.

Availability: Plentiful.

Price Range: Medium.

CHESTNUT (*Castanea dentata*)

Source: Formerly ranged over Eastern United States.

Color: Reddish-brown with lighter-colored sapwood.

Pattern: Low to medium luster; straight grain.

Characteristics: Coarse-textured; easy to work; highly durable.

Uses: Character-marked paneling and core stock.

Availability: Only as "wormy chestnut"; mostly as lumber; supply largely depleted by "Chestnut blight."

Price Range: Medium.

COTTONWOOD (*Populus deltoides*)—Eastern Cottonwood, Carolina Poplar.

Source: Most of continental United States.

Color: Creamy-white with dark markings.

Pattern: Slightly lustrous but not very distinct.

Characteristics: Numerous pores which are exceedingly small; lightweight; weak; works fairly well although stringy and does not split.

Uses: Woodenware; luggage interiors.

Availability. Veneer—plentiful.

Price Range: Inexpensive.

EBONY, MACASSAR (*Diospyros melanoxylon*)—Marblewood.
Source: East Indies.
Color: Dark brown to black; large proportion of the logs are streaked with yellow or yellow-brown.
Pattern: Rays are fine and very indistinct; the grain markings largely from the brown streaks on black background.
Characteristics: Dense; close grain.
Uses: Wall paneling, inlays, ornamental work.
Availability: Veneer—plentiful; lumber—rare.
Price Range: Costly.

ELM, AMERICAN (*Ulmus americana*)—Soft Elm, Water Elm, White Elm.
Source: United States, east of Rockies.
Color: Light brownish.
Pattern: Conspicuous growth pattern like ash.
Characteristics: Heavy; hard; strong; tough; difficult to split; coarse-grained; bends exceedingly well.
Uses: Widely used as veneers for containers; some for fine furniture.
Availability: Veneer—plentiful; lumber—available.
Price Range: Medium.

ELM, BROWN (*Ulmus rubra*)—Slippery Elm, Red Elm, Gray Elm.
Source: Canada and Middle West of United States from Canada to Gulf of Mexico.
Color: Dark brown to reddish-brown heartwood with thin, lighter-colored sapwood.
Pattern: Conspicuous growth pattern like ash.
Characteristics: Heavy; hard; strong; durable; very coarse-grained.
Uses: Wall paneling and furniture.
Availability: Veneer—plentiful; lumber—available.
Price Range: Medium.

GUM (*Liquidambar styraciflua*)—Heartwood and sapwood sold separately as:
1. GUM, RED (Heartwood)—Hazelwood, Southern Gum, Sweet Gum.
Source: Wide range in United States but commercial production is largely from lower Mississippi Valley.
Color: Reddish-brown.
Pattern: Dark streaks.
Characteristics: Moderately heavy; hard; straight; close-grained; not exceedingly strong. Red Gum, or the heartwood, is often selected for its attractive figure.
Uses: Outside and inside finish of houses; cabinetmaking; wooden dishes and fruit boxes.
Availability: Veneer—plentiful; lumber—available.
Price Range: Medium.
2. GUM, SAP (Sapwood of the same species)
Source: Same.
Color: Pinkish-white often blued by sap stains.

Pattern: Plain but not strong; usually watery.

Characteristics: Same as above except not as durable.

Uses: Plywood (interiors) and lumber for furniture, TV cabinets, etc. Architectural woodwork for paint. The most widely used species for veneers in the U.S.

Availability: Veneer—abundant; lumber—abundant.

Price Range: Inexpensive.

HICKORY (*Carya*)—There are some 16 species and 20 varieties in eastern North America of which the most important commercially is Shagbark Hickory (*Carya ovata*).

Source: From the Northeastern United States to the Southwest into Mexico.

Color: White to cream with inconspicuous fine brown lines and tan heartwood.

Pattern: Fairly indistinct but pleasing.

Characteristics: Extremely tough and resilient; quite hard and only moderately heavy.

Uses: As veneers—furniture, skiis, molded and bent plywood requiring extreme strength.

Availability: Veneer—plentiful; lumber—plentiful.

Price Range: Medium.

HOLLY (*Ilex opaca*)

Source: United States—Maine to Florida; the lower Mississippi region produces the limited commercial cut.

Color: Very white, turning brown with age and exposure.

Pattern: Very close-grained; almost no visible pattern.

Characteristics: Light; tough; not strong.

Uses: Cabinetmaking; inlay work.

Availability: Veneer—scarce; lumber—available.

Price Range: Medium.

LAUAN, RED (*Shorea negrosensis*)—Also called "Philippine Mahogany."

Source: Philippine Islands.

Color: Red to brown.

Pattern: Ribbon stripe; interlocking grain.

Characteristics: Coarse texture; large pores.

Uses: Furniture; doors and cabinetmaking.

Availability: Veneer—abundant; lumber—available.

Price Range: Medium to inexpensive.

LAUAN, WHITE (*Pentacme contorta*)

Source: Philippines.

Color: Light to grayish-brown.

Characteristics: Medium heavy; rather coarse texture.

Uses: Furniture; cabinetwork.

Availability: Less plentiful than Red Lauan.

Price Range: Inexpensive to low.

MAGNOLIA (*Magnolia grandiflora, Magnolia acuminata*)—Cucumber Tree.

Source: Southern United States, especially in the Appalachians.

Color: More dark streaks than poplar, sometimes with greenish cast.

Pattern: Fairly distinct.

Characteristics: Very much like yellow poplar but slightly harder and heavier.

Uses: About same as yellow poplar.

Availability: Plentiful.

Price Range: Inexpensive.

MAHOGANY, AFRICAN (*Khaya ivorensis*)

Source: Africa (Ivory Coast, Gold Coast, French Cameroon, Cape Lopez, Nigeria).

Color: Light pink to reddish-brown and tannish-brown.

Pattern: Although pores are distributed, this wood produces a very distinct, pleasing grain. The most lavishly figured mahogany offered in plain stripe, broken stripe, mottle, fiddleback, fine crotches, and faux swirl.

Characteristics: Available in great lengths and widths; milder-textured with slightly larger pores than other Mahogany species; relatively hard; works well; highly lustrous; polishes well; durable.

Uses: Interiors; furniture; accessories and art objects; boats, etc.

Availability: Veneer—abundant; lumber—abundant.

Price Range: Medium; for highly figured veneers—costly.

MAHOGANY, TROPICAL AMERICAN, including PERUVIAN and BRAZILIAN MAHOGANY (Swietenia macrophylla)

Source: Mexico, Brazil, Peru, and Central America (especially Honduras).

Color: Varies from a light reddish- or yellowish-brown to a rich, dark red, depending upon country of origin and situation. Tends to be yellowish-tan, changing on brief exposure to rich, golden brown.

Pattern: A considerable variety of figures, similar to African Mahogany except crotches are not readily available. Straighter grain generally.

Characteristics: Lighter and softer than Cuban; mostly straight-grained but even when interlocked is exceptionally stable; more mellow texture than Cuban (West Indian); extremely good strength properties; works well; stains and finishes well; durable and decay-resistant; Central America produces more figured logs for fancy veneers.

Uses: Furniture; paneling; fine joinery; boats and ships; pattern-making; exterior uses.

Availability: Abundant.

Price Range: Inexpensive to medium.

MAHOGANY, WEST INDIAN (*Swietenia mahogani*)—Cuban Mahogany, Jamaica Mahogany, Puerto Rico Mahogany, etc.

Source: Cuba and West Indies, principally Dominican Republic.

Color: Light red or yellow-tan when cut, darkens rapidly to deep, rich golden-brown or brown-red; exceptionally fine colors.

Pattern: Highly figured; mottled; fiddleback, crotches plus plain stripes.

Characteristics: Heavier and harder than other mahoganies; wears exceptionally well; extremely durable; close-grained; takes excellent finish; ideal turnery wood; takes an exceptionally smooth surface and fine silky texture; works well; high golden luster; good strength and bending properties.

Uses: Fine cabinetry.
Availability: Veneer—limited quantities.
Price Range: Costly.

MAPLE, HARD (*Acer saccharum*)—Bird's-Eye Maple, Northern Maple, Rock Maple, Sugar Maple.

> *Source:* Great Lakes States, Appalachians, Northwest United States; Canada.
>
> *Color:* Cream to light reddish-brown heartwood; thin white sapwood tinged slightly with reddish-brown.
>
> *Pattern:* Usually straight-grained; sometimes found highly figured with curly, blistered, quilted, bird's-eye, or burl grain, scattered over entire tree or in irregular stripes and patches.
>
> *Characteristics:* Heavy; hard; strong; close-grained; tough; stiff; uniform texture. Excellent resistance to abrasion and indentation.
>
> *Uses:* Furniture; interiors; fixtures; flooring; woodenware; cutting surfaces; decorative inlays and overlays.
>
> *Availability: Plain maple*—veneer—plentiful; *Figured maple* (including bird's-eye, butts, etc.)—veneer—rare.
>
> *Price Range: Plain Maple*—medium; *Figured maple*—costly.

MYRTLE (*Umbellularia californica*)—"Acacia" Burl, Baytree, California "Laurel," Oregon Myrtle, Pepperwood.

> *Source:* West Coast of United States, especially Southern Oregon and Northern California.
>
> *Color:* Golden-brown and yellowish-green. Wide range from light to dark.
>
> *Pattern:* Mixture of plain wood, mottle, cluster, blistered, stump, and burl figure with a scattering of dark purple blotches.
>
> *Characteristics:* Hard; strong; pores the size and distribution of walnut. A magnificent, highly figured veneer.
>
> *Uses:* Decorative panels for architecture and furniture; novelties.
>
> *Availability:* Veneers—plentiful; lumber—scarce.
>
> *Price Range:* Costly.

OAK, AMERICAN (*Quercus alba, Quercus rubra*)

> Except for source and color, Red Oak and White Oak, the two leading American species, are very similar. Characteristics they have in common are:
>
> *Pattern:* Quartered oak has a striking "flake" pattern caused by extremely large and wide rays that reflect light. Plain flat sliced or sawn oak has an attractive figure of stripes and leafy grain caused by the distinct layers of springwood and summerwood and the large pores, especially concentrated in the springwood. Rift-cut (half-round) oak has a fine pinstripe. Rotary-cut oak has a distinct watery figure with great contrast.
>
> *Characteristics:* A heavy, ring-porous hardwood with larger, more prominent pores in the springwood than summerwood; very strong and very hard; stiff and heavy; durable under exposure; great wear-resistance; holds nails and screws well. Because of its large pores, oak takes a great variety of fine filled or textured finishes.

Uses: Flooring (both solid and plywood tiles) ; furniture; paneling; and general construction; shipbuilding uses.

Availability: Veneer—plentiful; lumber—available.

Price Range: Medium.

OAK, ENGLISH BROWN (*Quercus robur*)—European Oak, Pollard Oak.

Source: England.

Color: Light tan to deep brown.

Pattern: Black spots, sometimes creating an effect much like tortoiseshell.

Characteristics: Noticeable figure and grain character.

Uses: Architectural woodwork; some in fine furniture.

Availability: Veneer—plentiful.

Price Range: Costly.

PALDAO (*Dracontomelum dao*)

Source: Philippines.

Color: Gray to reddish-brown.

Pattern: Varied grain effects usually with irregular stripes, some occasionally very dark. Occasional crotch or swirl.

Characteristics: Pores are large, partially plugged; fairly hard.

Uses: Architectural woodwork and furniture.

Availability: Veneer—plentiful; lumber—available.

Price Range: Medium.

PECAN (*Carya illinoensis*)

Source: Southern United States, east of Mississippi.

Color: Heartwood—reddish-brown with occasional darker streaks; sapwood—creamy white.

Pattern: Quite distinct, because of pores that are larger than hickory or walnut, two species that belong to the same family.

Characteristics: Close-grained; hard; very heavy; and strong.

Uses: Furniture and wall paneling.

Availability: Veneer—plentiful; lumber—available.

Price Range: Medium.

PINE, KNOTTY (*Pinus monticola*)—Idaho White Pine (a softwood).

Source: Idaho, Washington, Montana.

Color: Like Northern White. (Light brown or red.)

Pattern: Knotty.

Characteristics: Softwood but occasionally used as cabinet wood. Light; soft; not strong; close, straight-grained.

Uses: Used in construction and interior finish of buildings; some furniture.

Availability: Veneer—plentiful; lumber—plentiful.

Price Range: Medium.

POPLAR, YELLOW (*Liriodendron tulipifera*)—Tuliptree, Whitewood.

Source: New England to Michigan, Appalachians to Gulf.

Color: Canary color, sometimes with slightly greenish cast and occasionally with rather dark streaks.

Pattern: Even texture; straight grain.

Characteristics: Light to medium weight; strength; soft; easily worked.

Uses: As veneers—widely used for cross-banding and backs of plywood; as lumber—interior finish or fixtures (usually to be painted); boat building; core stock; woodenware.

Availability: Veneer (quartered, sliced, half-round, rotary, occasionally burls) —abundant; lumber—available.

Price Range: Inexpensive.

PRIMAVERA (*Cybistax donnell-smithii*)—Durango, Palo Blanco, San Juan. Sometimes misnamed "White Mahogany."

Source: From Central Mexico, south through Guatemala and Honduras into Salvador.

Color: Yellow white to yellow brown.

Pattern: Straight grain.

Characteristics: Odorless and tasteless; medium- to coarse-textured; straight to somewhat striped grained; moderately light in weight.

Uses: A fine, general-use cabinet wood.

Availability: Veneer—plentiful; lumber—available.

Price Range: Costly.

ROSEWOOD, BRAZILIAN (*Dalbergia nigra*)—Jacaranda, Rio Rosewood, Bahia Rosewood.

Source: Brazil.

Color: Various shades of dark brown—chocolate to violet; conspicuous black streaks.

Pattern: Streaks of dark brown or black pigment lines.

Characteristics: Rather large pores are exceedingly irregular both in size and position.

Uses: Furniture, pianos, wall paneling.

Availability: Veneer—abundant; lumber—available.

Price Range: Costly.

ROSEWOOD, EAST INDIAN (*Dalbergia latifolia*)—Bombay Rosewood, Blackwood, Malobar.

Source: Southern India and Ceylon.

Color: Dark purple to ebony; streaks of red or yellow.

Pattern: Small to medium pores in wavy lines; exceedingly fine rays; occasionally crotches and swirls.

Characteristics: Stands up exceptionally well under all conditions; texture is close, firm, and hard; requires rather a sharp tool to secure a smooth surface; very moderate shrinkage.

Uses: Wall paneling and fine furniture.

Availability: Veneer—plentiful.

Price Range: Costly.

SATINWOOD, CEYLON (*Chloroxylon swietenia*)—East Indian Satinwood.

Source: Ceylon and southern India.

Color: Pale gold.

Pattern: Rippled, straight stripe; bee's-wing mottled.

Characteristics: Hard; dense; interlocking grain; inclined to check.

Uses: Furniture.

Availability: Veneer—plentiful; lumber—rare.

Price Range: Costly.

SATINWOOD, WEST INDIAN (*Zanthoxylum flavum*)—San Domingan Satinwood.

Source: Puerto Rico, British Honduras.

Color: Creamy golden yellow.

Pattern: Wavy grain.

Characteristics: Fine grained; hard and quite heavy; works well with most tools.

Uses: Furniture; marquetry; inlaying; turnery.

Availability: Veneer—scarce; lumber—available.

Price Range: Costly.

TEAK (*Tectona grandis*)—Burma Teak, Rangoon Teak.

Source: Burma, Java, East India, French Indo-China.

Color: Tawny yellow to dark brown, often with lighter streaks.

Pattern: A great deal like walnut, sometimes mottled and fiddleback.

Characteristics: Strong; tough; oily. Except for oiliness, much like walnut.

Uses: Paneling; furniture; floors; ship decking.

Availability: Veneer—plentiful; lumber—available.

Price Range: Costly.

TULIPWOOD (*Dalbergia frutescens*)—Boise De Rose, Brazilian Pinkwood.

Source: Northeastern Brazil.

Color: Light background regularly streaked with red and yellow.

Pattern: Annual growth marked by dark rings. Rays are irregular, fine.

Characteristics: In line of the concentric layers, pores are fairly large and open with numerous, very small pores in the remainder of the layer.

Uses: Inlay, turnery, bandings.

Availability: Veneer—scarce; lumber—available.

Price Range: Costly.

WALNUT, AMERICAN (*Juglans nigra*)

Source: While walnut grows throughout the United States and southern Canada, its commercial range is confined largely to some fifteen Central States.

Color: Light gray-brown to dark purplish-brown.

Pattern: Plain to highly figured. This one species produces a greater variety of figure types than any other, approached only by mahogany.

Characteristics: Moderately heavy; very strong for its weight; exceptionally stable.

Uses: Furniture; architectural woodwork; gunstocks; novelties.

Availability: Abundant as veneers and plentiful as lumber.

Price Range: Medium to costly for highly figured types.

ZEBRAWOOD (*Microberlinia brazzavillanensis*)—Zebrano, Zingana.

Source: African Cameroon; Gabon, West Africa.

Color: Straw and dark brown. Exceptionally pronounced fine stripes.

Pattern: Striped; dark brown stripes; lustrous surface.

Characteristics: Heavy; hard; with somewhat coarse texture.

Uses: Veneer—wall paneling, inlays.

Availability: Veneer—plentiful.

Price Range: Costly.

Appendix B
FURNITURE ADHESIVES

ANIMAL GLUES

Also called hide or "horse" glues. The oldest type of wood glue. May be applied as hot or cold liquids. Good strength but poor moisture resistance. Set by drying. Tend to become brittle upon aging. Made from hides, hoofs, and bones of animals. Requires clamping. Good for loose-fitting joints because of thick glue line. *Typical Applications:* furniture, general veneer

CASEIN GLUES

Made from milk protein. Dry powders mixed with water for use. High strength and moisture resistance. Good for poor-fitting joints and oily woods. *Typical Applications:* wooden toys, furniture, general other wooden items, cardboard

CONTACT CEMENT

Has neoprene base. Instant setting, cannot be repositioned. Strong and water-resistant. *Typical Applications:* veneers, laminates, leather

EPOXY

Consists of resin and curing agent that must be measured and mixed. Excellent with nonporous materials and wood. Very strong bonds. Epoxy adhesives shrink little during cure, may be used in thick glue lines. Some expoxies are hard, filled adhesives; others are clear somewhat flexible materials. The flexible types are useful in bonding dissimilar materials. *Typical Applications:* wood, glass, tile, metals, some plastics, leather

HOT MELT

This synthetic resin adhesive is supplied in sticks which are used in an electric glue gun. It is easy to apply, and sets quickly, but parts cannot be adjusted after they are joined. Hot melt adhesive is solventless and nonflammable, and no clamping is required. Moderate strength and durability. *Typical Applications:* wood, leather, some plastics, metal

PLASTIC RESIN

Also called urea resin adhesive. Dry powders to be mixed with water for use. Easy to use. They produce a light-colored glue line, good resistance to heat and water. Strong but brittle. Not recommended for poorly fitted joints, thick glue lines, oily woods. *Typical Applications:* general furniture, veneer, large wooden surfaces

225

POLYVINYL WHITE RESINS

Milky white liquids frequently sold in plastic squeeze bottles. Bond by loss of water. Produce a clear, colorless glue line. Somewhat flexible. Moderate moisture resistance. Moderate strength. Resistant to oil, grease, and solvents. Excellent for repair of wooden items. *Typical Applications:* general furniture, wooden toys, cardboard, textiles, paper, wood

RESORCINOL

Two-part adhesives consisting of a dark-red or purple liquid and a curing agent. Produce high-strength joints for use outdoors or under severe service conditions. Cured adhesive resists water, oil, most solvents, and mold. Produces a dark-colored glue line. Requires a moderately thin glue line. *Typical Applications:* outdoor toys, furniture, wooden boats, wooden structures, fabrics

Appendix C
ABRASIVE PAPERS USED FOR REFINISHING

GRIT	GRADE #	DESCRIPTION	USE
80	1/0	Medium	Paint removal and rough shaping
100	2/0	Fine	Preparatory softwood sanding
120	3/0	Fine	Preparatory hardwood sanding
220	6/0	Very fine	Finish softwood sanding
240	7/0	Extra fine	Finish hardwood sanding
280	8/0	Extra fine	Finish hardwood sanding
360	9/0	Superfine	Polishing finishes between coats, usually wet

Silicon carbide or aluminum oxide papers are recommended for furniture work, with garnet acceptable for most work. Finer grades are usually backed by emery cloth for wet sanding.

Appendix D
SOURCES OF SUPPLY BY MAIL

These firms sell veneers and other cabinetmaking supplies by mail. Many also have antique hardware and specialized tools. Most have catalogs, some of them free. Write or phone for more detailed information.

Albrecht, Robert M.
8635 Yolanda Ave.
Northridge, CA 91324
(213) 349–6500

Constantine, A. & Son, Inc.
2050 Eastchester Rd.
Bronx, NY 10461
(212) 792–1600

Craftsman Wood Service, Inc.
3739 So. Mary St.
Chicago, IL 60608
(312) 842–0507

Exotic Woodshed
65 No. York Rd.
Warminster, PA 18974
(215) 672–2257

Homecraft Veneer
Box 3
Latrobe, PA 15650
(412) 537–3938

M & M Hardwood
5344 Vineland Ave.
No. Hollywood, CA 91601
(213) 766–8325

Minnesota Woodworkers Supply Co.
Industrial Blvd.
Rogers, MN 55374
(612) 428–4101

Morgan, Bob, Woodworking Supplies
915 E. Kentucky St.
Louisville, KY 40204
(502) 636–5000

Real Wood Veneers
107 Trumbull St.
Elizabeth, NJ 07206
(201) 351–1991

INDEX

INDEX

233

ABOUT THE AUTHOR

L. DONALD MEYERS is a member of the National Association of Home Workshop Writers. He is the author of the wood-finishing section of the *Popular Science Homeowner's Encyclopedia* and coedited the *Family Circle Do-It-Yourself Encyclopedia*. His articles appear frequently in national magazines.